A GUIDE TO
THE POLITICAL CLASSICS

A Guide to the Political Classics

PLATO TO ROUSSEAU

EDITED BY

MURRAY FORSYTH
AND
MAURICE KEENS-SOPER

OXFORD UNIVERSITY PRESS
1988

Oxford University Press, Walton Street, Oxford OX2 6DP

Oxford New York Toronto
Delhi Bombay Calcutta Madras Karachi
Petaling Jaya Singapore Hong Kong Tokyo
Nairobi Dar es Salaam Cape Town
Melbourne Auckland

and associated companies in
Berlin Ibadan

Oxford is a trade mark of Oxford University Press

Published in the United States
by Oxford University Press, New York

© *Forsyth and Keens-Soper 1988*

British Library Cataloguing in Publication Data

A guide to the political classics: Plato to Rousseau.
1. Politics. Theories, to ca 1760
I. Forsyth, Murray II. Keens-Soper,
H.M.A. (Harold Maurice Alvan)
320′.01
ISBN 0-19-824951-9
ISBN 0-19-824950-0 (Pbk.)

Library of Congress Cataloging in Publication Data

A Guide to the political classics: Plato to Rousseau / edited by
Murray Forsyth and Maurice Keens-Soper.
p.cm.
Includes index.
1. Political science–History. I. Forsyth, Murray Greensmith.
II. Keens-Soper, Maurice.
JA81.G85 1988 320′.09–dc19 88-10034
ISBN 0-19-824951-9
ISBN 0-19-824950-0 (pbk.)

Set by Eta Services (Typesetters) Ltd., Beccles, Suffolk
Printed in Great Britain
at the University Printing House, Oxford
by David Stanford
Printer to the University

Contents

Introduction

The Significance of the Classic Texts

THE EDITORS

THIS volume of essays is directed towards students of political philosophy who are approaching the great texts of the past for the first time. The intention is to help students to find their way into the texts and to get the most from them, and at the same time to encourage them to explore the texts further themselves. The essays are not summaries or substitutes but emphatically guides. Seven texts have been selected for examination, ranging in chronological order from Plato's *Republic* to Rousseau's *Social Contract*.

The essay form has been chosen primarily for practical reasons. In so many of the studies of the great political theorists of the past and their ideas, the chief texts, on which students ought to focus their attention, are absorbed into a general discussion encompassing the entire work of the thinker. The shape and unity of the text itself tends to become blurred. A difficulty of a different kind occurs when a particular text is subjected to so detailed an exegesis that the map becomes bigger—and sometimes more complicated and difficult to comprehend—than the original work.

In this volume we have tried to avoid both these extremes. The emphasis of the seven essays is firmly on the texts themselves: their setting, form, and content. At the same time, none of the authors has tried to say everything about the text, to push into every nook and cranny, to discuss every chapter, or to pretend that theirs is the ultimate word. Each essay is a selection and an interpretation geared to awaken the interest of the student to the potentialities of the work concerned and to helping him or her over what seem to be the biggest initial hurdles. We believe that in the end each student has to arrive at his own interpretation. There can be no escape from judgement.

Although the contributors have all sought to pitch their essays at roughly the same level, each has had to decide how best this was to be achieved bearing in mind the differences between the subjects they were considering. In respect of texts that range from what appear to be lecture notes (Aristotle's *Politics*), to a work of truly cosmic discursiveness (St Augustine's *City of God*), and from there to the systematic exposition of a new science (Hobbes's *Leviathan*), the common wish to render them more accessible can imply no uniform method of treatment.

This leads on to questions of deeper significance. Given the very different make-up of the works under discussion, and the very different circumstances in which they were written, what is it that links them together? Why are they called 'classics'? Why should present-day students, who in little more than a decade will be citizens in a new century, read these old books?

Clearly the answer to these questions can in the last resort only be given by the texts themselves. Books do not become 'classics' because some remote academic jury decides they have passed certain tests, but because they succeed—as other books do not—in reaching out beyond their age and stimulating the minds of later generations. If they continue to do this, they continue to be 'classics', and if they become incomprehensible or merely of antiquarian interest, they lose this status. The texts included in this volume have manifestly succeeded in provoking later thinkers over a very long period of time, and are called 'classics' for this reason. But it is always possible that they might fade into obscurity, and it is indeed the first assumption of this book that they should not be allowed to do so, that they continue to be worth the closest attention, and that even in our own hectically evolving era their ideas and arguments remain important.

Is it possible then to be more precise about the qualities that have enabled them to stand out and endure? The starting-point of any considered response must be that, despite the vast differences between them, these books are addressing a fact that is conterminous with human existence, the fact of rule or government. It is a commonplace that forms of rule or government have varied vastly in time and space: tribal units, Asiatic despotism, the *polis*, the 'estates-state', the 'modern state', and so on. That these are all developments of rule or government, or different expressions of a certain kind of human activity, few would deny. Man in this sense is a political animal, and with the exception of anarchists and those who have disowned the world, it is not rule or government that strikes terror or anger in the hearts of men, but its absence, abuse, or faulty construction.

What one is to make of this fact—what it reveals about our natures as moral beings—is the first impulse of political philosophy. For the self-evident fact of rule or government is not self-explanatory. It is interpretation that gives meaning to even the most rudimentary facts of life. Without interpretation there is no significance. And being men, the demand for explanation and understanding is inseparable from the impulse to transform ourselves and our world. The demand for explanation is thus no isolated or self-contained insistence. It is wedded to the fact that we are not passive subjects destined to accept impersonal fate but authors as well as actors, beings who create as well as submit to the necessities of life. The human significance of rule and government includes the world as we find it and the world as we would shape it.

The peculiarity of political philosophy is the assumption that it is possible, and indeed in some sense necessary, to respond to the fact of rule or government by exercising our reason. Reason is more than curiosity, and once engaged it is as relentless in its search for 'right rule' and 'right order' as is our need for rule upon which it dwells. Yet if political philosophy is human self-interrogation through reason, prompted by the demand to establish the significance of rule or government in its widest setting and most thorough implications, this sounds like a very tall order. It is. And it is precisely at this juncture that we glimpse what is meant by 'classics' of political philosophy, and why they are an education. What distinguishes the finest, the enduring works is precisely that they succeed in bringing the fact of rule or government into reasoned connection with the nature and ends of men. They unify our experience. Far from obscuring the practicalities of rule by placing them in their widest context, the greatest works persuade us that it is only in the answers we give to questions as to the nature of man, his faculties, and his ends that these peculiar features of our existence cease to be alien.

This conception of political philosophy has been challenged on occasion by the claim that the great texts are intelligible only when interpreted by reference to their own times. They are said to be significant as historical rather than as philosophical works. What they illuminate is said to be not a universal predicament but a particular set of circumstances.

In so far as this argument reminds us that authors such as those treated in this volume inhabited worlds notably different from our own, that they were often stirred to write by serious contemporary issues, and that they used terminology which may well have changed its meaning since their time, then there can be no quibble with it. It is one of the tasks of a guide like this, which is concerned with facilitating access to the thoughts of the classic writers, to try to indicate such contextual factors, and none of the contributors to it believes that the authors of the classic texts were disembodied minds using some immutable language of pure speculation.

If, however, it is argued that the purpose of studying the great texts of political philosophy is exclusively to show how they were influenced and moulded by the historical context in which they were written, and conversely to understand how they influenced the events of their own time, the error is profound. For in what does 'greatness' exist according to this perspective? If it is taken to mean 'the exercise of a great influence on contemporary events', then arguably we should be studying transient works that inflamed the multitude of the day rather than scholarly volumes like *Leviathan*. It is not the power to exercise an immediate impact on events that is remarkable about the works discussed in this volume but—to repeat it once more—the capacity to make us think long after historical circumstances have altogether changed. *Le divin Platon* inspired the young Rousseau two thousand years after the *Republic* was written. Why? Surely it was because from Plato's attempt to relate the perennial fact of rule to man's nature and end, Rousseau derived insights that aided his own efforts to bring them into accord.

The classics of political philosophy have thus achieved their status because they plumb most deeply the predicament of man's political existence, and it is because of this that they provide the best starting-point from which we, today, can derive our own answers to that unyielding predicament. They are not to be viewed as idols or icons, but rather as formidable whetstones for our powers of reasoning. Nor should the nature of the situation to which they are addressed be misjudged. To imagine that they contain prescriptions for current policy issues would be purest folly. It is with the larger issues of the nature and right ordering of the body politic that they are concerned.

It is not only the arguments of a particular text that can stir the minds of later generations. The dialogue between the authors of

vicissitudes

the great texts themselves, the ideas that they received from one another, and the convergence and divergence of their arguments over central issues provide an added source of stimulus to those who come later—an added inheritance. In other words, while the reduction of the great texts to the status of historical events enmeshed in their own times must be eschewed, the development of political philosophy over time, or the history of political thought, is an immensely valuable field of study. This kind of history is, at its best, philosophical reasoning exercised in and through the words and thoughts of a succession of earlier thinkers.

Does the span of philosophical argument that is covered in this volume reveal any persistent themes? Needless to say, there are *Themes:* many. Consider, for example, Plato's basic assumption that the *human soul* political order throws into high relief the various components of *personality* the human soul, or that men can see in the wider political order *reason,* the reproduction of their own individual desires, and spirit, and *character* reason. This vision of the state as a 'great person' recurs again and *"great person"* again in political philosophy—amongst the writers discussed in this volume, it can be seen in the theories of both Hobbes and Rousseau. Yet the differences that are expressed within this analogy or metaphor are as interesting as its continuity.

Another theme is that of the vicissitudes of what may be called the *polis*-idea, the idea of 'civil society' that was manifested in the *civil society* ancient classical republics, and which was presented and examined with such thoroughness by Aristotle. Plato is already the critic of this idea; St Augustine downgrades or deprecates it; Machiavelli expresses much admiration for it, but Hobbes seems to have none at all; Locke points the way to a new kind of 'civil society', very different from the ancient classic conception, while Rousseau finally seeks in his own particular way to revive the spirit of the ancient *polis*, turning his back on the new order of things implicit in Hobbes and Locke.

Perhaps the most interesting and deepest theme, however, is the contrast that can be seen reproducing itself in different forms over the centuries between those who seek to harness or subordinate the political order to a higher world of absolute and eternal moral rectitude, and those who insist that the political order is concerned with the mundane and practical world of human co-existence, and hence consider that the wish to implement absolute moral values may destroy such coexistence. This theme also helps to make plain the importance of the epistemological problem for political philosophy which will be evident in some of the chapters that follow. Is it possible for man to *know* absolute and transcendental moral truth, or is his knowledge necessarily limited and relative? The answer has profound political implications.

These are but some of the themes that are explored by the texts discussed in this volume. There has inevitably been a certain degree of arbitrariness in the selection of the texts for inclusion. It must not be concluded that the seven chosen represent a closed list of classic works for the period they cover, nor that we believe that the production of such classic works terminated abruptly on the eve of the French Revolution. The main aim has been to provide reasonably extensive treatment of certain works that students will be likely to encounter.

All the contributors to this volume have experience of teaching political philosophy, and all have connections with the Department of Politics at Leicester University. Christopher Hughes was formerly Professor in the Department, and has now retired. Bruce Haddock studied at Leicester and now teaches politics at the University College of Swansea. Andrew Lockyer also studied at Leicester and now teaches at the University of Glasgow. The remaining four contributors are currently members of the Department at Leicester.

Plato: *The Republic*

JOHN DAY

PHILOSOPHY began in classical Greece and reached its first splen-
did climax in the Athens of Socrates, Plato, and Aristotle. Plato
made immense contributions to many branches of philosophy.
His is one of the outstanding minds of Western civilization and he
was probably the most influential philosopher of all times. His
Republic (in Greek, *Politeia*—a less misleading translation would
be 'regime') was the first great work of political philosophy. In it
Plato elaborated arguments that were to affect profoundly subsequent discussions in Greece, Rome, medieval Christendom, and
the modern world about man, society, government, and morality.

The Context of the *Republic*

Political philosophy for the Greeks meant understanding the *polis*,
the unique type of community produced by classical Greece. In its
most fully developed form the *polis* prevailed in the Greek world
from around 550 BC until Philip of Macedon absorbed the *poleis*
into his empire in 338. The *poleis* were significantly different from
the monarchies and aristocracies from which they had evolved:
rulers no longer treated subjects almost as property and people felt
loyalty to the whole *polis* rather than merely to a clan or tribe.
The *poleis* varied in size and practice, but in essence they were
small, independent, and largely self-sufficient communities in
which the citizens ruled themselves. The number of people who
qualified as citizens varied considerably between different *poleis*,
so that in some the poor participated in government, whereas in
others they did not. The ideal of the *polis* was that all the citizens
fulfilled themselves as individuals by carrying out their duty to
the community.

Many people (of whom Plato was emphatically not one) have
regarded the democracy of Athens, in which many people were
citizens, as the highest point that the *polis* reached as a self-

determining community. Although the majority of those who lived in Athens, including women, slaves, and non-Athenian residents, were not eligible to be citizens and therefore took no part in governing the *polis*, the achievement of Athenian democracy (the rule of the people (*demos*)) remains impressive. Those citizens who chose to attend the Assembly helped to make decisions for the *polis*, so that the citizens as a body governed themselves as individuals.[1]

The eligibility of all citizens to participate in the affairs of the *polis* meant that government was in the hands of people who did many different jobs. The Athenians regarded this as a positive advantage, because the citizens as a whole brought to the task of ruling vast experience of other activities in the *polis*. In the *Republic* Plato, who believed that governing required special knowledge, blamed the amateur principle of democratic government for what he regarded as its serious deficiencies.

Plato was both a product and a theorist of the *polis*. Critical of the imperfections of the Athenian *polis* in practice, he sought in the *Republic* to create a perfect *polis* in theory. His principal purpose was to explain what justice is by discussing how just men would behave in a just *polis*. At the same time he was proposing remedies for the moral, social, and political ills of contemporary Athens. Paradoxically, Plato's ideal *polis* diverged fundamentally from the idea that the citizens should rule themselves, which lay behind the historical practice of the *poleis*. Aristotle later reacted against Plato's vision of a perfect *polis* remote from empirical reality and insisted that understanding the *polis* must be rooted in detailed examination of the actual workings of different *poleis*.

In the *Republic* Plato, while fiercely critical of Athenian democracy, incorporates into his model of the perfect *polis* elements that reflect the ideals of Sparta, Athens' great rival, to whom she eventually lost the Peloponnesian War in 404. The two *poleis* were opposed during the fifth century not only as military and

---

[1] It was similar to the ideal society of Rousseau's *Social Contract*. There the general will, which identifies the good of the community as a whole, can emerge only in an assembly of the whole community of citizens and only when they talk face to face. However, while the citizens in Rousseau's theory make the laws, they leave the routine of governing to delegated officials. In the classical age of Athenian democracy the citizens made few laws, having inherited their basic laws from past lawmakers like Solon, but they did make day-to-day decisions on policies that were to govern the *polis*.

naval powers but also ideologically. Whereas Athens stood for individualism and an open society, Sparta's aristocratic rulers favoured conformity and a closed society.

During and after the Peloponnesian War the Athenian *polis* suffered some moral decay and an increase of factionalism. Athenian democracy and civilization lost some of their vigour and self-confidence, although their decline tended to be exaggerated by contemporary critics. Athens did suffer from increasing internal discord and from a declining sense of civic responsibility, but her democracy still functioned and her cultural and intellectual life still flourished. Plato himself was a proof of that.

Plato was born in 428/7, a few years after the beginning of the Peloponnesian War, and died in 348/7, nine years before the *poleis* were absorbed into the Macedonian Empire. He had direct knowledge of Athens only during her relative decline after the period of her greatest glory. As an aristocrat yearning for order and stability, he was one of those who exaggerated the excesses of Athenian democracy. He was also profoundly affected by the death of Socrates, the great philosopher and teacher. Socrates was condemned to death in 399 for allegedly corrupting the youth of Athens, although he was in fact a strong patriot who prescribed moral discipline. For Plato the death of Socrates was unambiguous confirmation of the moral degradation of the Athenian democracy. The *Republic* was partly a reaction to what Plato regarded as the irresponsible individualism of undisciplined democracy. Living in an unstable world of war, factionalism, and political unscrupulousness, Plato sought in the *Republic* a permanent universe of moral truths.

He believed that some of the moral decadence that he perceived in Athens was encouraged by the Sophists, who taught philosophy in contemporary Athens and challenged traditional beliefs. In the *Republic* Plato tried to refute their arguments, which, he thought, undermined morality and stability. The Sophists were teachers of practical morality, but Plato condemned them for superficiality and alleged that they taught people merely to be clever talkers. Although the Sophists placed men at the centre of their enquiries and applied reason to ethics and politics, Plato thought that they argued for the sake of argument, without respect for truth and morality. Where Plato sought certainty, the Sophists encouraged doubt. By arguing that morals were the product of convention, not nature, the Sophists presented the case for moral relativism, which Plato hated.

The Opening Arguments of the *Republic*

The best way to study the *Republic*[2] is first to read it straight through without delaying over difficult passages, in order to gain an impression of the general shape, style, and content of Plato's argument; and then to reread it, examining in depth the most crucial parts of the argument. This commentary suggests that certain sections of the *Republic*, detailed references to which will appear below, are particularly important in the central enquiry into the nature of justice, although each reader is entitled to make his own judgement on this, especially as he becomes more familiar with the book. Plato, of course, intended the dialogue to form a continuous whole, but the modern reader nevertheless is likely to find some parts less worthy of close study than others if his primary purpose is to follow Plato's argument about what justice is. For example, the disquisitions on censorship of the arts and on the immortality of the soul, while not irrelevant to Plato's account of justice, are not vital to its definition.

The *Republic* is written in the form of a dialogue between Socrates,[3] Plato's teacher, and a group of his Athenian friends. The purpose of the dialogue is to discover the nature of justice.[4] In the first part of the book Socrates elicits from his friends some

---

[2] The edition specially recommended, because it is intended to be as literal a translation of the Greek text as possible, is: The Republic *of Plato*, translated, with notes and an interpretative essay, by A. Bloom (Basic Books, New York, 1968). A satisfactory alternative at a lower price is: Plato, *The Republic*, translated by A. D. Lindsay (Dent, London, 1984). See the bibliographical note for a fuller explanation of these recommendations. The quotations from the *Republic* in this chapter are from the Bloom edition. References are given in the text to pages in Bloom and to the section numbers common to most editions of the *Republic*. Where the section numbers in the text do not follow quotations, the page numbers in both Bloom and Lindsay are given in the footnotes.

[3] Scholars have debated how far the historical Socrates resembled the Socrates of the dialogue. However, the arguments in the dialogue are interesting in their own right, irrespective of whether Plato reproduced Socrates' opinions accurately or not. All references here to Socrates will be to the figure in the dialogue, without any implication that what he says is what Socrates would actually have said.

[4] Justice has remained a central concern of political philosophy since Plato. See, for example, Aristotle, Augustine, Hobbes, and, among our contemporaries, John Rawls, whose modern classic is called *A Theory of Justice*.

ideas on justice and demonstrates their inadequacies (327a–367a),[5] before proceeding later in the book to remedy those inadequacies by elaborating his own conception of justice. The ideas on justice that are put forward by the other figures in the dialogue are common-sense ideas that were widely held at the time and which have commanded much support since. The dialogue tries to show how to move from the imperfections of common understanding to the correctness that results from philosophical argument. Philosophy starts, therefore, as the elucidation of what the non-philosopher already knows implicitly, incompletely, imprecisely, and inchoately, although, as the argument in the *Republic* progresses, Plato envisages philosophy going beyond and above mere clarification and correction of common usage.

The first idea of justice to be considered in the dialogue emerges incidentally during an explanation of the value of wealth by Cephalus, for whom justice seems to be honesty in money matters. Socrates moves towards giving this notion more precision by asking if justice is 'the truth and giving back what a man has taken from another' (331c, p. 7). Socrates does not fully explain what this definition means before going on to criticize it, but it is implicit in his criticism that the definition under consideration is telling the truth and repaying what we have borrowed because we have promised to. Throughout history keeping promises has been regarded as a central part of justice, and for Hobbes keeping promises, or more precisely, keeping covenants, was the entirety of justice. Socrates, however, argues that it is not always just to repay debts and to tell the truth. If you borrow a knife from a man, you should not give it back to him if he has gone mad, presumably because he might attack you or other people with it. Similarly you should not tell such a madman the whole truth. If he asks you where you have hidden his knife, which you have refused to return to him, you should not tell him.

The basic argument that Socrates is advancing seems to be that there is no obligation to tell the truth and keep promises if very unpleasant consequences would follow. It is an argument that appeals to those for whom a good act is one that increases pleasure and decreases pain, but is unacceptable to those for whom the obligation not to tell lies and to keep promises is absolute. We can

---

[5] Bloom, pp. 1–44; Lindsay, pp. 1–46.

adapt an illustration that Kant uses[6] in order to demonstrate the weakness of Socrates' position. A man promises to execute the will of his friend, but nothing is written down, so that only the author and the executor of the will know its contents. When his friend dies, the executor discovers that those to whom his friend wished to leave his money are extremely rich and thoroughly evil, while he himself and his family are destitute and highly virtuous. The executor would receive more pleasure from the money than the intended heirs, who have more money than they know what to do with, and, in addition, the executor deserves some reward for his moral superiority. Yet a child of eight, according to Kant, would not think that the executor has any moral grounds for breaking his promise. Socrates by contrast seems in his first major intervention in the *Republic* to be undermining the sanctity of promises, which is ironic in view of his general stance in the dialogue (and in life) of defending pure virtue against short-term, hedonistic self-interest.

It is possible that Socrates is implying not that one should refuse to return a knife to a madman because unpleasant consequences would follow, but rather because the madman is 'out of his mind' and therefore not the same person to whom one made the promise. However, Socrates would not then be showing, as he intends, that it can be just to break a promise. For, in not returning the knife, one has not broken a promise: the promise was to return the knife to, let us say, Smith, but at present Smith does not exist and one cannot return the knife to him, since his body is now possessed by non-Smith, the madman, the non-person. The promise cannot be kept, but is not being broken.

The dialogue moves on to another formulation of justice when Polemarchus, defending the view of justice as keeping promises and telling the truth, suggests that this is part of a broader conception of justice, giving to each what is owed. This general, although imprecise, notion of justice would have commanded widespread acceptance in Plato's time and does so now. Yet Socrates is not happy with it. To show its imperfection he first persuades Polemarchus to translate the notion of what is owing or fitting into 'doing good to friends and harm to enemies' (332d, p. 8), which sounds more like partiality than justice. A further stage

[6] In *On the Common Saying: 'This May be True in Theory, but it does not Apply in Practice'* (in H. Reiss (ed.), *Kant's Political Writings* (Cambridge, 1970), pp. 70–1).

in the argument, however, redefines justice as doing good to those who are good, who are your real friends, and doing harm to those who are bad, who are your real enemies. This is recognizable as a commonly understood form of justice, which is used in enforcing moral or legal rules.

Socrates now launches a major attack on the idea of justice as doing good to the good and harm to the bad on the grounds that it cannot be just to harm anyone, since harming people makes them more unjust. This sounds odd. Socrates starts to defend this position by comparing men with horses and dogs. We shall take and elaborate the argument about dogs. Harming them makes them worse 'with respect to the virtue of dogs' (335b, p. 12). What is meant is that cutting a dog's hamstring, for example, makes the dog less good as a dog. The question arises: what makes a dog a dog? The zoologist might define dogginess differently from the hunter or the pet-owner. To make sense of our example about cutting a hamstring, let us suppose that the dog is a hunter. In this case, cutting a hamstring, which is harming the dog, makes him less good as a dog, whose dogginess consists in being a hunter and hence fleet of foot.

It is vital now to explore the concept of 'virtue' as it appears in the phrase 'with respect to the virtue of dogs', because 'virtue' does not mean what it usually means in modern English, namely, moral quality, and is a key concept in the *Republic*. The original Greek word is *arete*, which could be translated as 'specific excellence'. This is the quality that enables an animal or person (or object) to reach its intrinsic, essential fulfilment. Fleetness then might be the virtue of a hunting dog; and, according to Socrates, justice is the 'virtue' of a human being. As fleetness is the quality that enables a dog to become more dog-like, so justice is the quality that enables a human being to become more human. Therefore, as harming a dog, by cutting its hamstring, makes the dog less fleet, and consequently less dog-like, so harming a man makes him less just, and consequently less human.

The idea of justice as 'virtue' can be further elucidated by jumping ahead in the dialogue (352d–353e)[7] to the point where it is asserted that the soul (the Greek word is *psyche*, which incorporates not only man's spiritual side, but also his thoughts and

---

[7] Bloom, pp. 32–3; Lindsay, pp. 32–3.

feelings) has a 'virtue', justice, which enables it to do its 'work' (*ergon*—a common translation is 'function').[8] So, justice, rather than being the 'virtue' of a human being as a whole, as was implied earlier, is redefined more precisely as the 'virtue' of the human soul. The 'work' of each thing, including the soul, is 'what it alone can do, or can do more finely than other things' (353a, p. 32). 'Virtue' is the quality that enables a thing to do its work. In explaining the notion of work Socrates takes the example of the pruning knife. Its special work is to prune vines. A hammer could not do that work at all and a dagger would do it less efficiently. The 'virtue' of a pruning knife would be—this is my guess, Socrates does not specify this—the particular curve of its blade. Similarly, twenty-twenty vision is the 'virtue' of the eyes enabling them to do their 'work' of seeing; roundness is the 'virtue' of the ball enabling it to do its work of rolling; and fleetness is the 'virtue' that enables a dog to do its 'work' of hunting.

The 'work' of the soul, Socrates asserts, is 'managing, ruling and deliberating', and 'living'. Precisely what the soul manages and rules is not specified, but probably Plato meant that the soul should manage and rule the whole man, including his physical bits. The soul's work was partly to provide a life-plan for the total person. By deliberating the soul would work out the (moral) goals that one should move towards. Saying that the work of the soul is 'living' is not very helpful, but one can guess, on the basis of later arguments in the *Republic*, that Plato means living the good, or the moral, life, which reason dictates. Justice is the 'virtue' of the soul and as such helps the soul to do its work of managing and ruling the total person, deliberating, and living the good life. What precisely is the content of this justice that enables the soul to do its work remains at this stage of the argument unrevealed.

We can now return to the assertion that harming a man makes him less just (335c).[9] If you harm someone, you impair that quality, justice, which is necessary for his soul to perform those functions that make him a full human being. In a way, one can now understand why Socrates rejects a definition of justice that involves deliberately harming people. Yet Plato does not show precisely how harming a man by, for example, sending him into

---

[8] See p. 42 on Aristotle's use of this concept.
[9] Bloom, p. 12; Lindsay, p. 11.

exile will *necessarily* take away the faculty that would enable him to develop his full human potentialities.

One has, furthermore, to take on trust the assertion that the work of the soul is deliberating, etc. and that the 'virtue' of the soul is justice. Could one not argue either that the soul does not have any built-in ends or that they are not those that Socrates claims for it? Also, one could challenge the assertion that it is justice that is the 'virtue' of the soul, or at least, one could if one knew what justice was, and one could suggest instead that some other quality was the 'virtue' of the soul enabling it to achieve its ends.

Plato may seem open to the charge that he is merely asserting that justice is the 'virtue' of the soul and that the form of his argument against Polemarchus is only to replace one conception of justice with another. However, there is more to it than that: Plato believes that those who are superficially attracted to common definitions of justice like those of Polemarchus and the others in the dialogue will come to recognize that deep down they too believe in the one offered by Socrates.

Plato's denial that justice can entail harming those that are bad raises the difficulty that it seems to rule out the possibility of justly punishing anyone. Surely it is just to fine a convicted criminal, although to fine someone is to harm him. Part of the nature of punishment is to inflict harm, either as retribution, or to deter the criminal from further crime, or to reform his character. If harming people is unjust, retributive or deterrent punishment is certainly unjust, and therefore morally impermissible. Yet this conclusion would conflict with many people's moral convictions. Plato might wish to argue that reformative punishment does not harm a person, but only improves or helps him, although it is questionable whether an action done to a person purely in order to reform him is strictly speaking punishment at all.

Socrates, having dismissed to his own satisfaction the suggestion that justice is doing good to the good and harm to the bad, next takes on the Sophist Thrasymachus, who is less of a stooge for Socrates than the others in the dialogue and pugnaciously defends his own position. Thrasymachus states that justice is 'the advantage of the stronger' and 'the stronger' is taken to mean the 'ruling group' (338c–339a, pp. 15–16). The ruler decides which mode of conduct in his subjects will best advantage him, calls this justice, and demands that they conform to it. This approach to justice may seem cynical to some, but realistic to others, who think that it lets a breath of fresh air into the otherwise stuffy and impractical world of moral philosophizing. In alleging that moral talk is a veil for the ruler's self-interest Thrasymachus' discourse has a similar flavour to Machiavelli's *Prince*.

Against Socrates' assumption that justice can be objectively determined, Thrasymachus implies that justice is purely subjective. If rulers determine morality in their own interest, then morality may differ with different rulers. Thrasymachus thus interestingly anticipates Marx, who argues that governments usually act on behalf of a dominant economic class and support a morality designed to advance the economic interests of that class.

Socrates begins his refutation of Thrasymachus by persuading him to make his definition of justice more precise: justice is what the ruler commands when that is to his advantage and he makes no mistakes about what is to his advantage. Then Socrates goes a step further and claims that a ruler is a ruler in the strict sense only when he does not make mistakes, just as a doctor is only really a doctor when he is not making mistakes. According to Socrates, someone who in his field of expertise does not make mistakes we call a craftsman: when a craftsman makes a mistake, he is not at that moment acting as a craftsman. So Socrates edges Thrasymachus into accepting the statement that a ruler is a craftsman and at this point Socrates strikes to destroy Thrasymachus' definition of justice. Again Socrates presses the analogy between the doctor and the ruler. The doctor when he is acting as a doctor is concerned with looking after the sick. Similarly, the ruler when he is acting as a ruler considers the advantage of the ruled. The craftsman, whether doctor or ruler, is not, as a craftsman, interested in his own benefit, although as a private man he may seek good wages for doing his craft. A craft does not essentially consist in securing the advantage of the craftsman. A craftsman by definition is concerned with the 'advantage' of the subject-matter of his craft: the doctor with his patients, the cobbler, presumably, with his shoes, and the ruler with the ruled.

Thrasymachus makes a crushing reply: shepherds and cowherds do not fatten sheep and cows for the good of the sheep and the cows! Socrates' rejoinder is little more than to claim that indeed they do. The defence of his position might insist that strictly speaking the job of the shepherd is to improve the lot of the sheep by ensuring that they have plenty of succulent grass and that it is the craft of the butcher, not the shepherd, to kill the fattened sheep for meat. This would be of little consolation to the sheep, and the analogy would not prevent Thrasymachus from arguing that rulers, if they 'fatten' their subjects, do it only to tax them. In other words, one craftsman might be expert at both fattening and killing. Socrates' argument against Thrasymachus' claim that justice is the advantage of the stronger depends on the validity of the comparison between rulers and craftsmen such as doctors. Merely because it is important for both categories of men not to make mistakes does not in itself prove that rulers are by definition caring craftsmen.

After defending his contention that justice is the advantage of the stronger, Thrasymachus advances the unambiguously cynical proposition that injustice is virtuous and wise. Consequently, justice is 'very high-minded innocence' (348c, p. 26) and, if you can get away with injustice, it is wise to do so. Again there is a fore-shadowing of Machiavelli, who in the *Prince* states that 'by no means can a prudent ruler keep his word'.[10] Socrates' reply is elaborate and consists of three counter-arguments.

First, he argues that the just man does not want to get the better of everyone, but only the unjust. Socrates again brings craftsmen into the argument. He claims that a musician in tuning a lyre, for example, is not interested in trying to do better than another musician engaged on a similar job, but tries merely to perfect his technical skills, measuring his performance against a professional standard. It follows that not competing with fellow craftsmen is wise, and therefore good, Socrates assuming that what is wise is necessarily good. Then he argues that the just man, like the musician, does not wish to get the better of others like himself: the musician does not compete with other musicians trying to reach similar professional standards to his own; the just man does not compete with other just men trying to reach similar standards of justice to his own. The musician tries to get the better only of the unmusical, the just man tries to get the better only of the unjust. The just man in not trying to get the better of other just men is, like the musician, wise and good.

Socrates' second argument against Thrasymachus' defence of

---

[10] J. Plamenatz (ed.), *Machiavelli* (London, 1972), p. 107.

injustice is that injustice is inferior to justice because it is divisive. There are two subsections to this argument. The first point is pure common sense: the pursuit of injustice creates factions between men. The second point is that injustice makes a man 'not of one mind with himself' (352a, p. 31), in other words, 'at faction' with himself. Socrates assumes that the unjust man will be divided within himself, ambivalent and uneasy about his chosen course of action. The full explanation of this does not come till later in the dialogue where Plato shows that the soul has different parts. If a man were acting unjustly, his passions would be in conflict with his reason, which seeks justice.

The third argument against the wisdom of injustice we have already had cause to examine: the soul has a 'virtue', justice, that enables it to do its 'work', deliberating, self-management, and living well. If a man acts justly and thus enables the soul to do its 'work', that man will be happy (unlike the man rendered uneasy by the pursuit of injustice). Since justice is by definition 'virtue' of the soul, it is necessarily virtuous and its opposite, injustice, is not virtuous, contrary to Thrasymachus' assertion. Also, since justice enables the soul to lead the good life and since the man who lives the good life is happy, justice is wise, and not injustice, as Thrasymachus claimed. (What at this stage one has to take on trust is that the man who lives the good life is indeed happy. Why this is so, Plato explains later in the dialogue.)

The next person after Thrasymachus to engage Socrates is Glaucon, who invites Socrates to deal with the Sophist belief that justice, like gymnastics, is not good in itself, but good only for its effects. Glaucon puts forward two arguments to support this case, the first of which assumes that men are naturally selfish (Plato will later deny this) and therefore ready to act unjustly if they can get away with it. However, since 'the bad in suffering injustice far exceeds the good in doing it' (358e, p. 36), men decide that it is in their interest to avoid a situation in which they could inflict injustice on others but others could inflict injustice on them. They make a compact not to do any injustice and 'name what the law commands lawful and just' (359a, p. 37). Glaucon's argument here bears some resemblance to Hobbes's reasoning in *Leviathan*.

The second argument that Glaucon floats is that men may have the sense to calculate whether justice is advantageous or not, and that such a calculation might well show that an unjust man with a reputation for justice wins more wordly success than a just man with a reputation for injustice. So it is appearances that bring rewards. This second argument that Glaucon advances, like the first, assumes that men are inherently self-interested. They are concerned only with whether just and unjust actions will increase their happiness, not whether an act is right. Machiavelli in the *Prince* seems to advocate a similarly amoral morality: 'for a prince, then, it is not necessary actually to have all the above-mentioned qualities, but it is very necessary to appear to have them'.[11]

The first part of the dialogue in which Socrates and his companions discuss popular notions of justice concludes with an argument from Adeimantus in support of the proposal by Glaucon that men should calculate carefully whether to act justly or not. Glaucon has argued that injustice may be more profitable than justice, provided that the unjust man appears to be acting justly. Adeimantus, on the other hand, starts by suggesting that justice is valuable for the reputation that it brings. If you win a good reputation, material rewards will follow. Then Adeimantus acknowledges that, on the other hand, a just life may prove to be unprofitable and asks Socrates to give a profit and loss account of acting justly.

Justice in the City and the Soul

Socrates prepares to answer the questions raised in the dialogue up to this point about the nature of justice and the benefits that it brings by an investigation into what the just city (*polis*)[12] would

---

[11] Plamenatz, *Machiavelli*, p. 108.

[12] *Polis* is sometimes translated as 'city-state', but Bloom renders it as 'city', on the grounds that to include the word 'state' 'implies that our [modern] notion of state is somehow contained in that of the *polis*, although only half-consciously' (p. 439). However, it is doubtful whether the use of 'state' in fact does suggest a *very* close resemblance of the *polis* to the modern state. If the phrase 'city-state' indicates *some* significant similarities between the *polis* and modern concepts of the state, that is arguably useful, since the idea of the *polis* has strongly influenced modern thinking about the state. In principle, the *polis* was the sole source of law and had authority in all spheres of human behaviour, thus foreshadowing notions of sovereignty in modern theories of the state. Furthermore, the same sort of objection that Bloom makes to the translation of *polis* as 'city-state' could be made to his translation, 'city': the word 'city' conveys notions associated with the modern city, whereas the Greek city was significantly different. 'City' has come to mean a large town where a large number of people live close together, whereas for the Greeks it signified a special form of social and political organization. Bloom's translation 'city' also has the disadvantage, as 'city-state' does, that it takes no account of the rural population, who were the majority of the citizen body.

be like (367e–427c).[13] People have different needs, and in the just
city everyone by using his special ability will help to satisfy
others' needs. Each person has a particular nature (*physis*),[14]
which fits him for a particular kind of 'work' (*ergon*) (370a).[15]
Those who guard the city, the guardians, would by nature be
'spirited' (the word is a central one in the dialogue) and hence
courageous, and lovers of wisdom, or philosophers (philosopher
literally means 'lover of wisdom'—what kind of wisdom the
guardians must love is explained later in the dialogue). There are
two types of guardian, the full guardians, whose work is to be
philosophers, and the younger guardians, whom he calls auxiliaries, whose work is to be soldiers.

After a long section on the education and style of life that the
guardians need in order to develop their philosophic and spirited
natures (376c–427c),[16] Socrates elaborates in a crucial passage his
own understanding of justice (427c–445b).[17] He starts by discussing those qualities that are vital to the good city: wisdom, courage, moderation, and justice. The modern reader might well find
this a somewhat arbitrary list and want to make some amend-
ments to it, but Plato is here merely reproducing what were
regarded as the essential civic qualities in ancient Greece. These
four qualities together form the 'city's virtue' (433e, p. 112), by
which it is able to do its 'work' (these concepts we examined
above in looking at justice as the 'virtue' of the soul).

Wisdom, Socrates says, is a special 'kind of knowledge that
counsels . . . about how the city as a whole would best deal with
itself and the other cities' (428c–d, p. 106) and is only to be found
in the philosopher guardians, who form the smallest group in any
city. Plato has a very particular form of knowledge in mind
which he explains later in the dialogue. (See below the section on
philosophy and philosophers.)

Courage, the meaning of which one might think would be
obvious, curiously is said to be preserving 'the opinion about

---

[13] Bloom, pp. 44–105; Lindsay, pp. 46–113.

[14] See p. 42 for a discussion of Aristotle's use of this concept.

[15] Bloom, p. 46, has 'job' here, although in the passage about dogs he has 'work', while
Lindsay, p. 48, who has 'function' in the dogs passage, has 'work' in this passage about
nature!

[16] Bloom, pp. 54–105; Lindsay, pp. 57–113. The education of the guardians is also discussed further in 521c–541b; Bloom, pp. 200–20; Lindsay, pp. 214–37.

[17] Bloom, pp. 105–25; Lindsay, pp. 113–35.

which things are terrible' (429b–c, p. 107). The precise significance of this phrase is difficult to fathom, but Plato may be referring to the fact that a person cannot be accounted courageous if he
is not conscious of the dangers that he is facing. As wisdom is to
be found exclusively in the philosopher guardians, courage is the
special characteristic of the auxiliary soldiers (although the philosopher guardians are also courageous).

The third quality, moderation, is the harmony of all parts of
the city that comes from mastery of the desires of 'the many',
those who are not guardians or auxiliaries, by the desires and prudence of 'the few', the guardians and the auxiliaries. Plato does
not regard conflicts of interest as an inevitable feature of society
and consequently does not regard the handling of such conflicts as
a principal task of the rulers. Rousseau was to agree with him.
They both believed that if people recognized what their real ends
were, a harmonious society without conflict would result.

Socrates is now ready to reveal the nature of justice, since, he
claims, justice is the means of achieving harmony, or moderation,
in the city. The final revelation is an anticlimax: justice is 'the
minding of one's own business' (433a, p. 111) and not interfering
with that which others are best fitted to do. Each of the three
main groups within the city, the philosopher guardians, the soldier auxiliaries, and the money-makers (all the other people in the
city, including farmers, craftsmen, merchants, traders, and
labourers) must each do what it is by nature fitted to do and must
not try to do what the others can do better. The guardians must
rule, the auxiliaries must be soldiers, and the rest of the citizens
must do whatever they are specially able to do, like mending
shoes, growing vines, or selling knives. If each keeps to his own
'work', harmony will prevail in the city, but if any meddle in
things in which they have no natural competence, there will be
disorder and injustice. The worst injustice occurs if the money-
makers meddle in what the soldiers and the rulers are naturally
skilled at, for this will destroy the city. In other words, democracy
is unjust.

The four cardinal qualities of the city depend on each other. If
the guardians exercise their wisdom and the auxiliaries their courage, they will rule and defend the city and hence will be acting
justly. If the money-makers do not interfere with the work of the
guardians and the auxiliaries, they will be acting justly. From the

just behaviour of all the citizens moderation, or harmony, will ensue.

Minding one's own business is not what Plato's contemporaries immediately thought of as justice and intuitively we may want to insist that it is not what we mean by justice. However, there is a sense in which Plato's idiosyncratic definition of justice does have some connection with one of the traditional ideas of justice that Socrates earlier in the dialogue has considered and dismissed, namely giving each what is owing to him. Encouraging each person to do what he is specially fitted for is one way of giving people what is owing to them. Whatever doubts one may have about Plato's definition of justice, his defence of each doing what he is best fitted for by nature deserves sympathetic consideration. There would be something perverse about a skilful cobbler spending his life inefficiently soldiering or a clever administrator devoting himself to making ill-fitting shoes, although some liberals would defend a person's right to do whatever he chooses, whether he did it well or not and whether or not there was any demand for whatever he produced (e.g. bad government, uncomfortable shoes). Also, Plato assumes that each person will have only one special skill, so that it will be easy to find what is his natural occupation. However, people may be equally skilled at several activities, for example, at philosophy, cooking, and horse-riding. If a person has more than one special aptitude, should he not be allowed to choose whether he becomes a philosopher guardian or a shoemaker, or whether to do a bit of ruling and a bit of cobbling?

After defining justice in the city, Socrates proceeds to argue that there is a comparable justice in the soul (we now discover more precisely why justice is the 'virtue' of the soul). This idea depends on there being three parts in the soul, just as there are three groups in the city. The parts in the soul are the reasoning part, the desiring part, and the 'spirited' part. The rational part can come into conflict with the desiring part, which is, according to Socrates, irrational. In such an internal conflict the 'spirited' part sometimes enters on the side of the rational part. (Is it always true, as Plato asserts, that the 'spirited', angry part always supports the rational rather than the desiring part? Temper might seem a more natural ally of the passions.) Just as the guardian philosophers should rule those who are unphilosophical, so the reasoning part of the soul, which can plan for the future, should rule the non-reasoning, desiring part of the soul, which is interested only in immediate gratification. When the reasoning part, aided by the 'spirited' part, rules the desiring part, there is moderation within the soul, just as there is moderation within the city when the guardians, aided by the auxiliaries, rule the money-makers. When each part of the soul minds its own business, there is justice in the soul, just as there is justice in the city when each of the three groups of citizens minds its own business. In both city and soul injustice prevails when the parts interfere with each other's specialisms: the money-makers must not rule, nor must the desires.

Socrates is now able to deal with the suggestion made earlier in the dialogue that injustice is wise and profitable. Justice entails the mastery by reason of the desires, which, Socrates asserts, is in accordance with nature. Since justice ensures this right balance in the soul, there can be no doubt that it is wise and profitable for all individuals. A man can fulfil himself and enjoy internal calm only if he is just. Only if a man behaves justly, will he be completely happy. Justice, then, is good for the happiness that it brings to those who practise it, as well as being good in itself.[18]

Plato's notion of justice in the soul is unique and curious. Justice has come to be conceived as establishing right relations between men. A just man is someone who behaves correctly to other men; for example, he keeps promises, he treats equals equally, he gives others their due. For Plato justice is concerned not only with the ordering of relations between men, but also with the ordering of the parts within a man. Is his argument convincing? Certainly he shows parallels between justice in the city and justice in the soul, as he conceives them. However, the parallels are persuasive only if there really are three distinct parts in the soul, as there are three distinct groups in the city—and both divisions could be challenged.

The tripartite division of the soul may seem a crude theory of human psychology, especially if compared with more sophisticated, empirically based theories worked out in the twentieth century. Yet there are interesting similarities between Plato's theory of the mind and Freud's. Is it too fanciful to see Plato's reasoning part corresponding to Freud's super-ego, the internalized parent

---

[18] Later in the dialogue Plato again takes up the theme that the just man is the happiest (588b–592a; Bloom, pp. 270–4; Lindsay, pp. 290–5).

laying down norms of behaviour, with Plato's 'spirited' part resembling the Freud's ego, the assertive self, and Plato's desiring part anticipating Freud's id, the libidinous instinct? Whether this is convincing or not, Western civilization has followed Plato in making a clear distinction between reason and the passions. Hobbes, for example, can be seen doing so in *Leviathan*. Many thinkers have accepted Plato's belief that reason alone could decide what was morally good and his conviction that one should support reason against the desires, which are portrayed as selfish, but self-destructive. Rousseau, for example, demanded that 'individuals must be obliged to subordinate their will to their reason' and claimed that 'to be governed by appetite alone is slavery'.[19]

Plato's arguments for the dominance of reason have been influential, but have not gone unchallenged. His claim that the desires are necessarily short-sighted, self-indulgent, and destructive of true humanity needs to be subjected to scrutiny. The opposite view can be represented by the novelist D. H. Lawrence, who saw cold, analytic reason as destructive of good human relations and placed great faith in the creative power of one particular 'desire', love. Some philosophers, like Augustine and David Hume, have stressed the limitations of reason, arguing that only desires can move men to act. Reason by its very nature can only show logical relationships and facts, neither of which provides motives for action. Reason, for example, can show that driving drunkenly causes death on the roads, but that is not a motive for driving soberly. The motive for driving soberly comes from the desire to avoid killing people. Reason merely tells one how to satisfy this desire.

One important question raised by Plato's treatment of justice is how precisely justice in the city is related to justice in the soul. It seems as if justice in the city depends on justice in the soul. If men had unjust souls and therefore allowed their desires to govern their conduct, they would not, presumably, recognize the need to do only what they were good at and would meddle in others' affairs. Money-makers would dabble in ruling and injustice would swamp the city. In this sense, justice in the soul is more fundamental than justice in the city: justice in the city is almost a reflection of justice in the soul.

---

[19] *The Social Contract*, ed. M. Cranston (Harmondsworth, 1968), I, ch. 8 and II, ch. 6.

A problem arises from this analysis. If, as Plato indicates, reason predominates in the souls of the philosopher guardians, 'spirit' in the souls of the auxiliary soldiers, and desires in the souls of the money-makers, how could anyone other than the philosophers have just souls and how could there ever be a just city, which rests on *all* the citizens having just souls? The answer would seem to lie in arguing that the money-makers, although in danger of being dominated by their desires, which form the largest part of their souls, can (perhaps with some guidance from the guardians) ensure that their small stock of reason nevertheless is in control of their souls. They need just enough reason to recognize that they have insufficient reason, unlike the philosophers, to rule either themselves or the city well. Similarly, the auxiliaries presumably have the rational capacity to recognize their rational short-comings. Plato can be optimistic that the philosophers, well-endowed with reason, will use that reason to govern their souls, but he might have to acknowledge that the many whose reason is weaker are likely often to let their passions take over and to insti-tute the reign of injustice.

For Plato justice is the primary moral value and is intrinsically linked with other essential moral qualities. It is vital for order within the soul and within the city. It is essential if the individual and the city are to reach their full potentialities. For the individual justice entails rationality and self-restraint and guarantees fulfil-ment and happiness. In the city justice requires wisdom and spiritedness in the guardians and it results in moderation, or harmony, for all.

Philosophers and Philosophy

In the just city the philosopher guardians are particularly suited to rule. In a passage that is crucial for understanding Plato's concep-tion of justice he explains precisely the nature of the wisdom that philosophers love and the reason why possession of this particular kind of wisdom qualifies them to rule (473c–521b).[20]

The philosopher by definition loves *all* wisdom, not just some, and consequently no falsehood. He is interested only in the pleasures of the soul, not those of the body, and therefore has no

---

[20] Bloom, pp. 153–200; Lindsay, pp. 166–214.

use for money. Since he contemplates the whole of time and being, he regards his own life as relatively unimportant and he is unafraid of dying. Although philosophers ought to become kings, not all those with philosophical inclinations would wish to become rulers. Some potential philosophers would give up philosophy because they were corrupted by the unphilosophical. Some true philosophers would ignore politics because they found distasteful the 'madness of the many' (496c, p. 176), which causes bad government. Those philosophers who did rule in the just city would have to possess a particular kind of wisdom. When Plato says that philosophers must be kings, he is not only saying that rulers should have some considered theory of knowledge, he is saying that they should have true knowledge, a knowledge of what *is*, permanently, not merely of what *appears* to be, momentarily.

The proper philosophers' knowledge is of 'forms', which may be interpreted as essences or ideals. These forms are found by reason and are to be contrasted with appearances, which are apprehended by 'opinion' (or 'belief', *doxa*). A quality or a thing has many appearances, but only one form. To illustrate this theory of knowledge we can take the idea of justice (although Plato does not at this stage in the argument). For Plato there are many appearances of justice, which are not the real thing; for example, the different notions of justice discussed early in the *Republic*, the many formulations of justice that have been accepted in different societies throughout history, and the manifestations of justice in particular just acts. None of these is justice itself; each is a fleeting and distorted reflection of real justice, of the form or essence of justice. The form of justice is, according to Plato, minding your own business.

By 'opinion' Plato means a kind of superficial understanding that stands between true knowledge (of forms) and total ignorance. Under 'opinion' he would include 'knowledge' of facts (this is not real knowledge, since it is not of forms) and common-sense moral beliefs. To take again the example of justice, 'opinion' would embrace factual 'knowledge' of magistrates acting justly in lawcourts and notions of justice like the award of gold stars to children for good behaviour.

Whereas 'opinion' grasps only ephemeral events, genuine knowledge apprehends unchanging forms. Reason transcends the world of mere appearances with which 'opinion' is concerned and discovers the forms, or ideal types, or basic models, from which the objects of our experience derive their intelligibility. Thinking about our everyday experience of justice, for example, and analysing our everyday usage of the word 'justice', the philosopher can reach upwards to an ideal or perfection of justice that makes sense of the previously unordered and not fully understood experience and usage. We have seen in the *Republic* itself the elements of this process of using 'opinion' as a platform from which to discover knowledge. The forms in some way always have existed and always will exist, ready to be discovered by reason, or, to put it another way, whenever philosophers use reason, they will come to the same conclusions about what the forms are. Since reason does not change, the forms do not change. In a world of flux the forms remain constant. The philosopher can escape from the shifting sands of the world he experiences to the fixed forms of the world that his reason can discover. It is not an escape from reality, for it is the forms that are real, because they are rational and permanent, while the 'real' world of experience is ultimately illusion.

It is not just moral qualities like justice that have forms: there are forms of, for example, chair, or university, or blueness. The Platonic philosopher might seek the form or essence of 'chairness'; he would look for the form of the chair that makes intelligible our application of the word 'chair' to a variety of different objects. What is the essence of chairness? What is merely accidental or incidental among the qualities of the chairs that we know of? Chairs may have four legs, or three, or none; some chairs are made of wood, others of metal or plastic; some chairs are brown, others white, or black. None of these characteristics of chairs—the number of legs, what they are made of, their colour—tells us what a chair essentially is. The philosopher might eventually come to the conclusion that what is essential to 'chairness' is its function: it is made to sit on, as distinct from a table, for example, which is made to put things on. So there is a form of a chair, its being made to sit on, which exists for reason to discover. You cannot lift or smell the form of the chair, for it is the product of reason. None of the chairs that you can lift or smell tell you what the form of the chair is: the form is distinct from any appearance, it exists only in the mind of the philosopher. But the form of the chair is real and unchanging, whereas the chairs that we see and kick are not real and have a limited life, they will disappear one day from destruction or decay.

The concept of form is central in Plato's theory of knowledge, but he also uses in the *Republic* another key concept, 'idea', which has a similar meaning. It is open to interpretation whether 'idea' is just another name for 'form', or whether it is something subtly different. Plato uses the notion of idea in the phrase, 'the idea of the good' (505a, p. 184).[21] This is the ultimate object of the philosopher's search; the idea of the good is greater than the form of justice. In some not clearly specified way the idea of the good is 'beyond' the forms such as justice and necessary for their full understanding. The idea of the good is like the sun. Just as the eyes need light from the sun in order to see colour, so souls need light from knowledge of the idea of the good in order to have full knowledge of the forms, including that of justice. Plato does not explain what the idea of the good is, nor how the philosopher will find it. Presumably one cannot understand it without undergoing the long and elaborate education that he lays down for his philosophers. The idea of the good does not seem to bear the same relation to the forms as they do to appearances: the good does not seem to be a distillation of the just and the moderate and the other moral forms. Reason is supposed to be crucial in the discovery of the idea of the good, as it is for the discovery of the forms, but there does at this point in the argument seem also to be almost an element of mysticism. The idea of the good is beyond explanation. After long processes of reasoning the philosopher is supposed to have an intuition, his mind makes a leap from an understanding of the forms to understanding of the idea of the good. The argument has a hiatus. Perhaps God could fill it. It is interesting that some Christians, including Augustine, became neo-Platonists.

In order to elucidate his theory of knowledge and its relationship to the duty of the philosopher to rule, Plato offers two allegories or analogies, first of the Line and then of the Cave. With each of these allegories Plato unfolds more details of the theory that he has already outlined in distinguishing between knowledge and 'opinion'.

---

[21] Lindsay, p. 198, actually translates it as 'form'.

The Line is divided into four sections, each corresponding to one level of understanding. The two lower levels of understanding together constitute 'opinion', which apprehends the 'visible world'. The very lowest level of understanding grasps only superficial appearances and mistaken moral beliefs. People operating at this level would believe as a result of their uncritical and uninformed observation that each morning the sun rises, and they would uncritically accept crude moral slogans like 'an eye for an eye and a tooth for a tooth'. The second lowest level of understanding grasps empirical 'reality' (it is not reality for Plato, of course, but it is for the man in the street or for the scientist) and the more or less correct moral beliefs (which still fall short of the moral knowledge which the philosopher has). This is the world of common sense. A modern man with this level of understanding might be aware that the sun does not rise, but the earth moves round the sun: he has progressed beyond the most elementary acceptance of appearances, although without moving away from what he can see to what he can work out by reason. This type of understanding would also lead a man to the sort of moral belief that Cephalus puts forward early in the dialogue, broadly sensible up to a point, but not able to stand up to searching philosophical analysis.

The two higher levels of understanding together apprehend the 'intelligible world' through reason. The higher of the two higher levels of understanding is knowledge (of forms), the lower is mathematical thinking. This is a qualitative step forward, according to Plato, from 'opinion', but not at the exalted level of knowledge, for which it is a necessary preparation. Mathematical thinking gives practice in abstraction. The philosopher will want to abstract the form of justice from its various visible manifestations, the mathematical student will be identifying the nature of triangularity by examining a variety of triangles that he has observed. The triangles will be of various sizes, some isosceles, some equilateral, some with different-sized angles and sides, but the mathematician will be looking for the essential qualities of all triangles. The essence of the triangle, its three-sidedness, etc. cannot be drawn, but can be held in the mind of the mathematician. The difference between mathematical reasoning and full knowledge is that mathematics reasons from hypotheses (logic would do the same), whereas knowledge is about the real, unhypothetical world, a world that is not just in the head of the thinker, but is outside him. The reality of knowledge is in the forms and it gives meaning to the apparent 'reality' of everyday experience.

In the elaborate allegory of the Cave Plato again explains aspects of his theory of knowledge and shows its applications to the central thesis of the *Republic* that philosophers should be rulers. Men are first imagined to be sitting chained in a cave so that they can see only the flickering shadows cast by objects being passed in front of a fire. Since the chained men cannot see the objects or the fire, they think that the shadows constitute reality. This is the lowest level of understanding, as explained in the division of the Line: men at this stage accept appearances quite uncritically. Then they are released from their chains and see at the back of the Cave the fire and the objects passed in front of it. They now learn that their first level of understanding was mere illusion based on ignorance. When men look at the objects and the fire they have a more sophisticated grasp of the world around them. This is the second level of understanding in the division of the Line, a less mistaken type of apprehension than the first, but still men are in the Cave, in relative darkness, not beyond the level of common sense. Then Plato envisages some men, the potential philosophers, climbing out of the Cave. This passage is difficult, quite different from the experience of the Cave, and may be equivalent, although Plato does not say so, to the level of mathematical understanding in the division of the Line, where the potential philosopher gains practice in abstract thinking. Eventually the men climbing out of the Cave reach daylight and the real world. They had supposed that the experiences in the Cave were the totality of life, now they find a bright new world. At first they are dazzled by the strong light, they cannot understand the real world that philosophy opens out to them. When they become accustomed to the light, they see the forms (including the form of justice): they are using their reason and obtaining knowledge. Eventually they are able to look up and see the sun which provides the light that illuminates the forms. That sun is the idea of the good. The philosophers, having seen the light, now return to the Cave. Just as they were dazzled on first coming into daylight, now they are confused on re-entering the darkness of the Cave. Their immediate desire is to escape from this darkness, the life of the city, and return to the light, philosophical speculation, but they recognize a duty to help those wallowing in ignorance in the Cave by using their knowledge of reality, which they have seen in their journey out of the Cave.

The story of the Cave, as well as underlining the importance of philosophers becoming kings is valuable for showing the connections between the different levels of understanding and the ways in which some men may progress from one stage to another. The sort of thing that Plato has in mind may be illustrated by imagining some examples of progress in understanding. Those at the lowest level, chained in the Cave to watch mere shadows, see lightning as no more than mysterious flashes in the sky or perhaps believe that God is hammering on his anvil. Those who turn round in the Cave to see the objects that produce the shadows may understand the causes of lightning and explain it according to scientific laws. The philosopher who leaves the Cave understands the nature, the essence, the form of lightning. The 'shadows' of justice in the Cave are rigged trials, the condemnation to death of Socrates himself, the penalty of death for stealing a loaf in early nineteenth-century England, and the cynical theories of justice of Thrasymachus. Turning away in the Cave from mere shadows, but still in the realm of 'opinion', a man accepts common-sense notions of justice like that proposed by Polemarchus, giving to each what is owing to him. Then the philosopher, seeing the form of justice illuminated by the sunny idea of the good, realizes that justice is minding your own business. (Particularly in the context of the myth of the Cave this formulation seems too prosaic to satisfy the expectations that Plato raises about the content of the forms.)

To give the feel of the spiritual, as well as the intellectual, progression that Plato imagines his philosophers making we shall take the case of a person coming to know the music of Bach. To the chained man in the Cave the music is merely strange and strident sounds. When the man is released from his chains he enjoys the music in a sensuous way. Climbing out of the Cave he masters harmony and counterpoint. In the light, contemplating the forms and the idea of the good, he is spiritually uplifted by the music, finding within it not only pleasure and order, but reaching through it to the beauty of man, God, and the universe.

Plato's argument that most ideas and expressions of justice are merely distorted reflections of the form, essence, or perfection of real justice, which the philosopher's reason can discover, is open to serious objection. The theory states that there can be only one correct definition of justice and that that remains correct in all times and places. However, an alternative theory of knowledge, which the Sophists endorsed, denies that there is any way that one definition of justice can be adjudged the correct one and all the others wrong. Instead, one can argue, there are various legitimate conceptions of justice, for example, those of Cephalus, Polemarchus, and Socrates, which may or may not overlap each other. 'Justice' then is not a kind of rational higher 'thing' to be discovered and identified, but a label that is attached to sets of ideas and phenomena that have sufficient in common to be given the same name. The philosopher's work is not to find essences, but to explore the persuasiveness and intelligibility of various definitions and to investigate their relationship to each other.

Those who disagree with Plato's contention that there is only one true idea of justice would disagree with him over what constitutes reality. For Plato the essences or forms are real and the experiential world is mere appearance, but for his opponents what we experience and what we feel are real, while the pursuit of essential meanings is vain. 'Justice' to such thinkers is not an essence or form, but merely a name or label that we attach to a set of our thoughts.

The Degeneration of Governments

After telling the story of the Cave, Socrates conducts a long discussion of the natural degeneration from the best kinds of government to the worst, and of the types of government that result when men with particular types of soul govern (543a–588a).[22] He starts with the philosopher and the ideal city that he has described in the *Republic*. The best kind of soul is that which loves wisdom and the best kind of government, here called aristocracy, which means the rule of the best, is that in which philosophers, the lovers of wisdom, rule. The first stage of political decline is to timocracy, government by those who love honour, which results from their having too much 'spiritedness' in their souls (Sparta's military regime would probably have been an example). Such a

---

[22] Bloom, pp. 221–70; Lindsay, pp. 238–90.

soul is clearly inferior to one dominated by love of wisdom. A man with an over-spirited soul would presumably be suitable as a soldier, but is not an ideal ruler. Timocracy declines into oligarchy, which strictly means rule by the few and which Socrates uses to mean rule by the rich. These rulers are men mainly motivated by love of money. Their souls are therefore under the sway of a desire, which makes them less admirable than souls governed either by love of wisdom or by love of honour, yet, according to Socrates, this particular desire, for money, is the best of the desires (how could he justify this assertion?). Oligarchy declines into democracy, the rule of all the people, which Socrates interprets as a regime that gives way to all desires. This was how Plato interpreted the experience of democracy in his own city of Athens. The democratic soul is similarly the one that is governed by whatever desire happens to be strongest at the time. The final stage of degeneration is to tyranny, where a ruler exploits his subjects because he is a slave to the worst desires, such as for sex and alcohol. According to Socrates, the happiest men are the lovers of wisdom, while the tyrants are least happy, for those with tyrannical souls are at the mercy of their ever-sprouting desires and those who are tyrants ruling cities are constantly fearful of betrayal by their dependants.

A Pattern laid up in Heaven

Although Socrates explains justice by describing the ideal city, he does not believe, as he reveals almost incidentally, that there is any more than a remote chance that it will come about. The philosopher is therefore very unlikely to have the opportunity to rule in an ideal city. The main value of the ideal city seems to be that it is a 'pattern' (or standard) laid up in heaven to guide the philosopher who wants to perfect himself personally (471c–473c, 592a–b).[23] The *Republic*, which had seemed to be a blueprint for an ideal city, seems suddenly to be no more than a moral inspiration to the philosopher. Perhaps it is not surprising that Socrates has constructed an ideal city that will probably not be realized in actuality, since he is interested primarily in forms, which exist beyond actuality and can be fully apprehended only by philo-

---

[23] Bloom, pp. 151–3, 274–5; Lindsay, pp. 163–6, 294.

sophers. In the *Republic* he has sketched the form of justice and the form of the city. Since the forms alone have ultimate reality, whether they can ever be even approximately realized on earth is relatively unimportant. Philosophers do have a duty to go into un-ideal cities (return to the Cave) to persuade the many to accept their authority and their vision of how the city should be ordered, but Plato was not optimistic that they would succeed. To the unphilosophical politician operating in the actual world, Plato's ideal city may seem impracticable, since it can serve as a model only to philosophers: unphilosophical rulers cannot come close to the ideal. So Plato presents us with a puzzling paradox about the apparent disjunction between theory and practice.

Conclusion

Many have found Plato's political philosophy strange, idiosyncratic, or incomplete. His notion of justice may seem, at least at first sight, remote from the common usage and intuitive understanding of any age. Nor does Plato's account of politics focus on certain issues that some later thinkers were to regard as central to politics, such as sovereignty and the management of conflicting interests. Yet Plato is important in the history of political philosophy because he was the first to elaborate and to articulate a vision of politics as the activity of moral beings pursuing exalted purposes, who seek by their nature to go beyond what is merely transient or concerned solely with the satisfaction of material wants. In this way Plato started the debate on political philosophy, throwing out a challenge to which subsequent political philosophers have continually responded.

Bibliographical Note

A major decision to be made in approaching the study of any work of political philosophy written in a foreign language is which translation to use. The purposes to which translators of Plato give priority vary significantly. Some translations of the *Republic* attempt to *interpret* ambiguous passages, rather than allow the reader to make his own decisions on what Plato meant. Other translations place emphasis on rendering Plato's Greek into harmonious English, even if this entails losing the precision of the original. Such translations sometimes erect barriers between Plato and the English reader, instead of trying to come as close as possible in a different language to Plato's actual thought.

The edition recommended here is that by A. Bloom (The Republic *of Plato* (Basic Books, New York, 1968)), because he aims to translate the text as literally as possible, 'insofar as possible always using the same English equivalent for the same Greek word' (p. vii), and provides scholarly notes on the nuances of key terms such as *polis*, *arete*, and *doxa*. The translation by A. D. Lindsay in the cheaper Everyman edition (Plato, *The Republic* (Dent, London, 1984)) is similarly direct and is accompanied with a useful introduction by R. Bambrough. For those who wish to go back to the Greek of the *Republic* the Loeb Classical Library edition is useful, as it has a good English translation by P. Shorey facing each page of Greek: Plato, *The Republic* (2 vols.; London, 1946).

Of commentaries on the *Republic*, one nineteenth-century work remains a classic: R. L. Nettleship, *Lectures on the* Republic *of Plato* (London, 1962). A very good modern commentary is J. Annas, *An Introduction to Plato's* Republic (Oxford, 1981), which contains invaluable bibliographies on particular sections of the argument in the *Republic*. Other recommended commentaries on the *Republic* include: R. C. Cross and A. D. Woozley, *Plato's* Republic: *A Philosophical Commentary* (London, 1979); N. R. Murphy, *The Interpretation of Plato's* Republic (Oxford, 1951); N. P. White, *A Companion to Plato's* Republic (Oxford, 1979).

Two controversial books, written under the shadows of Nazi Germany and Stalin's Russia, interpreted the *Republic* as a philosophy of totalitarianism: R. H. S. Crossman, *Plato Today* (London, 1937) and K. R. Popper, *The Open Society and its Enemies*, vol. i (London, 1945). The scholarly debate on Popper's interpretation is contained in R. Bambrough (ed.), *Plato, Popper and Politics* (Cambridge, 1967).

Many of Plato's other books bear on points that he made in the *Republic*. These works may be conveniently consulted in E. Hamilton and H. Cairns (eds.), *The Collected Dialogues of Plato* (Princeton, 1961). A most succinct introduction to Plato and his thought is R. M. Hare, *Plato* (Oxford, 1982). Another useful account of Plato's philosophy as a whole is C. J. Rowe, *Plato* (Brighton, 1984), which contains a good guide to recent literature on Plato. Two books are helpful for their discussion of all Plato's political thought, including *Politicus* and the *Laws*, as well as the *Republic*: R. W. Hall, *Plato* (London, 1981) and G. Klosko, *The Development of Plato's Political Theory* (London, 1986).

For the historical background of Plato's philosophy the literature is immense. Amongst the large number of readily available paperback books on Greek politics and history the following may be recommended: H. D. F. Kitto, *The Greeks* (Harmondsworth, 1969); M. I. Finley, *The Ancient Greeks*

(Harmondsworth, 1977); T. R. Glover, *The Ancient World* (Harmondsworth, 1944); A. Andrewes, *Greek Society* (Harmondsworth, 1971); V. Ehrenburg, *The Greek State* (London, 1969); J. K. Davis, *Democracy and Classical Greece* (Glasgow, 1978); W. G. Forrest, *The Emergence of Greek Democracy* (London, 1966). The latter is surely the wittiest book on Greek politics.

2

Aristotle: *The Politics*

ANDREW LOCKYER

ARISTOTLE'S *Politics* has been described both as a post-mortem on the Greek city-state and as a textbook for constitution makers. There is an element of truth in both these judgements.

One of the problems of offering a pithy characterization of Aristotle's *Politics* is the composition of the text itself. If it is regarded and read as a systematic treatise, then it will inevitably be found wanting.[1] What we have inherited, on the best guess, is a compilation of notes based on Aristotle's lectures given perhaps over his period of thirteen years at the Lyceum, ranging from general political theorizing to detailed description. Understanding the character of Aristotle's *Politics* requires some grasp of the purpose of the political education provided by Aristotle's school.

The Context of the *Politics*

When Aristotle established his school outside Athens in 335 BC the decline of the Greek city-state was fully evident. The high point of achievement of the intimate, independent, self-governing political communities of classical Greece is a matter of debate. The fourth-century Greek writers, like Aristotle, identified it with the early fifth-century *polis* and the collective Greek spirit that repulsed the Persians. Modern admirers have regarded fourth-century Athens as the zenith of democratic achievement. There is no doubt that Aristotle witnessed the demise of the city-state, whether it was through internal weakness, as he thought, or because of the irresistible power of Macedon.[2]

The economic development of the Greek states in the later part

[1] References to the *Politics* are to Ernest Barker's translation (Oxford, 1946).

[2] Aristotle came from Stagira on the borders of Macedonia. His father was a physician at the Macedonian court, and Aristotle is reputed to have briefly tutored the young Alexander. This association brought him hostility at Athens in his later years and some commentators have suggested that the Macedonian connection casts doubt on his endorsement of the *polis*. For the relevant historical background see Barker's introduction, pp. xi–xxvi.

of the fourth century led to internecine rivalries that were paralleled within states by growing class conflict. The established aristocratic families were increasingly being challenged from below. The Peloponnesian Wars were a contest not only between the advocates of the competing ideologies of democracy and aristocracy, but also between the traditional insular and military values of Sparta and the new imperialist commercial values of the Athenian League. It is not surprising that members of the Athenian educated élite, whether native like Plato or foreign like Aristotle, had more sympathy with traditional Sparta than modern democratic Athens.

An underlying theme of the *Politics* is the degeneracy of the times. Aristotle's conception of the good life is an idealization of the civic morality of the past. It is contrasted with the acquisitiveness associated with the pleasure-seeking philosophies in contemporary Athens. Commentators who have called the *Politics* 'bourgeois' could not be wider of the mark. If labels are useful, Aristotle can be called both 'conservative' and, in the original Greek sense, 'revolutionary'. The only means of conserving the classical Greek way of life was to 'revolve' or return the *polis* of the past. Aristotle agreed with Plato that Athens in particular, and Greece in general, had become too corrupt to be saved either by individual moral example (as Socrates had attempted), or by statesmanship; the hope lay in the education of a new generation of men who might advise on the establishment of new constitutions, or on re-forming existing ones. In retrospect, Aristotle's teaching may appear as a post-mortem analysis of the Greek city-state, but it was inspired by the hope of regeneration. Aristotle's *Politics* must be read in large part as a defence of classical Greek values, and in particular of those which make citizenship central to the good and rational life of man which came to be embodied in the classical republican tradition.

Aristotle subscribed to the adage that 'good laws make good men'. The Greek idea of law (*nomos*) included both what we call customary morality and a conception of social justice. For Aristotle the laws thus conceived require to be incorporated into a 'right constitution'. (This notion will be discussed·later.) A lawgiver must be understood therefore not only as a creator of a legal order, but also as one who can encapsulate customary morality within political institutions. The lawgiver must formalize a people's way of life into a political and ethical order; he must aim to realize the goal which Plutarch attributes to Lycurgus, who reputedly gave the Spartans 'the best laws they were capable of receiving'.[3]

Notwithstanding the customary nature of law, the conception of the creative role of the lawgiver was critical to the idea of the *polis*. The myth of foundation served to invest the *polis* with the status of a rational and chosen political and ethical order superior to the natural order of kinship associations. In actuality the formation of the original city-states was based on an amalgam of tribes whose local loyalties remained strong. The authority of the *polis* (its god and its laws) had to be asserted over kinship associations— families and tribes (their gods and their lore). The traditional or 'original' lawgivers had themselves to be attributed with god-like qualities to elevate their laws above the merely human. The Greeks had no difficulty with the double status which allowed them to deify lawgivers while at the same time regarding the *polis* as a human creation. (In this way they were better equipped than ourselves to endow constitutional law with superior authority.) As they came in time to view the gods as less involved in human affairs the need to deify lawgivers diminished. By the time of Plato and Aristotle it was possible to conceive of constitution makers as mortal, even though they had to be highly educated, preferably at the Academy or the Lyceum. The founders of both schools accepted the task of constitutional adviser to various rulers in Greece and Asia, as did some of their students: the role of lawgiving by the fourth century BC was not entirely defunct, impossible, or imaginary.

If good laws make good men what makes good lawgivers? Although Plato and Aristotle agreed about the need for lawgivers, they profoundly disagreed about the nature of the education required. This is because they fundamentally differed about the nature of politics itself.

The Nature of Politics and its Study

At the beginning of his major work on *Ethics* Aristotle proclaims

---

[3] The term 'lawgiver' has been used throughout in preference to 'legislator', in the belief that the former suggests more the role of proposing than enacting laws. The lawgiver may be an adviser without possessing any authority, still less supreme power.

that politics is the master science: it includes the aims of other sciences in having as its end 'the good for man' (*NE* I. 2, p. 3).[4] It is typically Greek for ethics and politics to be thus integrated. Later in the work Aristotle says that action directed towards the ends of human life requires 'practical wisdom' (*phronesis*). This he defines as 'the reasoned state of capacity to act with regard to the things that are good or bad for man' (*NE* VI. 5, p. 124). The practically wise man knows not only the things that are worthy of pursuit, he knows how to achieve them—how to bring good about for himself and for others. He must have knowledge of particulars as well as general knowledge. His reasoning is 'deliberative' rather than 'demonstrative', deliberation is prior to action. The practically wise man is essentially a 'doer', a moral and political actor.

Aristotle pointedly contrasts practical wisdom with 'theoretical science' and 'philosophic wisdom'. His examples of the former are mathematics and geometry, whose truths are necessary and demonstrable. Philosophic wisdom combines theoretical science with intuitive understanding (*nous*). Both philosophy and theoretical science are conceived by Aristotle to be non-practical. They are concerned with the pursuit of universal and eternal knowledge, rather than what is particular and can be usefully applied. Politics of course is a matter of practical rather than philosophic wisdom. It is an inexact deliberative, rather than a demonstrable, science. This is where Aristotle diverges crucially from Plato. Plato's disregard or rejection of practical wisdom, certainly in the *Republic*, led him to prescribe theoretical scientific education for rule, and ultimately to assimilate politics to philosophy.[5]

Given that politics is a practical activity and an inexact science, it cannot be demonstrably taught. Aristotle's method in the *Politics* (and *Ethics*) reflects the nature of the subject-matter. The student of politics must consider the 'phenomena' (*phainomena*)— the 'things that appear'. The *Politics*, as it comes to us, begins with the words 'Observation tells us . . .'. Aristotle's reputation as the first great empiricist rests here. Ascertaining and recording the facts about actual states was an important part of the study of politics at the Lyceum. Information on over 150 states was reportedly collected. The school is the first we know to have a 'library'.

---

[4] *NE* refers to Aristotle's *Nicomachean Ethics*. The edition used is translated by W. D. Ross (Oxford World's Classics, 1954).

[5] See pp. 25–6, above.

This aspect of Aristotle's approach to politics is in keeping with his research method in other empirical fields; he was a great collector and classifier of 'the facts'. His background in medicine and biology is usually cited at this point. However, two qualifications are necessary: the facts that appear in politics and ethics cannot be left at the face value of appearances; and 'facts' include 'opinions'.

In announcing his approach to a subject of deliberation Aristotle says we must begin by considering the 'common opinions', or at least 'the most authoritative of them' (*NE* I. 4, p. 5). His method is firstly to outline the common opinions, the range of views, or sometimes what particular authorities say. Next he notes areas of agreement and disagreement, and identifies problems or difficulties. Then he attempts to resolve them. He adopts what is surely the best lecturing technique in the 'inexact sciences', he allows his own position to emerge from a discussion of the range of views, but without assuming there is always a right answer. It is Aristotle's method that makes him an unequalled source of information on the breadth of Greek views on a subject.

How, we may ask, does the method of teaching relate to the practical activity of politics and the art of lawgiving? The first point is that lawgiving, statesmanship, and being a good citizen all need practical wisdom. Although they require to different degrees the ability to generalize from different types of experience, they equally require knowledge of particulars and the development of 'right judgement' (*NE* VI. 12, pp. 154–8). For the would-be lawgiver, a comparative knowledge of the laws of a number of states is not enough. Aristotle criticizes those Sophists who purport to teach politics as if it can be learned without experience (*NE* X. 9, p. 275). He says studying a collection of laws is only useful to those who can judge the best, or the best in particular circumstances. A textbook of laws no more makes a lawgiver than a medical textbook makes a physician. What is required in both cases is right judgement, which is part of practical wisdom. Whether in medicine, morals, or politics this judgement is acquired only by experience.

Aristotle says (*NE* I. 4, p. 5) that only those who already have practical wisdom will benefit from lectures on politics. Politics cannot be taught to the young, though they can readily become mathematicians (*NE* VI. 8, p. 148). The acquisition of sound judgement can only come from right upbringing and good habits; it is intimately linked with the development of moral character. In essence, Aristotle subscribes to the common view that moral and political education is a matter of what we call 'socialization'. The element of circularity here is recognized by Aristotle. His school was an attempt to halt the downward cycle of degeneracy, but formal study could be no complete substitute for right upbringing. It could only be hoped that some had not been too corrupted by existing institutions and the prevailing morality. What had to be avoided was the pitfall of Plato's Academy (perhaps of all academia); the school itself should not become a way of life. Aristotle's students were not allowed to forget that political education was chiefly acquired in the *polis* and was to serve the *polis*, where the good life must be lived.

Aristotle's Conception of Man

In book I of the *Politics* Aristotle says that man is by nature a political animal. Barker's translation runs 'man is by nature an animal intended to live in the polis' (I. ii. 9, p. 5). While investing nature with intention is going a little beyond the text, the translator does highlight the special weight which attaches to Aristotle's underlying concept of nature (*physis*).

The nature of something is its 'end', or what it is when fully developed: '. . . What each thing is when its growth is completed we call the nature of the thing, whether it be a man, a horse or a family' (I. ii. 9, p. 5). The nature of a thing is also identified with its 'soul' (*psyche*), with its purpose (*telos*), and sometimes with its 'function' (*ergon*).[6] The examples above suggest that Aristotle has living things in mind when conceiving of what is natural. It is indeed the case that organic nature provides the paradigm for the entire natural world for Aristotle. Everything in the universe is part of nature (*physis*) in so far as it has 'life', or is the source of its own organizing form and motion. Equally, all things have their own 'soul' if their elements and substance are informed from within. What is natural is contrasted with what is made: the arte-

---

[6] The English terms of course are approximations to the Greek. For *ergon*, 'function' is preferred to 'work'; sometimes what men are 'fitted for' serves to render the meaning better. The connotation of instrumentality is not always appropriate.

fact is given its function and purpose from without, it has the 'soul' of its maker.

Aristotle's teleological conception of nature is a critical advance on Plato's ontology. Plato contrasts the 'real' unchanging eternal world of the forms with the contingent and decadent world of the senses, but according to Aristotle he fails to explain the principles of change at work in the world. As Aristotle sees it, the dynamic relationship between form and substance explains both the composition of nature and the causal forces at work. The function and purpose of the form is the source (agency and end) of change. At all times things are coming into being and passing away; the movement is from potentiality to fulfilment, and beyond to decay and transformation. The cycles of life in nature can be known by 'reason' that does not change. (That is *nous*, the 'intuitive understanding' in which both men and the gods share.)

Why, it may be asked, does Aristotle single out political life to characterize what is distinctively human in man's nature? Why is he not equally defined as having a philosophical or a social nature?

In book x of the *Ethics* Aristotle says that 'reason more than anything else is man' (*NE* x. 8, p. 226); to live according to reason is therefore the best and most fulfilling form of life. At this point Aristotle deals with one of the great issues in classical thought. It is the dilemma posed by the competing ways of life presented by politics and philosophy. (Plato's choice of philosophy was in part a response to Socrates' heroic failure to marry the ideals.) As Aristotle at first depicts it, there appears to be a choice between the life of the *polis* or the exercise of practical wisdom involving moral virtues, and the contemplative life involving the intellectual virtues and the pursuit of truth. At one point Aristotle puts the case for the contemplative life of philosophy. Contemplative reason is the highest form of activity. Being unrelated to the practical world it is self-sufficient activity; that is, pursued for its own sake and not for some other good. It is the activity of the gods who 'lack nothing' and are reputed to be the most happy.

Although we are not gods and our share of reason may be small, we should 'strain every nerve' to strive to realize what is divine within us. The philosophical life, it seems, is being endorsed. But Aristotle proceeds, 'such a life is too high for man' (*NE* x. 8, p. 265); men are gregarious and need friends to be happy and to fulfil themselves. The life according to reason for man must include intellectual pursuits, but philosophy alone cannot be a replete way of life for a human being. It is practical wisdom, the capacity for moral judgement and the life of political action, that differentiates men from gods. Men must live according to all that is good in their natures.

Aristotle's man is a social animal—indeed the most sociable of all animals, but this is not his distinguishing characteristic: it is not what he is peculiarly 'fitted for' (his *ergon*). Bees and other gregarious animals are also sociable. 'Man alone of the animals is furnished with the faculty of language', and it is this which makes him capable of 'declaring what is just and unjust' (i. ii. 11, p. 6). Men uniquely have the capacity to live in moral communities of which the *polis* is the highest and most complete form. Men are superior to other animals in their 'purpose' and 'function'; when they fail to live according to reason and to their moral and political capacities, they become the worst of all creatures (i. ii. 16, p. 7). Men are neither beasts nor gods; though they share some attributes of both.

There are a number of difficulties which the modern reader will encounter with Aristotle's conception of 'man'. We are familiar with the double meaning which arises from the application of the word both to the whole of humanity and specifically to the male adult. For Aristotle the general application coexists with an even more selective reference.

It will be noted that the teleological conception of human nature is both descriptive and prescriptive. (It transcends what is sometimes called 'the naturalistic fallacy', in that it permits the derivation of what ought to be from what is.) There is a sense in which the potential within all nature demands to be realized—the seed ought to become a plant—but for agents with the capacity to choose and to act, and therefore go 'against nature' the development of (good) human potentialities is a categorical imperative. The normative sense of 'being a man' is not unfamiliar to us. Also we accept that species potential is not realizable in all people—for instance the incurably infirm, geriatric, and insane. None the less, the equal status of being human, despite our differences, has come to us as a self-evident normative truth, but it has not always been so regarded. For Aristotle, and possibly all his contemporaries, the divisions amongst human kind were as morally significant as those between men and the gradations of the animal world.

Aristotle adheres to the belief in a biological continuum which places the other species below man; but human beings are the most variable. Taxonomically, they are equivalent in range to 'birds' rather than 'ostriches'. The difference between human beings in their 'natures' and attainments are sometimes greater than the difference between lower men and the higher animals. It is worthy of note that the species characteristics of human beings which accord with their natures, 'upright posture, speech, and rational action', all have to be learned.[7] The teleological conception of man facilities gradation, since 'humanity' is a potentiality which may be more or less fulfilled.

What is hard for us to accept is that the general species nature of man admits of further division such that full humanity is beyond the natures (or potentiality) of some none the less human beings. Being more or less human for Aristotle is conditional not only on performance and achievement, but also upon differences in the function of our natures. The obvious difficulty, pointed out by most commentators, is in distinguishing between differences arising from nature (differences in human potential) and those of performance which result from upbringing and opportunity. The common criticism is that Aristotle treats cultural and conventional differences as those of natural potential. It is often suggested that this is because biology is the basis of his schema of nature. The problem remains, how in principle do we distinguish between the two?

Another facet of Aristotle's theory that gives difficulty is the ascription of functions and purposes to 'man' in the abstract, irrespective of individual choice. This suggests a belief in a superior purpose, or grand designer, which has made possible the Christian appropriation of Aristotle. It would be wrong to deny any monotheistic element in Aristotle, but it would be a mistake to ground his conception of human nature upon it. Aristotle's man is preeminently his own man, his *telos* is to act according to his own purposes, albeit in concert with others and in fulfilment of a given but extendable potential. The life that men are 'fitted for' (their *ergon*) is at best pursued in a world of their own intellectual and practical creation.

---

[7] S. R. L. Clark, *Aristotle's Man*, pp. 17 and 27. This section is generally indebted to Clark's work.

The Household and the *Polis*

The distinction that Aristotle makes between the household and the *polis* is of seminal importance to his political theory. It coheres with his conception of man as both animal and rational.

'All associations are instituted for the purpose of attaining some good' (I. i. 1, p. 1). We know that the nature of these associations will be defined and classified in terms of their ends. The household has the purpose of sustaining life, while the end of the *polis* is the pursuit of the good life. Aristotle says that the *polis* is the most 'sovereign and inclusive of all associations', because it is directed towards the highest of human purposes;[8] it alone is 'sufficient' for men in that it provides the conditions in which the good life can be lived. The *polis* is a 'whole' which includes households and aggregates of households (villages) as constitutive 'parts' (I. ii. 14, p. 6). For Aristotle the relationship between *polis* and household can be characterized as the juxtaposition of freedom and necessity that is a reflection of the human condition.

The relationships within the household that Aristotle identifies are of three sorts; those of parents and children, husband and wife, master and slave. They are characterized by different sorts of rule based on different degrees of natural subordination, but they have in common the necessary structure of the association. They are essentially relationships between unequal parties and as such are to be contrasted with the relationship between freemen in the *polis*. The paradigm of the latter is that between equal citizens, where there is reciprocity of 'ruling and being ruled by turn' (III. xiii. 12, p. 134); where reason rather than hierarchical status is the governing principle. (This generic account of political rule as we shall see is at odds with the variety of constitutions which Aristotle finds in actuality.) The political rule of the *polis* is the antithesis and sequel of the authoritarian rule of the household. The equal citizen must first be a 'monarch' in his own home (I. xii. 2, p. 32). The implication is clearly that only heads of households are in a position to be citizens and that other members of the household do not directly participate in the political arena. Children, women, and

[8] Barker translates *kyrion* 'sovereign'. This might be regarded as anachronistic since the doctrine of sovereignty, on one view at least, arises with the theory of legal supremacy and the legislative power of the modern state. Barker is aware of this. However, *to kyron* does imply the authority to deliberate and initiate. The body in the *polis* which exercises this power (the *politeuma*) can be regarded as 'sovereign', even though ruling was not typically legislating. See Barker's notes Y and Z, pp. 127–8.

slaves have their ends met within the household, which means not only their biological needs are catered for, but they can fulfil themselves in this sphere.

Aristotle discusses economics under the heading of the 'art of household management'. The business of the household is principally concerned with the right use of household property, but Aristotle recognizes with some reluctance that 'acquisition' (*chrematistic*) must be its proper concern. Here he distinguishes between natural and unnatural acquisition (I. ix., pp. 22–7). The former involves forms of life connected with farming, including fishing and hunting, which make use of resources whose purpose is to serve the ends of material life. The accumulation of 'wealth' in this form is naturally limited and is morally acceptable to Aristotle. However he contrasts this with unnatural acquisition arising out of exchange for the purpose of profit making, where 'money' or 'unnatural wealth' is pursued for its own sake. The latter is unlimited, unrelated to the true ends of the household, and morally unjustifiable. Aristotle clearly associates the pursuit of 'unnatural wealth', particularly concerned with the retail trade, manufacture, and usury (I. x–xi, pp. 27–31), with the acquisitive tendency which he saw as a corrupting influence in his time.

Aristotle's view of the household is never far removed from the reality of Greek life. He is fully aware that kinship associations based on households were 'prior to the *polis*' both in terms of historical antecedence and in relation to each person's upbringing. Although the power exercised by the patrician families was in time diminished (in Athens by the reforms of Cleisthenes for instance), the authority exercised within the private sphere of the household was still formidable. The household remained the primary unit of personal identity for the Greeks. The *polis* was an association of households rather than of individuals and membership was a pre-condition of citizenship. Aristotle also reflects the general truth that the household was the central institution of economic life. However, there is substance in the view that his conception is modelled on the traditional aristocratic households of the fourth century rather than on what was typical in contemporary Athens.[9] Evidence of this is that he regards the inclusion of slaves as integral, while on the best estimate, most citizen house-

[9] This is argued most forcibly in E. M. Wood and N. Wood, *Class Ideology and Ancient Political Theory*, pp. 209–37.

holds were without domestic slaves in fifth-century Athens. Equally, an agrarian economy based on landownership and subsistence farming underpins his discussion of household management. He assumes the family land can provide the means of life (an unwarranted assumption for many Athenian citizen families after the Peloponnesian Wars). Minimal, necessary trade is just acceptable, but 'production' (making things), retailing (buying and selling), commerce (borrowing and lending), all in order to make money, are deemed morally debilitating, inimical to the good life and, in the ideal *polis*, incompatible with citizenship (VII. viii–ix, pp. 298–303).

The importance of the distinction which Aristotle makes between the sphere of politics and domestic life is worth reviewing: it is one which is central to an understanding of the classical heritage. The political and public are contrasted with the economic and private. The former delineates the exclusively human realm in which men exercise their freedom and rationality. For those capable of this life, being confined to the private domestic sphere is a 'privation', being 'deprived' of the opportunity of winning honour and reputation amongst equals.[10]

The parallel distinction of interest to us is that between political man and economic man. The former is a category of human achievement not attainable by all, while 'economic man' is an inherent universal status (including women, children, slaves, and anyone else living under despotism). Whereas political man engages in moral activity (*praxis*), speaking, deciding, fighting, in the service of the public good as well as his own, economic man is conceived primarily as a passive 'consumer' rather than producer. Economic activity appears never to have achieved among the Greeks a status commensurate with full humanity.[11] It could not (as for Marx) distinguish man's species activity, for the reasons that Aristotle makes clear. There is no doubt that Aristotle's distaste for 'production' is indicative of the prejudice of his class, but the ethical ground of his objection transcends this. It derives from the perception that economic activity is self-centred (even

[10] Pericles' funeral oration in Thucydides, *The Peloponnesian War* (Penguin Classic ed.), bk. 2, pp. 34–47, is a famous statement of the ethos. Hannah Arendt's *Human Condition* (New York, 1959) is the modern classic on the subject.

[11] Wood and Wood suggest otherwise. They argue that the prejudice against manual work and trade is a preoccupation of aristocratic Greek political philosophers. This view does not stand full scrutiny, *Class Ideology*, pp. 64–81.

though the 'self' is identified with the communal family); it is concerned with the pursuit of private 'goods' rather than the higher public good. The life devoted to money-making is to Aristotle finally not only immoral but irrational.

The values of the Greek civic ethic which Aristotle portrays are implicitly a challenge to many of our views; in particular, the conception of rationality grounded on the view of man as a self-centred infinite consumer, which underlies much modern economic and political theory.

Property

Aristotle's theoretical account of property in relation to its function is located within the theory of the household. Property consists in the instruments available to serve the ends of the household; 'each article of property is an instrument for the purpose of life . . . property in general is the sum of such instruments'. It includes both animate and inanimate instruments; the slave being the most useful 'animate article of property' (I. iv. 1–2, pp. 9–10). However, Aristotle recognizes throughout the *Politics* that the distribution of property has a critical part to play in the composition of actual states, and reflects their different conceptions of justice. Even though the management of property is deemed a household affair, its distribution is a political and constitutional matter.

For the Greeks, as traditionally for ourselves, the politically and socially significant form of property was house and estates. (The Greek term *oikos* links 'property', 'house', and 'family'.) The importance of this form of property is more than economic; primarily it provides the fixed and permanent territorial location of the person and family. For this reason the inheritance of fixed property has often been used historically as the basis for citizenship. For the Greeks, whose primitive religion was founded on ancestor worship, family land, the burial place of ancestors, originally had a sacred significance. The enhanced sense of belonging that attached to the shared patrimonial place, amongst the noble families at least, survived the replacement of the familial by the civic religion.[12]

[12] Fustel de Coulanges, *The Ancient City* (London, 1916). Also W. K. C. Guthrie, *The Greeks and their Gods* (London, 1968).

There are a number of factors to bear in mind in Aristotle's discussion. First, the notion of absolute ownership was foreign to the Greeks. There were always legal and moral constraints upon the transfer of property. Since household property was a collective rather than individual asset, the head of the household had power of use rather than disposal. (The idea that ownership is characterized by the right to dispose of or 'alienate' possession, is Roman rather than Greek in origin.) Secondly, following this, the role of the *polis* in relation to property holdings was considerable. The maintenance of households was always seen as the business of the *polis*, not only for their private good, but because the strength and political stability of the *polis* depended upon it.[13] Since the *polis* was nothing other than its citizen households, their collective assets were deemed to be available for civic purposes, especially in time of acute public need.[14] It is against this background that the distribution of property and political power are conceived by Aristotle to be a matter for lawgivers. Aristotle recognizes that the distribution of property is critical to the character of actual states, that disputes about property are a source of civil strife and therefore a subject for the would-be lawgiver. At a number of points he suggests that lawgivers who attempt to redress the distribution of property are dealing with the symptom rather than the disease. Plato's advocacy of communism is an example.

Aristotle's rejection of Plato's communism is of interest for its inclusion of some arguments that are characteristic of liberal individualism, but it is misleading to leave the matter there. Aristotle argues against common ownership of property but in favour of private ownership and common use (II. v, pp. 48–55). His three objections to common ownership are (*a*) that it will cause discontent if the lazy and the industrious equally benefit; (*b*) that the pleasure of owning and giving will be lost; (*c*) that the exercise of the virtues of 'temperance' and 'liberality' which consist in the right use of property would be excluded. Of these arguments he gives the latter the most weight, but by implication the more general objection, which he only partially sees, is that commun-

---

[13] Aristotle's *Athenian Constitution* informs us that the Archon Eponymus had the duty to watch over the preservation of families and property; the task that had earlier been performed by the Council of Areopagus. (Everyman ed., pt. II, ch. 56, pp. 296–7 and pt. I, ch. 4, p. 249.)

[14] P. Vinogradoff, *Historical Jurisprudence*, vol. ii (Oxford, 1922), p. 228.

ism requires the abandonment of separate households. Plato's *polis* he depicts as one big unfeeling household (II. ii.–iv, pp. 40–7).

One of the problems with Aristotle's discussion is that he is not generally clear about the difference between 'ownership' and 'use', but the arrangement he favours is plain enough. It is where 'the property of each is made to serve us all, in the spirit of the proverb which says "Friends' goods are goods in common"'. He cites with approval the Spartan example where citizens make use of their neighbours' property on a journey 'as if they were their own', as needs require (II. v. 7, p. 49). Communal use clearly embraces the principle of free-sharing for Aristotle. This morally worthwhile activity promoting fraternity is only possible when citizens control household property and also have a public-spirited attitude to its use.

The right attitude to property is a function of seeing it in proper relation to the end of the *polis*. This perspective is nowhere more apparent than in his critique of Phaleas' scheme for the equal distribution of land as a solution to 'civil discord' (II. vii, pp. 62–8). Aristotle says that equalizing property is no solution, it is 'more necessary to equalize men's desires than their properties'; crime results not only from 'lack of necessities but for the sake of superfluities' (II. vii. 20, p. 67). The solution to civil discord is to be found in right upbringing under laws which teach a true sense of values.

Property ownership is essential to citizenship. This for Aristotle, of course, is a functional rather than legal relationship. Since typically in Greek law only citizens could own fixed property, it would be a mistake to suggest that property ownership came first. Historically, citizenship was largely by descent as was the relevant property inherited, the exception being the few occasions when a constitutional reform created new citizens and redistributed land, which were part and parcel of each other.[15]

The formal entitlement to participate in public affairs qualifies a man to be a citizen; however it is only those who do take part in political life that are active citizens (III. ii. 5, p. 97). Property is

[15] Unlike the Romans, the Greeks seldom extended citizenship to non-citizen families. When an exception was made, it required also the granting of private rights (a property holding) and integration into the tribal or deme organization (Vinogradoff, p. 45). To extend citizenship on any scale required a reorganization and redistribution like that performed by Cleisthenes. See Forrest, *The Emergence of Greek Democracy* (London, 1966), pp. 191–224.

the necessary condition in practice because it provides the required free time for the citizen to engage in politics. Aristotle says, 'citizens must have a supply of property in order to have leisure' to devote to public concerns (VII. ix. 7, p. 302). 'It is generally agreed that leisure, or in other words freedom from necessity, should be present in any well-ordered state' (II. xi. 10, p. 86). Leisure is contrasted not only with necessary work but with necessary 'play', which is relaxation from work. Leisure, we are told, is a higher pleasure involving the cultivation of the mind: it includes political, moral, and intellectual activity (VIII. iii. 1–10, pp. 335–7).

There are two dimensions to the relationship between leisure and citizenship within Aristotle in which the emphasis upon fact and value are different. Firstly, the facts of Greek life meant that in practice the 'leisure' time available to devote to politics and the higher pursuits was limited by the demands of economic life. We might conceive of there being a limited economic 'surplus' of leisure, which could be spread widely or concentrated in the hands of the few. Aristotle is aware, especially in his discussion of types of democracies, that the extent of political participation will depend on material conditions. Those entitled by descent to share in public life may only do so in practice 'when they are able to find the necessary leisure' (IV. vi. 3, p. 171). Aristotle suggests that in fact only agriculture provides the surplus to give a citizen sufficient leisure.

However, the second more overtly prescriptive dimension is that only the agrarian way of life appears to be ethically acceptable for citizens. Aristotle returns to his distaste for mechanical pursuits, 'the term mechanical (*banausos*) should properly be applied to any occupation, art, or instruction, which is calculated to make the body or soul or mind, of a freeman unfit for the pursuit and the practice of goodness' (VIII. ii. 4, p. 334). It is not the physical nature of the work that is debilitating, although this is a factor emphasized by other classical authors,[16] it is occupations 'for the sake of gain' that keep men's minds 'too meanly occu-

---

[16] Xenophon for instance gives these words to Socrates in a dialogue on 'economics', 'those arts which are called handicrafts are objectionable, and justly held in little repute in communities; for they weaken the bodies of those who work at them or attend to them, by compelling them to sit and live indoors; some of them too, to pass whole days by the fire; and when the body becomes effeminate, the mind loses its strength'. *Xenophon's Minor Works*, trans. J. S. Watson (Bohn's Classical Library, London, 1882).

pied'. Aristotle approves the sentiment of the best Victorian nanny, in saying that the amount of useful knowledge imparted to children should never be large enough to make them mechanically minded (VIII. ii. 3–6, p. 334). The underlying economic assumption that only land can generate a surplus gives way to the traditional aristocratic notion that trade and manufacture lower humanity.

The Justification of Slavery

In all nature there are ruled and ruling elements, and just as it is natural and beneficial for the soul to rule over the body in the individual, so it is for men to rule over animals, and for the naturally superior human beings to rule over inferior ones. Aristotle says, 'We may conclude that all men who differ from others as much as the body differs from the soul, or an animal from a man (and this is the case with all whose function is bodily service . . .) all such are by nature slaves, and it is better for them . . . to be ruled by a master' (I. v. 8, p. 13). The nearest there is to an argument here is a recital of the natural order of things. Aristotle is aware that an appeal to the existence of the institution of slavery does not prove his case. Those who are slaves might be slaves by convention (*nomos*); that is, by human laws only, and this would not make them justly slaves. Indeed, he concedes that in practice some have the body and soul of freemen, and are therefore slaves 'contrary to nature'. Yet he does not doubt that some human beings are by their 'make-up' fitted for slavery.

How to identify natural slaves raises the question of just acquisition. He says that when slaves are justly acquired it is 'part of the art of war and hunting' (I. vii. 5, p. 18). He discusses two views about enslaving prisoners: some take the view that the victors in war are necessarily superior in virtue (perhaps like the Spartans they value only military virtues); others believe that the victor may or may not be morally superior; both parties agree that 'superiority in goodness' ought to be the criterion. He takes issue with those who argue that the law determines right and the victors make the law. Only if the war is just and the just are victorious will this be so. It transpires that only prisoners taken in a just war can be legitimately enslaved, and a 'just war' turns out to be a war waged against barbarians (I. vi. 5, p. 15). Greeks ought not to enslave fellow Greeks even if they do take them prisoner; the practice should be confined to those non-Greeks who are fitted by nature to be despotically ruled (I. vi. 6, p. 16 and VII. xiv. 21, p. 319).

Let us briefly look at some of what we know about slavery as it existed in the Greek world.[17] There were many persons of inferior status to citizens, resident aliens and 'metics' for example, who were not slaves even though they lacked significant freedoms. Slavery entailed some sort of 'bondage' either to another person, or to the *polis*. Amongst those who were regarded in law or public opinion as slaves, there was great variety in the degree of freedom exercised in relation to dwelling, movement, occupation, income, and wealth. We can classify the following types. (1) The domestic servant (*oiketes*) male or female, closely integrated in the citizen's household. This was the main traditional form. (2) The Spartan Helots and Thessalian Penestae described as 'serfs', who were not individually 'owned' but who were collectively bound to labour on the land. In the Spartan case they were a subjugated people giving forced service to their military conquerors. Somewhere between public and private slaves, they were most like the communal Egyptian slaves (though not used for vast public works). (3) Public slaves who worked for the city bureaucracy in Athens; they kept accounts and constituted the police force (the Scythian 'bowmen'). (4) 'Mechanic slaves' of various types. These ranged from skilled and responsible jobs, to a large number who laboured in the silver mines at Laurium. In this category were 'pay bringers', who were hired out by citizens (sometimes to the slaves themselves) in order to make a profit. There are widely varying estimates of the numbers in all categories: it seems likely that Athens in the mid-fourth century had the largest number, between 60,000 and 100,000, which is 3 or 4 per citizen household, but they were concentrated in the hands of the wealthy. It has been estimated that two-thirds to three-quarters of Athenian citizens owned no slaves.[18] The large increase of numbers in Athens that took place in the fourth century was principally of 'mechanic slaves'.

There were a limited number of ways by which someone

---

[17] The best single source is M. I. Finley (ed.), *Slavery in Classical Antiquity* (Cambridge, 1968).

[18] A. H. M. Jones, *Athenian Democracy* (Oxford, 1957), p. 17.

became a slave. (1) Debt slavery. This was probably always rare and officially ended at Athens by Solon. (2) Captives in war, including mass enslavement. This was traditionally the most important. In the fifth century when the enemies were largely non-Greeks, this was apparently unquestioned; Aristotle reflects the qualms felt when the warfare became internecine. (3) Being born into slavery. This became by far the most likely origin: by Aristotle's time almost all slaves in Athens would have known no other status from birth. It was possible for slaves to buy themselves out of bondage or receive their freedom as a gift (as Aristotle's will granted his own). Although evidence suggests that the status which this would bring was not highly sought after.

Let us consider Aristotle's position in relation to Greek practice. The first point to note is that he only justifies the one traditional form of household slavery. The purpose of the household is life: 'Life is action (*praxis*) not production: and therefore the slave being an instrument for the purpose of life is a servant in the sphere of action' (I. iv. 5, p. 10). Action requires deliberation, thus the role of the master is essential to the slave. There is no case for the use of slaves outside or beyond the purposes of the household. He does not justify using slaves for production, for hire, or for working in mines. He is against communal slavery: the Helots will always be liable to revolt and the Spartans and Thessalians will always be at war against their native populations and their neighbours (II. ix. 3, p. 74). His arguments could not justify non-citizens owning slaves; nor, on the face of it, public slaves. (Although he does allow them a place in his ideal *polis*.) These forms of 'slavery' are unacceptable from the point of view of the slaves' interest, because they provide no guidance or instruction from the proximate rule of a rational master. Aristotle's conception of slavery is essentially paternalistic. His emphatic opposition to the use of slaves for production or mechanic purposes is an attack on the practice of the time.[19]

The only form of acquisition to which Aristotle gives any credence is again the traditional form of taking prisoners. He expressly casts doubt on the expectation that the children of slaves will necessarily be of a slavish nature. They should be educated

[19] W. L. Newman, the great nineteenth-century commentator, is one of the few to see that, 'the limitations that Aristotle imposed on slavery would probably have attracted most contemporary comment', *The Politics of Aristotle*, vol. i, p. 152.

and given the chance of manumission (VII. x. 13, p. 306). We know that Aristotle was unhappy at the prospect of one Greek state making slaves of fellow Greek prisoners. The traditional arguments for being entitled to enslave prisoners would be known to him. The heroic view that allowing yourself to be taken prisoner rather than dying a freeman is evidence of a slavish nature had lost some of its bite, especially when there was the prospect of a civilized exchange or ransom rather than a life of servitude. In the end for Aristotle only defeated barbarians deserve to be enslaved.

Surely Aristotle accepts what is no more than a narrow xenophobic Greek prejudice against foreigners who are racially distinct and therefore appear to be different? This is largely true. The fact that slaves taken in the Persian Wars were physically different was a significant factor in the Greeks' perception of natural differences. There is one substantial reason, however, why the Greeks in general and Aristotle in particular believed themselves justified in regarding barbarians to be inferior. Persians, Egyptians, and Macedonians, despite their great works, apparently chose at home to be ruled by absolute despots. They make no distinction between household and *polis*, Aristotle says, because 'there is no ruling element amongst them' (I. i. 4, p. 3). In this condition there is not only an absence of politics, but no place for philosophy, noble conduct, or even true friendship. Their lack of native freedom is thought to be evidence of lack of rationality. They would be better off with Greeks as their masters. We need not approve the sentiment, indeed our own history teaches us to be wary of it, but it is important to our understanding of their citizen ethic to know why the Greeks believed themselves superior.

Citizens and Constitutions

Book III deals with the general theory of citizenship in relation to constitutional types. His famous classification of types spans the range from the ideal, to the actual, from good to bad; it therefore forms an important bridge between the differently orientated books in the *Politics*.

There are four terms derivative from 'polis', that together underlie Aristotle's analysis: they are constitution (*politeia*), citizen (*polites*), ruling body (*politeuma*), statesman (*politicos*).[2] In one sense the *polis* is made up of its citizens, but how they are 'composed' depends on the *politeia*. The constitution is more than the legal political structure, it embodies the principles upon which the *polis* is founded: it is its 'soul'. Generically, the *polis*, as we know, has as its 'end' the good life, but the particular constitution defines the nature of the good way of life. Aristotle identifies the constitution with the *polis*' conception of 'justice' (III. ix. I, p. 117). The constitution will determine who are citizens, and what citizenship amounts to in terms of the distribution of duties and rights (in that order for the Greeks). The ruling body (*politeuma*) refers both to the ruling 'offices' and the class of citizens who occupy them. The ruling offices or body of citizens placed in power by the constitution (*politeia*) is the same as the sovereign (*kyrion*), Aristotle says (III. vi. I, p. 110). Finally, the constitution will provide the conditions for 'office' or 'honour' (*time* means both), which will allow some citizens to distinguish themselves as leaders or statesmen (*politicoi*).

Aristotle's classification of constitutions is initially in terms of two criteria: the number of the ruling body and whether or not the rule is 'right' or 'perverted'. He distinguishes the latter by whether the ruling body rules in the public interest of all citizens, or in its own personal or class interest. The right forms of the one, the few, and the many are kingship, aristocracy, and 'polity'; their perversions are respectively, tyranny, oligarchy, and democracy (III. vi–vii,, pp. 110–15). By the standard of 'absolute justice', the rank order from best to worst is kingship, aristocracy, 'polity', democracy, oligarchy, and tyranny. One of the ways in which Aristotle distinguishes the right forms from their corruptions is whether office holding is regarded as a duty which should be shared, or as a private benefit to be hung on to. He identifies the former attitude, with the right forms of the past and the latter attitude, with the corruptions of 'today' (III. vi. 9–10, p. 112).

The definition of a citizen arrived at in book III is 'a man who enjoys the right of sharing in deliberative or judicial office'; and this coheres with the 'common-sense' view that civic life is 'ruling and being ruled in turn' (III. xiii. 12, p. 134). Aristotle however is aware that the generic definition does not fit equally well with all types of constitution. The duties and rights of citizens will depend

[20] See Barker's note S on this terminology, p. 106.

on the nature of the constitution, therefore, the 'good citizen' is relative to the constitution (unlike the good man defined by the standard of absolute justice).

Aristotle clearly recognizes that there is a particular problem of the standing of those citizens under corrupt constitutions who are excluded from the ruling body. Not only are they non-participants in the ruling offices but their interests appear to be excluded from the *polis*. It seems that they are citizens in name only. The problem for the generic definition however goes deeper. It is not only in the perverted forms that full citizenship, in the sense of sharing in the ruling offices, is not attainable by all citizens. In kingship and probably aristocracy there is a difference between being a citizen and being a member of the ruling body: some citizens never having 'a turn' at ruling. Only if 'sharing in rule' is now to be understood as sharing in the benefits of rule, and the equality of citizenship being the equality of the rule of law rather than political participation, does the general definition apply. Aristotle appears to concede at one point that democracy comes closest to the general definition of *politeia* (III. i. 11, p. 95): this term is also used to denote the least good 'right' type (the convention is to translate it in this context 'polity'); its claim to be *the* generic type will be discussed. In so far as sharing in rule and in being ruled in a community of equals is indeed the condition of rational political man, Aristotle's endorsement of kingship and to a lesser extent aristocracy is problematic.

Aristotle's ranking of constitutions is an application of his general theory of justice. His uneasy endorsement of monarchy is in part a consequence of this, in part a derivation from the Platonic heritage. The principle of distributive justice as outlined in the *Ethics* (*NE* v. 3, pp. 112–14), requires that everyone gets 'what is due to them': the key concept here is that of 'proportionate equality'. In relation to office, the relevant criteria for honour or reward is provided by the 'end' of the *polis*. Since the purpose of the *polis* is the 'good life' of the citizens, contribution to that end should be the basis of merit (III. ix, pp. 117–20). If one man is superior to all others in the excellence of ruling, such that he is not only individually best, but better than all others collectively, then absolute justice demands that he should be king. Most of what Aristotle says on the subject in the *Politics* (III. xiv–xviii, pp. 137–52) and the *Ethics* (*NE* VIII. 10–11, pp. 209–12) suggests that true kingship is a theoretical possibility only. In practice there are various forms of kingship which fall well short of the ideal. Aristotle does not class them as tyrannies because, unlike other classical authors, he confines this term to those who have no intent to rule in the interest of their subjects. Actual forms of kingship are better in practice when their power is less than absolute and the rule of law is instituted rather than rule by personalized judgement (which he concedes would have to be best in the case of a true king). The true king is sufficient to himself and has no equals, he therefore has no true friends with whom to share the burden of office, nobody to devolve responsibilities to (III. xv–xvi, pp. 145–8). By implication Aristotle is criticizing Plato's notion of a community of philosopher kings. If there were such superior beings, it would be unjust to banish them for being too good for the *polis*. (This was the classical solution; supposed to be the origin of the institution of ostracism.) However, Aristotle does suggest they would do best to lay down laws to establish a constitution fit for lesser mortals.[21]

The student legislators at the Lyceum should not propose laws on the assumption that there will be god–philosopher–kings (they in any case have no need of lawgivers). Aristotle's ideal, discussed in books VII and VIII, is an aristocracy. His model constitution is based on the supposition that a lawgiver could choose the most favourable circumstances. This is not entirely unrealistic because in setting up a colony, it might just be possible to choose both the geographical location and the social composition. Aristotle's schema is to be compared with that in Plato's *Laws*, which makes the same assumption, rather than with the ideal of the *Republic*. Aristotle's ideal is no great inspiration. The most important point about the aristocratic constitution is that the rule of 'the best' (*aristoi*), or most meritorious, is in itself the end or good of the *polis*. The ideal *polis* is one which is constituted to facilitate the best way of life for its citizens; in serving the ends of the *polis* therefore they pursue their own purposes and happiness. Of the various functions that must be performed within the *polis* those assigned to citizens are done by turns, when they are best able to

[21] Aristotle does not propose self-banishment after the setting-up of a constitution but there was a popular tradition that the truly god-like might follow this course. Lycurgus is reputed to have set the example. 'Life of Lycurgus', *Plutarch's Lives* trans. J. Langhorne (London, 1879).

perform them: military duties are performed by the younger citizens, deliberating and judging by the middle-aged citizens, religious duties by the elders. This reminds us that the virtues amongst citizens are various and those appropriate to particular offices are predominant at different times of life. Thus rule by the best is incompatible with permanent office holding; the best at the moment might permit all to rule at some time. In Aristotle's ideal there appears to be no class of citizens permanently excluded from ruling offices, unlike actual aristocracies (which approximate to the ideal). Ideal aristocracy could be compatible in theory with all citizens sharing in rule. In practice of course the citizens would need to be few with substantial property. This is no doubt the presumption underlying Aristotle's aristocratic ideal.

However, while his ideal might meet the requirement that all citizens share in rule and in being ruled, it is at a cost to the coherence of the general theory. This is because in his ideal some functions that are necessary to the *polis*, which were largely performed by citizens in actual states, are relegated to jobs for non-citizens (VII. ix. 7–8, pp. 302–3). Aristotle says that those who provide necessary services in manufacture, trade, and agriculture are 'necessary conditions' rather than 'integral parts' of the *polis*. It is the most serious weakness in the theoretical ideal that a 'necessary part' of the *polis* is not integrated into the whole, as it must be, according to the general theory in book I. As a result, this category of persons has no theoretical place or justification in the *polis* at all. The anomaly arises in part at least from Aristotle's honesty. Although he deplores the fact, he has to admit that the economic functions performed by non-citizens beyond the ambit of the domestic household have become indispensable to the modern city-state. His unwillingness to accept that citizens could engage in any sort of productive work in his ideal is a measure of the extent to which Aristotle remains a defender of 'aristocratic' values, in the colloquial sense. How far he believed these to be shared by his audience is another matter. What was practically possible in his time he saw to be very different.

The Actually Possible

According to Aristotle, most contemporary city-states embodied elements of democracy and oligarchy. Ideologically, they repre-

sent competing conceptions of justice. In practice, actual constitutions will often be a mixture of the two, or somewhere on a continuum between extreme oligarchy (approaching tyranny) and
extreme democracy (approaching anarchy), with the mid-point
of 'polity'. In short, Aristotle's typology is flexible enough to
cover any combination of institutions and social composition.
Much of the middle books of the *Politics* is devoted to an absorbing discussion of the merits of the varieties of actual constitutions.
We must focus on the broad theoretical features.

In terms of absolute justice both oligarchy and democracy fall
short, but there is something to be said for the principles of each.
Both embody a partial conception of justice. Democrats believe
that because men are equally 'free-born' citizens they are equal in
all things; oligarchs believe that because wealth makes men superior in some respects they should be treated as superior in all respects (III. ix. 4, p. 118). Only in so far as free birth and wealth do
have a bearing on a person's contribution to the good life of the
polis are they relevant to true justice. Both make the error of judging persons by the criteria of their class, rather than their personal
merit (III. ix, pp. 116–21).

Aristotle says that in fact the real difference between the two
types is not number but the class which rules: democracy is the
rule of the poor who are usually many and oligarchy by the
wealthy usually few (they are usually also the well born) (III. viii,
p. 115). Although a truly just constitution must recognize the
merits of individuals, Aristotle does identify certain virtues with
classes. As might be expected, the qualities of leadership required
of statesmen would be associated with the wealthy and noble,
who have sufficient leisure. The particular virtues of the many and
poor are recognized to have some collective weight. The free-
born poor have the combined capacity to elect magistrates and to
call them to account. They possess what Aristotle calls 'the aggregate quality of number' when they judge in the assembly and
lawcourts. Being on the receiving end, 'they know where the
shoe pinches' so to speak; they have the wisdom of collective experience (III. xi, pp. 123–7). By implication, the case is made for
democratic majority-rule; which is what there is when the assembly and courts are sovereign. This is not to say that Aristotle
endorses the democratic case, but he concedes it has some justice
when not 'pushed too far'.

Aristotle discusses various types of democracy and oligarchy, always showing a preference for the most moderate and law-abiding. The most favoured oligarchy is one where wealth and noble birth are combined with merit, so there is an element of aristocracy in them. Similarly, the best form of democracy seems to come close to a 'polity'. In general Aristotle suggests that democracies are more stable than oligarchies because more people have an interest in their maintenance (v. v–ix, pp. 214–34). However, the distance between the extreme form of democracy and the most moderate is enormous. Aristotle's account is at one with the conservative oligarchs' view of contemporary Athens. The most moderate form of democracy could be an account of Athens in 'the old days, before the war'.

Aristotle's portrayal of extreme democracy contains many of the classic objections to direct democracy. This form of democracy almost fails to be a constitution at all because of the lack of respect for law and order; public affairs are not even confined to legitimate citizens. Extreme democracy is identified with the pursuit of absolute equality and liberty becoming licence. 'The democrat starts by assuming that justice consists in equality: he proceeds to identify equality with the sovereignty of the masses; he ends with the view that "liberty and equality" consist in "doing what one likes"'. Each man lives '"for any end he chances to desire"' (v. ix. 15, p. 234). In such a *polis* there is no discipline, temperance, or regard for merit. Politics is characterized as 'mob rule' leading to flattery and demagogy, where the emotions of the demos are given full rein. This picture of political disorder caused by the predominance of the urban poor represents the real fear of well-to-do Athenians after the Peloponnesian Wars. As a result of the war many who sought protection or had been dispossessed remained to swell the numbers in and around Athens, where casual employment could be found. No doubt the lawlessness of the city then as now was an exaggeration, but it has a potent place in anti-democratic ideology. The image of fifth-century Athens, like that of the later Roman Republic, makes a firm association between the city, democratic assembly, and lawlessness. Aristotle's objection to democracy owes more to a stereotype of demos man and the corresponding social order, than to a critique of democratic political institutions.

Aristotle contrasts extreme democracy with the moderate

rural-based democracy where most citizens live and work on their farms. They have relatively little leisure to attend the city and therefore meetings of the assembly must be limited (VI. iv. 1–15, pp. 263–5. Participation of the demos in politics will largely be confined to electing and examining magistrates, who will need to meet a property qualification for office. If the free-born poor are to rule in their class interest, they had better not be the abject urban poor. They had better be rural farmers with something for the law to protect, and whose interest is in conserving the *polis* and not in dispossessing the wealthy. Since in this form of democracy a large part of public affairs is assigned to the few, it in fact approximates to a 'polity'.

The remaining form of constitution described by Aristotle is the most important from the point of view of his contribution to political analysis. This is so because it represents a compromise and reconciliation between the general theory and the facts of political life as he found them. Polity is the only 'right' constitution that is possible when men in politics are corrupt, when in practice they put their own or their class interest before the good of the whole. Polity also turns out to be the only form of constitution where there is some sort of proportionate political equality so that all citizens can certainly share in the ruling offices whatever their particular qualities or social classification. The general requirement in functional terms of 'the citizen' can be fulfilled in polity by all, such that it is named appropriately 'the constitution' (IV. vii–xiii, pp. 174–86).

When the social composition of a *polis* is predominantly poor or wealthy, then its constitution will naturally be a democracy or oligarchy; only the imposition of an external force can change this. There is no point in the would-be lawgiver in his audience prescribing laws which ignore the reality of the existing distribution of power. (This in itself is a far-reaching Aristotelian insight in political science.) However, when neither extremes of wealth and poverty naturally dominate, and preferably when there is a preponderance of citizens in the middle with a medium amount of property, then a polity is both possible and desirable (III. xi. 20, p. 133). Aristotle regards polity as 'the practically best possible' for most city-states. The principles of democracy and oligarchy can be combined by making some ruling offices open to all free-born; typically, electing, judging, and deciding in assembly; and some offices requiring a property qualification; typically magistrates, perhaps military commanders. In this way the common good is served by giving no class of citizens the power to rule only in their own interest, thus by institutional compromise the corrupt forms together constitute a right form of constitution.

From one perspective, polity involves an institutional solution to the problem of class conflict. It is the form of government most suitable to a divided citizenry, when holding office is going to be used for promoting sectional interests rather than the collective good. Certainly the idea of giving opposing classes, or parties with opposing notions of justice, some share of political power is an important theoretical innovation in constitutionalism. However the idea of institutional balancing of political extremes, despite the use made of the idea by those who followed Aristotle, is not at the heart of Aristotle's conception of the balance aimed at in 'polity'. Rather his design is to shift political power away from both the extremes of rich and poor class interests. Thus he extols the virtue of those in the 'middle class' (any connection with 'bourgeoisie' must of course be expunged from the modern reader's mind). For the Greeks the most important property classifications were those connected with office holding and, more particularly, forms of military service. Those with sufficient property to equip themselves to fight on foot (the hoplite) Aristotle identifies most strongly with the middle class (IV. xiii. 10–11, p. 188). However, more generally he has in mind the citizen who is not committed by class loyalty to take sides but is amenable to reasoned argument. Taking the balanced view or the middle way corresponds to Aristotle's view that virtue consists in 'the mean' between extremes.[22] Similarly, the constitution of the best possible state must aim to avoid the excesses of wealth and poverty and give a significant place to those of 'a moderate and adequate property', who are without envy, and are governed by reason rather than passion (IV. xi. 9–14, p. 182). Even though in practice Aristotle is forced to acknowledge that class divisions amongst citizens do exist and must be taken into account by constitution

---

[22] The role which Aristotle assigns to a class between the opposing interests of rich and poor is taken up by many proponents of consensual political theory. Often the group is identified with the intelligentsia, who have sufficient means to be educated, but no pressing material interest to cloud their balanced judgement. See for instance the role assigned to the 'enlightened' minority in J. S. Mill's *Representative Government* (1859).

makers, he places his faith in laws which depend upon the stereo-
typical 'citizen'. The balanced citizen has an important a part as
the balance of the citizenry.

Aristotle's Legacy

What has been presented here is a selection from Aristotle's teaching on politics. It is also an interpretation, as any systematic selection must be. It is made from the perspective of Aristotle's
contribution to the classical republican tradition. This involves
taking not only a particular view of Aristotle and Greek politics,
but also of the historical importance of the legacy of this tradition
in political theory, which it is beyond the bounds of this exercise
to attempt to demonstrate. It may be none the less worth rehears-
ing in summary the Aristotelian foundations of classical republicanism.

The central core of classical republicanism depends upon the
conception that man is by nature a political animal and that only
where the opportunity exists for a citizen to take part in government can his human potentiality be realized. Aristotle's man is the
basis of what is called the 'civic humanist' conception of man
which underpins classical republicanism. First and foremost, the
citizen is a free agent, a chooser and actor in the public arena; as
Homer puts it, he is a 'speaker of words and a doer of deeds'. He
must know how to act morally; being beneficent to subordinates,
sharing with friends and equals, honouring the worthy. Personal
fulfilment should be derived in turn from being honoured by
fellow citizens for service to the community. Since the moral and
political are improved by the intellectual and aesthetic, the good
citizen will pursue the higher pleasures of beauty and truth
through the 'muses' and philosophy. Physical training and a life-
style compatible with military service are an equal concomitant of
civic duty. Political and civil service require the means of life, but
necessary work is not an essentially human activity to be valued as
such. Property ownership is understood as a pre-condition of
political freedom, most fundamentally because it makes a citizen
economically and therefore politically independent, but it is no
more than a means.

The civic humanist conception of man as a citizen allows
there to be distinctions amongst equals. Aristotle's notion of

proportionate equality facilitates the defence of a distinct role for the virtuous few amongst the many. Thus classical republicanism is able to incorporate the reality of class division, so long as it is limited and contained by a constitution that contrives the promotion of the common good. At worst the few can be constrained by the many, at best they will willingly serve them. Aristotle lays the foundation for a workable compromise between democracy and aristocracy, which is able to take account both of what citizens might be and of what they actually are.

Classical republicanism combines the optimistic aspirations of civic humanism and the classical pessimism of degeneracy in human affairs. The key conception is that political decay, corruption, class warfare, and political revolutions can be checked or at least postponed by laws which secure a constitutional balance. Aristotle's conception of the constitution (polity) is the basis of the idea which takes root in Polybius' account of the Roman constitution, and is passed to seventeenth-century Englishmen via Italian Renaissance thinkers (prominent amongst whom was Machiavelli) to eighteenth-century Scots and Americans. If wildly simplified historicism is permissible in the concluding remarks of an essay, it can be said that the fruits of classical republicanism are found in the mixed or balanced British Constitution of 1688 and the American Constitution of 1789.

The modern conception of democracy which recognizes the division between the few and the many in occupying different but countervailing roles is deeply indebted to the tradition. It is however an equivocal inheritance because at the heart of classical republicanism is a conception of citizenship which has expectations of political participation much beyond that of modern democratic societies. The Greek experience requires us to set aside the excuse that political life like philosophy is 'too high for man'; we are challenged to ask whether it is not after all our institutions and values that inhibit the realization of true human potentiality.

Bibliographical Note

The main English translations of Aristotle's *Politics* are as follows: B. Jowett (Oxford, 1885); H. Rackman (Cambridge, 1932); E. Barker (Oxford, 1946; paperback edition, 1978); J. Warrington (London, 1959); and T. A. Sinclair

(London, 1962). The Everyman edition by Warrington is *The* Politics *and* Athenian Constitution; the additional text is worth having. Sinclair's Penguin Classics edition is obviously an attractive purchase, but all other editions are second-best to Barker. Barker's treatment pays due regard to the fact that the Greek text is not a full narrative; his notes and introduction are invaluable.

Aristotle's *Politics* is not overburdened by commentaries in English. The introduction and detailed notes which accompany the Greek text of W. L. Newman, *The* Politics *of Aristotle* (Oxford, 1887–1902) is valuable for detailed textual scrutiny. The three most accessible commentaries are E. Barker, *The Political Thought of Plato and Aristotle* (London, 1906); R. G. Mulgan, *Aristotle's Political Theory* (Oxford, 1977); and J. B. Morrall, *Aristotle* (Political Thinkers Series, London, 1977). Useful chapters on Aristotle's political thought are found in C. I. McIlwain, *The Growth of Political Theory in the West* (London, 1932) and in T. A. Sinclair, *A History of Greek Political Thought* (London, 1951).

Amongst works related to the politics, S. R. L. Clark, *Aristotle's Man* (Oxford, 1974) involves speculations upon Aristotle's anthropology, which are formidable but insightful. See also Clark's article 'Aristotle's Woman', *History of Political Thought* 3:2. (1982), for balance. Lord Carnes, *Education and Culture in the political thought of Aristotle* (Oxford, 1982), argues the case for the 'good life' to found in the 'muses'. Hannah Arendt, *The Human Condition* (Chicago, 1958), expounds on the civic ideal in Aristotle in the course of propounding her own view. From the opposite pole E. M. Wood and N. Wood, *Class Ideology and Ancient Political Theory* (Oxford, 1978), give a scholarly Marxist historical perspective on Plato, Socrates, and Aristotle. J. P. Lynch, *Aristotle's School: A study of a Greek Educational Institution* (London, 1982) is interesting background.

The student of the *Politics* might choose to expand his or her understanding of Aristotle either by acquaintance with his other works, or by finding out more about Greek life and history. My advice is to take the latter course first and the books listed at the end of the chapter on Plato's *Republic* are relevant here too.

Of those other works of Aristotle which relate to the *Politics*, the *Nicomachean Ethics* is the most important. The edition used here is translated by W. D. Ross (London, 1954). There are numerous commentaries on the *Ethics*; W. F. Hardie, *Aristotle's Ethical Theory* (Oxford, 1968) should suffice. Aristotle's *Athenian Constitution* is an important source on Athenian history. In addition to the Everyman edition mentioned above, there is the Hafner edition translated by Kurt von Fritz and Ernst Kapp (New York, 1966) in paperback. Aristotle's *Rhetoric* was required reading in past generations when training in rhetoric was part of liberal humanist education (its place has been taken by Management Studies in our universities). The *Rhetoric* is worthy of study; some of its subject-matter overlaps with the *Politics*. R. C. Jebb, *The* Rhetoric *of Aristotle* (Cambridge, 1909).

For a general overview of the corpus of Aristotle's works any of the following might be consulted. W. D. Ross, *Aristotle* (Oxford, 1949); W. Jaeger, *Aristotle* (Oxford, 1948); A. E. Taylor, *Aristotle* (London, 1943); G. R. G. Mure, *Aristotle* (Oxford, 1964); G. E. R. Lloyd, *Aristotle: The Growth and Structure of his Thought* (Cambridge, 1968). None of these general studies it should be said comment much on his political science.

For further reading on the theme of Aristotle's contribution to the classical republican tradition: Z. Fink, *The Classical Republicans* (Evanston, 1945), reviews the authors who have contributed to the tradition; J. G. A. Pocock, *Machiavellian Moment* (Princeton, 1975), develops the theme historically and schematically.

3

Saint Augustine: *The City of God*

BRUCE HADDOCK

AUGUSTINE'S *City of God* has always posed special problems for
political theorists approaching the work for the first time. Not the
least of these difficulties concerns the organization of the text
itself. Written in instalments between 413 and 426, the work is
both immensely long and discursive. Far from following a consistent line of argument throughout, Augustine gives us absorbing
accounts of a host of issues which preoccupied him. He shifts, for
example, from a sensitive discussion of whether or not any sin
should attach to the conduct of the poor women raped by invad-
ing barbarians (I. 16), to detailed examinations of such issues as the
rites and practices involved in the worship of the pagan gods
(II. 4), the role of poetry and drama in Greek and Roman society
(II. 9, 11–14), and the part played by demons in disrupting the
day-to-day conduct of life (II. 25–6).[1] All this is grist to the historian's mill, for whom Augustine comes to resemble a veritable
encyclopaedia of late Roman culture. But what of the political
theorist? How is he to gain some purchase on an argument which
studiedly avoids addressing political issues directly?

What has to be accepted from the outset is that Augustine did
not set himself the task of writing a treatise on political theory.
His principal concern was rather to highlight the gulf which
separated two world-views, Christian and pagan, at a time when
there was still a tendency to treat Christianity simply as an ambiguous offshoot from the common stock of classical culture.
This, in itself, was a task with profound political implications.
The *polis* had, after all, been the key institution in the Greek
world. Even where citizens were not directly involved in making
political decisions or assuming public responsibility, their sense of
their own identity was nevertheless conferred upon them by their

---

[1] The *City of God* is divided into 22 books. References are to book and chapter numbers
common to all modern editions, followed by page references to the Penguin edition in the
case of specific quotations. See the bibliographical note for further details.

polis. And in those polities where there was more widespread participation, the performance of one's role as a citizen was seen as a sacred duty, distinguishing a free man from a slave, barbarian, or beast.[2] In the Roman world, too, the role of law lent a significance to public institutions and procedures which dominated the conception of what it meant to be a Roman. Public life could thus be seen as an end in itself. For Augustine, however, the political world had no such intrinsic significance. He regarded the state itself (and the various institutions of social life) as a series of constraints imposed upon men because of their sinful natures. The truly significant relationship in any individual's life was not between himself and the state but between himself and God. One's appraisal of political institutions, in this scheme of things, could not be in terms of their intrinsic merits but rather in terms of their providential role in the fulfilment of God's design for men.

This attribution of a limited and derivative significance to political life is Augustine's distinctive contribution to political thought. We should be clear, however, that in reacting against the state or *polis* as the ideal focus for men's actions and deliberations, he was not simply denying the validity of secular institutions. Unlike the Stoics, Cynics, and Epicureans, Augustine was not arguing for a radical individualism. It was not only that the state could not embody all that men had it in them to hope for or aspire towards; but rather that human reason itself was an inadequate instrument for the fashioning of a way of life. Men needed the state and its institutions to restrain them, reprehensible though the values of the state might be. Given their predicament, men could not flourish without the state; neither could they find fulfilment in it. What they needed, above all, was to see the state aright, in relation to matters of permanent value. And it was just such a perspective that Augustine sought to provide in the *City of God*.

The contrast at the core of the *City of God* is between the eternal values enshrined in God's ordered universe and the transience and fickleness of all human endeavour. What makes the

---

[2] See the essays on Plato and Aristotle above for discussions of Greek views of the significance of politics in general and political participation in particular.

City of God so distinctive as a theological treatise, however, is its penetrating account of human motivation. Men are portrayed as wretched creatures tossed by impulses which they can struggle to subdue but will never finally master. The lust for power and sex are given special prominence. But even in the finer details of life men are liable to find their judgement distorted by greed, envy, or vainglory. In his portrayal of the darker side of human nature, Augustine draws very much upon his own observations of affairs. Indeed, as a stylist he has often been praised for the vividness and realism of his descriptions. It gives his writing an immediacy which is lacking in later scholastic theology. For the political theorist who might not trust his hand at theology, it is some comfort to know that he will recognize the individual portrayed in the *City of God* as a close relation of the creature he has come to know and love in Machiavelli, Hobbes, and Hume.

Noting the affinity between Augustine's account of human nature and that of later (more secular-minded) pessimists is no more than a beginning. What has to be grasped is that the distinctive cast of political pessimism in the Western tradition has theological roots; and Augustine's remains the most authoritative statement of the view that has come down to us. Here was a man straddling the pagan and Christian worlds, thoroughly versed in Roman literature, who was anxious to specify precisely where Christianity stood in relation to classical culture. It is a measure of his achievement that Christian writers would approach Greek and Roman philosophy within his frame of reference for the next 800 years. Indeed, his reading of Plato as the classical philosopher who had most nearly grasped the essentials of the Christian position persisted until the eighteenth century (VIII. 5–11; XXII. 26–8). All this must be borne in mind when we come to consider Augustine's importance for the student of political thought. It is something of a commonplace to describe the Western tradition as a synthesis of classical and Christian culture. But if we want to understand that tradition, it is essential that we grasp precisely how the two cultures were mutually absorbed. Seen in this light, Augustine assumes a double significance: not only is his synthesis of pagan and Christian thought worthy of attention in its own right, it also set the parameters for Christian reactions to the classical world.

The conflict between paganism and Christianity was brought

to a head in the most dramatic fashion with the sack of Rome by Alaric in 410. The Roman Empire had not, of course, crumbled with the one assault. But a symbolic shock had been administered which obliged both pagans and Christians to re-examine some of their most fundamental assumptions. For pagans, the Roman Empire had come to be identified with civilization itself. And the very idea that it could be successfully assailed by barbarians led men to ask themselves why a vigorous (and seemingly invincible) society should now be so weak and divided. A convenient scapegoat could be found in the Christian religion. The conversion of the Empire to Christianity by imperial edict had led to a neglect of traditional pagan rites and practices; and it was no accident that the administrative and military prowess of the Empire should reach its nadir as the influence of Christianity approached its zenith. What we see among the far-flung Roman aristocracy is a self-conscious return to the roots of pagan culture, a cultivation of habits of mind which had never, in fact, been wholly abandoned.

That this movement represented a direct challenge to Christianity is clear. What is less obvious, however, is that Christians should find the decline of Rome difficult to accommodate within their own scheme of things. The conversion of the Empire to Christianity had seemed to fit perfectly with a providential view of history, extending the influence of the Church to the furthermost limits of the civilized world. With the demise of the Empire now an imminent possibility, Christian thinkers had to seek a fresh understanding of the Church's relationship with the secular world. Not only had they to exonerate themselves from the charge that their beliefs and practices had undermined the foundations of the Empire; but they had to discern a meaning or significance in the traumatic events which had shaken the civilization they had all taken for granted.

Augustine was ideally qualified to address these tasks. As the product of a mixed marriage, with a pagan father and Christian mother, he had a solid grounding in both the secular and religious dimensions of the Roman tradition. Indeed, before his baptism in 387 (at the age of 33), he had been thoroughly eclectic in his intellectual and spiritual tastes, flirting at different times with Stoicism, Manichaeism, and neo-Platonism. In his professional career, as a teacher of rhetoric, he had shown outstanding promise, earning advancement to a prestigious post at Milan in 384. After his baptism, however, all his intellectual energies would be marshalled in the cause of the Church. By the time he was consecrated as bishop of Hippo in 395, he had a considerable reputation as a philosopher, theologian, and controversialist. Uniquely among his contemporaries, he had mastered both the pagan and Christian intellectual traditions. When he came, then, in the *City of God*, to state the case for Christianity against a resurgent paganism, he could exploit an insider's knowledge of Roman culture in order to expose its shortcomings.

Augustine begins his account with a detailed rebuttal of the pagan view that the safety of the city could be secured through the propitiation of household gods. Such devices had signally failed to protect Troy (i. 3); and the Romans themselves had not seen fit to spare the temples of conquered cities (i. 6). Seen in this light, the misfortunes which had befallen Rome following Alaric's assault upon the city should require no especial explanation. The conduct of the barbarians had been in accordance with the normal conventions of warfare (i. 7). Atrocities had always attended the sack of a city. What really required explanation, however, was the fact that the ferocity of the barbarians should assume an 'aspect of gentleness' when confronted by the spectacle of basilicas filled with people seeking refuge (i. 7, p. 12).

Augustine's strategy in these opening sections is clear: to establish a providential framework which could enable a positive significance to be discerned in a series of events that had shaken the confidence of Christians and pagans alike. Behind his concern with the historical record lurked a larger philosophical purpose. His intention was not only to highlight the futility of hoping to influence the course of events through ritual practices but to sever the connection in conventional attitudes between virtue and desert. The virtuous and the wicked are equally vulnerable in the face of the vagaries of experience. The distribution of worldly felicity between individuals was something that simply had to be accepted as a datum, susceptible of neither theoretical nor moral justification. But there was a lesson to be learned from men's responses to fortune. The proper reaction to life's variable prospects was a disdain for the goods it provided. One could, of course, seek comfort and well-being; but it should not have a moral significance attached to it. This was the flaw at the heart of pagan religious culture. The equation of practical success with civic or religious virtue had led to an undue importance being attributed to occurrences which would always be beyond human comprehension. Men would exult in the world's goods or be overwhelmed by its ills, thereby identifying their conceptions of themselves with the shifting fortunes of daily life. Yet there was an alternative view. The apparent unfairness of events could be seen as a sufficient reason for seeking one's criteria of significance elsewhere, in a world of eternal values disclosed by reason or faith (II. 8–11). Such a perspective had the obvious merit of accepting the transience of affairs without relapsing into scepticism. Not the least of the advantages of what is usually regarded as a thoroughly 'other-worldly' philosophy is in fact the psychological support it lends to the individual in his daily pursuits, struggling to do the best he can for himself in intractable circumstances.

A systematic devaluation of the temporal sphere was a central concern of the *City of God*. But Augustine had not endorsed a neo-Stoic position. He was not intent upon dismissing all involvement with secular affairs as corruptive and irrelevant to one's spiritual life. Indeed Christianity is distinctive among the welter of religious and philosophical ideas which flourished in the later Roman period in its emphasis on the historical disclosure and ultimate triumph of its doctrine in time. Christianity had presented itself as an historical philosophy, with elaborate criteria for appraising the secular world it was confronting. Augustine had thus to combine his critique of pagan worldliness with the rather more subtle task of estimating the significance of successive civilizations.

Rome itself presented him with his most sensitive problem. It was a comparatively straightforward matter to show that Rome had suffered calamities long before Christianity had displaced the pagan gods, thus exonerating Christianity from any direct responsibility for the decline of the Empire (II. 3, with detailed historical illustration throughout III). In Augustine's account, pagan religious practices had undermined Rome's civic culture from within, condoning sacrilegious and obscene entertainments and failing to sanction a doctrine of right living (II. 4–6). And Roman philosophers, gifted though they might have been in technical respects, were not equal to the task of sustaining a flourishing civic and moral culture (II. 7).

Nor is the failure of the philosophers an incidental consideration. Human weakness is a dominant theme throughout the *City of God*. Men's moral and intellectual fallibility is such that reason alone can never serve as the foundation for a way of life. Augustine's strictures against the philosophers should thus be read in the context of his larger case against the autonomy of the secular sphere. The fact remained that Rome had once flourished and had subsequently come to grief. It was crucial, given the context in which he was writing, for Augustine to give some account of this remarkable train of events. Indeed the fortune of Christianity had become so inextricably commingled with the history of Rome that he could not effectively address his more narrowly theological concerns without some discussion of its fate. In the event, Rome served him as a paradigm case, illustrating both the significance and the limits of political society. And it was through reflection on the corruption of Rome that he was enabled to counterpoint the transcendent purposes of the Heavenly City.

The corruption of Rome, in fact, presents Augustine with much less of a dilemma than its manifest success at its zenith. An empire which had been coextensive with civilization itself in men's imaginations could not be without some merit or significance. Augustine was not content with the rather facile teleological view which looked beyond Roman institutions to the role of the Empire in fostering and sustaining the Church. Instead he attributed Rome's success to the wisdom of her institutions and the austerity of her public and private morals in the early days. Quoting Scipio from Cicero's *De Republica*, he likens 'concord in a community' to 'harmony in music', with 'different classes, high, low and middle', united, 'like the varying sounds of music, to form a harmony of very different parts through the exercise of rational restraint' (II. 21, p. 72). The crucial element in this 'harmony' or 'rational restraint' is, of course, a notion of justice. Augustine again draws upon Cicero for his initial definition. A community is seen not simply as 'any and every association of the population, but "an association united by a common sense of right and a community of interest"' (II. 21, p. 73). It follows from this 'that a commonwealth only exists where there is a sound and just government', leading inexorably to the conclusion that a tyranny of any kind (whether rule is by one, a few, or the many) is tantamount to the dissolution of the community (II. 21, p. 73).

Augustine does not wholeheartedly endorse this contractualist position.[3] Later in his argument he will be at some pains to demonstrate that a true sense of justice presupposes the realization of the ends enshrined in Christian doctrine (XIX. 21 and 24). But he was equally reluctant to accept a position which would not only deny that Rome was a commonwealth properly so called but would also exclude the very possibility of a just polity being established. Even in a hypothetical Christian polity, a distinction between the elect and the reprobate would persist, leading to division and conflict between groups and individuals and to a need for institutional procedures for the pursuit of purely secular ends. A revised contractualism served well enough to account for the limited agreements men made in order to further their practical interests. According to these more modest criteria, Augustine could endorse the commonly held view that Rome 'was better ruled by the Romans of antiquity than by their later successors', without thereby compromising his central contention that the political world in general had only a relative significance in relation to the wider ends of human communities (II. 21, p. 75).

Accounting for the decline of Rome was a much more straightforward affair. Augustine had no need to revise the standard accounts of Rome's degeneration to be found in Sallust or Cicero. If it was moral probity that had once sustained an empire, it was moral corruption which finally sealed its fate. Instead of glorying in a reputation for public service, Romans began to 'lust for power' for its own sake (I. 31, p. 42). The moral restraint which had enabled the country to flourish and secure its liberty gave place to unbridled greed and sensuality. Public office, which had once been regarded as a sacred duty, was now seen as a private perquisite, significant only as a means of satisfying one's appetites. Under pressure of this kind, it was only a matter of time before the Empire would collapse. Anxious to ensure that no responsibility for the decline of public spirit should attach to Christianity, Augustine could let the story of Rome's cultural inanition speak

[3] One should be clear that Augustine's adoption of contractualist arguments never extends as far as the formal use of the idea of a social contract as a means of designating the proper limits of a legitimate polity. His concern is rather to highlight the community of interest between rulers and ruled which distinguishes a commonwealth from a tyranny. He is not concerned with the question of how a community of interest might express itself, nor with specific institutional procedures for resolving arguments about the character of that interest. For contrasting uses of the idea of social contract see the essays on Hobbes, Locke, and Rousseau below.

for itself. Impeccable Roman authorities were sufficiently vehement in their condemnation of the later Empire to serve his purpose. It remained for him simply to augment their accounts with particularly vivid illustrations of the decadence which had been tacitly supported in pagan religious practices, pausing always to highlight the rectitude of Christian doctrine by contrast.

We should be clear, however, that (for Augustine) Rome's decline is not to be explained in terms of a concatenation of contingent circumstances. The moral corruption which had sapped the vitality of her culture could not be reversed simply by men taking stock of their situation and remedying such abuses as came to their notice. Augustine's point is much more far-reaching. His contention is that any moral, religious, or political theory which attributes undue significance to worldly felicity will be rendered absurd in the face of the misfortunes that necessarily befall men in the course of their practical engagements. Some of these problems will appear to be self-inflicted, with ambition, greed, and lust for power upsetting the most carefully devised plans; others will be the product of natural disasters which could not (in principle) have been foreseen; but misfortunes of both sorts will always be a feature of the human condition.

Nor can men discern a pattern in the misfortunes which afflict them. Good and bad are equally vulnerable, unable either to understand or guard against life's calamities. Yet there is an order to events. What might appear to be random or fortuitous is actually 'in accordance with the order of events in history, an order completely hidden from' men, 'but perfectly known to God himself' (IV. 33, p. 176). Earthly dominion, for example, which is generally counted among life's boons, is given to both good and evil precisely in order that men might be weaned away from ephemeral values. The very fact that Rome had once flourished so mightily thus makes it a perfect example for Augustine of the transience of the things of this world. One has either to accept that human life is wholly unintelligible or have recourse to the larger fideistic framework afforded by the *City of God* for an account which lends a positive significance to men's overwhelming sense of bewilderment.

The fortune of Rome thus served to illustrate the heights and depths of secular achievement. In the early days, the sound moral character of the ancient Romans could justify the extension of their dominions. A real concern for the public interest could be seen at work within a ruling élite, leading men to put the honour and glory of serving the commonwealth before their private advantage (v. 12). And if this love of praise was itself a vice, it could yet counterbalance other (and greater) vices (v. 13). Since everything that occurred in the world was ordained by God's universal providence (v. 13), it followed that the worldly success of the Romans could be construed as a reward from God for their qualities of character (v. 15). Augustine even allows that citizens of the Eternal City, in their pilgrimage in this world, have something to learn from the achievements of the Romans, with their contempt for their own material interests, their disinterested concern for their country, their respect for the law, and their resistance to the temptations of avarice and sensual indulgence (v.16).

But the felicity of the Romans could not last. It was compromised (crucially) by its reliance on wordly ambition, 'the hope of glory in the sight of men' (v. 16, p. 205). And though there was 'a clear difference between the desire for glory before men and the desire for domination', there was nevertheless a 'slippery slope' which led from 'excessive delight' in the one to 'burning passion' for the other (v. 19, p. 212). Once the lust for domination predominates in men's deliberations, self-restraint is effectively at an end. Men stoop to the 'most barefaced crimes' in order 'to accomplish' their 'heart's desire', becoming 'worse than the beasts' in their cruelty and self-indulgence (v. 19, pp. 212–13). The type of rule associated with this new disposition is personified in Nero, for whom public office was simply a means of private gratification. A tyranny on Nero's scale nevertheless remains a part of God's order, designed to chastise a wayward people and to encourage the wise to seek their salvation elsewhere.

So much, at least, can be gathered of God's plan for men from an examination of the rise and fall of empire. But Augustine is clear that this is only to scratch the surface. What God's ulterior purpose might be is always beyond human comprehension. Yet the supposition that there is a rational design behind appearances, in the civil no less than in the natural world, serves Augustine as a regulative assumption in his account of the limitations of practical and theoretical endeavour. The postulation of an altogether different manner of association in the Heavenly City functions as a criterion in his explanation of the darker side of human nature. As a political theorist he is concerned with the forces which impel human beings to contend with one another for status and reward—ambition, greed, lust for power—in disregard of the wider ties that bind communities together. In order to understand the specifically political dimension of his thought, however, it is essential to grasp at least the lineaments of the theological views which inform his position. Two issues, in particular, need to be addressed before we can examine his central political arguments. In the first place, given that Augustine is concerned (among other things) to justify institutional restraint in terms of the deficiencies of human nature, we need to ask ourselves how responsibility for actions is to be understood in a scheme of things based upon the presupposition of an omniscient and omnipotent God. And secondly (and relatedly) we must establish precisely what significance should be attached to the evil which institutions are designed to counter.

On the question of the relationship between God's foreknowledge and man's free will, Augustine found himself trying to steer a middle course between a fatalistic determinism on the one hand and a radical indeterminism on the other. Both positions were incompatible with crucial aspects of Christian doctrine. A universal determinism would equate God's providence with fate or destiny, leaving no scope for the special relationship which set men apart from the rest of God's creation. Men were dependent upon God; but they had the capacity to share in God's reason, understanding something of the nature and limits of their own conduct. If they felt themselves to be distant from God in their current predicament, this was no more than a consequence of their sinfulness. By sinning, they had destroyed an original harmony. Henceforth their reason would be swamped by the conflicting demands of the passions, undermining any sense they might have had of their own integrity as individuals and pitting them against their fellows. The crucial point for Christian doctrine is that the pitfalls and calamities of practical life should be construed as self-inflicted wounds. Without this assumption, God would appear to be little more than a perverse or spiteful tyrant. In Augustine's view, however, the misfortunes which God visits upon men are a necessary means of their redemption. Suffering actually fosters self-awareness. It enables men to enjoy God's grace without sacrificing their position as self-conscious agents.

If a providential determinism denying the reality of free will was thus unacceptable to Augustine, it did not follow that he should commit himself to a view which simply acknowledged God's providence while exempting the human will from its sway. Augustine took particular exception to Cicero's treatment of the issue in *De Divinatione* and *De Fato*. Cicero had supposed that granting God's foreknowledge involved acceptance of the view 'that everything happens according to necessity' (v. 9, p. 190); and this would leave our understanding of human life in disarray since we would have no grounds for making moral judgements. There would be 'no point in making laws, no purpose in expressing reprimand or approbation, censure or encouragement'; nor, in the sphere of justice, would there be grounds for 'establishing rewards for the good and penalties for the evil' (v. 9, p. 191). According to Augustine, however, such a view was based upon a false dichotomy, as if allowing some scope for free will necessarily involved the denial of God's foreknowledge. He argued, on the contrary, that man's free will was actually a part of God's pre-ordained order. There was no need to belittle the significance of men's agonizing about how they should behave simply because God happened to know from the outset what the outcome of their deliberations would be. Nor did God's foreknowledge make him a cause of their conduct. As Augustine put the point succinctly, 'the fact that God foreknew that a man would sin does not make a man sin' (v. 10, p. 195). Responsibility, on this view, remains with man; it is the consequence of sin which manifests an inexorable inevitability.

It cannot be claimed that Augustine's attempt to balance the notions of free will and determinism is, in the final analysis, successful. The emphasis in his argument is always on grace rather than desert, relegating the individual to something of the role of a marionette. And, indeed, later workings of an essentially Augustinian doctrine, especially in the forms of Calvinism and Jansenism, were treated with hostility or suspicion by the Catholic hierarchy. Orthodox theologians of the sixteenth and seventeenth centuries were troubled specifically by the implications of the doctrine of predestination for an understanding of man's free will. But the issue had, in fact, surfaced in Augustine's own day, in his controversy with Pelagius. Whether or not Augustine's view is defensible, however, it tells us a great deal about the character of his political thought. His stress on grace rather than human endeavour in the redemption of mankind was predicated upon a profound conception of sin. Men were moulded in Adam's image and tainted by his original folly. Their sinful natures set clear limits to what could (in principle) be achieved in the secular sphere. All that could be expected from social and political institutions was a moderation of the consequences of sin. The realization of men's finer possibilities was deferred to another realm.

How, then, is evil to be understood in Augustine's thought? In his earlier days, while still a follower of the Manichaeans, Augustine had conceived of good and evil as two independent principles, locked in cosmic conflict. And it is true to say that certain remnants of Manichaean doctrine continued to inform his mature thought. Indeed the fundamental division in the *City of God* between spiritual and earthly realms can be traced back to Manichaean sources. The dualistic account of good and evil, however, could no longer be accommodated to his conception of God. A God whose attributes included not only goodness but also omnipotence and omniscience could not be portrayed as in any way vulnerable to the force of evil. But this, of course, left Augustine with the task of explaining how such a God could tolerate the existence of evil.

Augustine's response to the dilemma was to deny the reality of evil itself. Everything in nature had been created good. What we call evil was not, in fact, a separate entity or principle but 'merely a name for the privation of good' (XI. 22, p. 454). It could best be understood, given men's limited intelligence, by analogy with the harmony of nature, where even the loss of an eyebrow on a human face would detract from the beauty of the whole. And even (apparent) want of harmony should be interpreted in a positive light, fulfilling some aspect of God's design which men had failed to discern.

Such a view could account for the paradox that food and drink are regarded as goods yet 'are experienced as harmful when used without restraint and in improper ways' (XI. 22, p. 453). Restated in secular terms, Augustine's doctrine would appear to amount to little more than a claim (familiar since Aristotle) for the functional interdependence of all natural and social phenomena. But that is only half the story. What is distinctive about Augustine is his treatment of human sinfulness. Men, like all other natural creatures, had been faultless in their original creation. They had enjoyed a perfect harmony in their faculties and dispositions. All this had been destroyed, however, by an act of will (XI. 17). Adam and Eve (whatever specific misdemeanours they might have committed) chose not to follow God's instructions. They had undermined the original harmony of their existence through dis-obedience, exchanging the effortless enjoyment of God's goods for pain, hardship, and death (XIII. 14). Thenceforth they would know no tranquillity. Their minds would be tossed by incompat-ible desires, leading to deep anguish as reason and will were set in opposition to one another.

Nor did men have sufficient resources to redeem themselves by taking thought. The corruption of their natures was such that their unaided efforts would only deepen their misery. Human ingenuity had become a slave to the passions which tore men apart; the more they sought to disentangle themselves from the myriad snares of practical life, the more complete their slavery would become. The wise man, no less than the fool, was trapped in a vicious circle of sin and degradation. What had occurred at the Fall was wilful, a deliberate 'falling away from the work of God' (XIV. 11, p. 568). Whatever ends men might have pursued as a consequence of the Fall 'were evil because they followed the will's own line, and not God's' (XIV. 11, p. 568). Hence the will itself should be seen as the root cause of evil, 'the evil tree which bore evil fruit' (XIV. 11, p. 568). Hope for men, in these circum-stances, lay in turning away from themselves. The choices they made would be genuinely free when their subservience to sin had been eradicated. And this could only be achieved through acknowledging their total dependence upon God's grace.

Here we see the beginnings of Augustine's fundamental distinc-tion in the *City of God*. While all men pursue happiness, they do not necessarily follow the same path to their goal. Some, blissfully unaware of their corruption, will insist on living 'by the standard of men'; while others, acknowledging their weakness and degra-dation, will accept that they must live 'by the standard of God' (XIV. 4, p. 552). At issue here is a choice between the paths of false-hood and truth, sin and righteousness. To persevere in following men's standards is, in fact, to embrace a contradiction. Since our principal objective is to promote our own welfare, our motive in sinning must be to promote that end. The upshot of sin, however,

is always an exacerbation of the internal conflicts which undermine our best endeavours, leaving us wretched and vulnerable
even in a moment of (apparent) delight.

What distinguishes the life of the righteous is not a more successful pursuit of earthly happiness but an acceptance that such
happiness is simply unattainable (XIV. 25). While 'death, decep-
tion and distress' disfigure human life—all three consequences of
sin—men are denied the enjoyment of the happiness which their
natures crave (XIV. 25, p. 589). The righteous, instead, fix their
sights upon an image of heavenly bliss. By setting the possibilities
of practical life in a proper perspective, they are given peace of
mind. But, more important in the context of political theory,
they are also enabled to see a positive significance in institutions
and arrangements which might otherwise seem irksome and unnecessary.

To Augustine, then, the crucial division in the history of social
and political life is not between separate territorial units or rulers
and ruled but between the righteous and reprobate. He had set
himself to discuss 'the rise, the development and the destined ends
of the two cities, the earthly and the heavenly, the cities which we
find ... interwoven, as it were, in this present transitory world,
and mingled with one another' (XI. 1, p. 430). And, significantly,
he traces the source of the two cities not to sets of incompatible
principles but to 'two kinds of love: the earthly city was created
by self-love reaching the point of contempt for God, the
Heavenly City by the love of God carried as far as contempt of
self' (XIV. 28, p. 593). The one city 'glories in itself', looking 'for
glory from men', the other 'glories in the Lord', finding 'its highest glory in God, the witness of a good conscience' (XIV. 28,
p. 593). In the earthly city, 'the lust for domination lords it over
its princes as over the nations it subjugates'; while in the Heavenly
City, 'those put in authority and those subject to them serve one
another in love, the rulers by their counsel, the subjects by
obedience' (XIV. 28, p. 593). What is at issue is whether men
should live according to the transient standards which regulate the
affairs of this world or according to the eternal standard enshrined
in God's providential order. And though men might not have the
intellectual capacity to discern the rationale of God's order, they
are nevertheless enjoined to follow his injunctions as an act of
faith.

We should be clear, however, precisely what Augustine is claiming for his distinction. He is not suggesting that the earthly city and the Heavenly City correspond with any actual communities or institutions. Though he had drawn his models from his reflections on the Roman Empire and the Church, he never wavers in his contention that good and evil are intermingled in all human institutions. Even the Church, which might have been supposed to be exempt from the limitations imposed on human institutions by men's sinfulness, is seen as a human contrivance. Though inspired by God's will, it is nevertheless made a reality by men's endeavours. And, like any other institution, it is open to use and abuse by men whose motivation is purely selfish. Indeed Augustine was in no doubt that Christianity's acceptance as the official religion of the Roman Empire had compounded the difficulties involved in identifying the Church as the expression of God's will. Once status and influence had been accorded to the Church as an institution, it was clear that it could be regarded by the ambitious as a convenient means of self-advancement. Both the elect and the reprobate were thus involved in the life of the Church, swimming 'without separation, enclosed in nets until the shore is reached' (XVIII. 49, p. 831). The Church certainly served God's purpose and was a vehicle for the ultimate triumph of the Heavenly City but, as a temporal institution, it suffered from the inevitable distortions and trials associated with human corruption.

Nor was Augustine oblivious to the positive benefits which the earthly city could confer. Even though, earlier in his argument, he had described kingdoms without justice as 'gangs of criminals on a large scale' and criminal gangs as 'petty kingdoms', he was not concerned to deny that standards of some sort were employed in the earthly city (IV. 4, p. 139). A criminal gang itself should be understood in terms of certain principles of association ('a group of men under the command of a leader, bound by a compact of association, in which the plunder is divided according to an agreed convention'). All that distinguished a criminal arrangement from a kingdom was the scale of villainy, 'the title of kingdom' being conferred not as a consequence of the 'renouncing of aggression but by the attainment of impunity' (IV. 4, p. 139). And, despicable though order secured by such means might appear to be in relation to the natural harmony which had been sacrificed through sin, Augustine is adamant that it has something to contribute to the realization of God's purpose.

It would thus be misleading to interpret Augustine's portrayals of the Heavenly and earthly cities as a stark contrast between the principles of good and evil. Nothing in God's creation could be dismissed as wholly evil. Even the devil, in so far as existence was one of his attributes, enjoyed a semblance of goodness. But it did not follow that the terms in which pagan thinkers had characterized goodness and the good life could be accepted. What was wanting in their analyses was any recognition of the limitations of human understanding and endeavour. In Stoic thought, for example, reason itself was seen as a sufficient instrument to overcome human foibles. It was not supposed, of course, that all men could be redeemed through reason. There would always be the fool for whom immediate pleasures were far more arresting than the intangible advantages of a settled mind. Yet there was no obstacle, in principle, to the attainment of virtue and happiness.

This was precisely the view that Augustine was concerned to reject. He was nevertheless faced with a problem. He could not identify worldly wisdom with evil (in the manner of the Manichees) without undermining his own view of God's providence. What he had to do, instead, was to highlight the shortcomings of pagan notions of virtue in relation to Christian doctrine, while making clear that pagan social and political order was a necessary requirement for the final triumph of Christianity.

Yet this was a position fraught with difficulty. In attempting to steer a middle course between pagan and Manichaean conceptions of the good life, Augustine left himself exposed to criticism both from Christian thinkers who rejected worldly values altogether and from the perspective of traditional Greek and Roman notions which located the highest good in either the individual or the community. His own view, which might best be described as a theory of degrees of goodness, occupied him throughout book XIX of the *City of God*. In what is his most sustained statement of political doctrine, he defended a view of *de facto* authority which political theorists have often compared with Hobbes. The affinity in their arguments on the specific question of obedience, however, disguises a wider divergence in their justifications of authority. Where order for Hobbes is justified in utilitarian terms,

Augustine values earthly peace as a necessary but not sufficient condition for the emergence of the *summum bonum* in the Heavenly City. Indeed it is axiomatic for Augustine that consideration of value (in whatever sphere) must be in terms of God's providence. Thus any attempt to examine the political ideas of book XIX in disregard of the central theological arguments of the *City of God* is seriously misleading. In the last resort, Augustine's treatment of social and political order is intelligible only as an implication of his conception of sin.

Augustine begins his detailed criticism of pagan doctrine with a discussion of Varro's typology of moral philosophy (XIX. 1–2). Varro had distinguished 288 possible positions on the question of the supreme good and supreme evil in human life, taking into account such issues as whether or not virtue can be taught, whether it is to be sought for its own sake or because of the pleasure it brings, whether pleasure itself is to be understood in spiritual or physical terms, and so on. From this plethora of arguments, Augustine narrows down the issues to focus on the specific view endorsed by Varro (XIX. 3). Varro had identified virtue with happiness as a means of enhancing the spiritual and physical well-being of mankind. This happiness, moreover, had been seen as a social phenomenon, extending through different levels of association (from the household, through the city, to the universal society of nations, and finally embracing the universe as a whole). In each sphere, virtue builds upon certain 'primary blessings of nature' (XIX. 3, p. 850). And while these blessings precede moral teaching and the acquisition of virtue, they are given a positive moral connotation as the necessary foundation for a flourishing way of life.

In Varro's scheme of things, as for the Platonic tradition as a whole, virtue is a corollary of a proper understanding of the foundations of social life. For Augustine, however, the equation of virtue and reason was the cardinal error which divided citizens of the earthly city from the elect. The sin that had originally set men apart from God was precisely to follow their own reason and inclinations. The ultimate good ('eternal life') could only be attained by living rightly (XIX. 4, p. 852). But, having sinned, men no longer enjoyed an intuitive understanding of the good life. Given that 'we do not yet see our good', it followed that we had 'to seek it by believing' (XIX. 4, p. 852). It was not reason, but faith, which disclosed the course of virtue to men. Indeed reliance upon reason without the restraint of faith was a symptom of pride rather than wisdom and would only confirm men in their sinfulness.

It is not only the role of reason which Augustine objects to in Platonic ethics. The idea of virtue building upon a beneficent natural foundation was itself wholly misconceived. The 'primary blessings of nature' were neither good nor bad in themselves. Such resources assumed a moral significance only in relation to the uses made of them by men. And, indeed, human conduct itself only became problematic after the Fall. The exercise of virtue was not a matter of maximizing men's natural and social advantages but rather of struggling to overcome the consequences of sin. Augustine sees the cardinal virtues (temperance, prudence, justice, and fortitude) as attempts to combat evil. Far from virtue and happiness being complementary notions in our earthly condition, the significance we attach to virtue is actually a testimony to the pervading evil in our midst. Happiness should certainly be the goal of our endeavours; but, in this life, the best we can hope for is the patience and courage to endure misfortune.

Augustine's rebuttal of Varro was thus couched in terms of a contrasting view of human nature and its possibilities. He had not sought to expose the internal flaws in Varro's argument so much as to question the nature of his enterprise. And when he goes on to defend his own postion in detail, his approach is deeply revealing of the character of his thought. He seeks to persuade not through formal argument but rather by appeal to our ordinary experience of life. The pitfalls of social life, for example, are illustrated in terms of the frustrations and misunderstandings which anyone would have encountered within the family or among friends (XIX. 5); the folly of relying upon human judgement is highlighted in a portrayal of the agony of a judge in a criminal case, deciding the fate of an individual on the basis of (necessarily) imperfect evidence (XIX. 6); and the unavoidable divisions between communities are brought home to us as a consequence of the diversity of languages (XIX. 7). Nor would such 'rhetorical' means of resolving philosophical questions have seemed strange to Augustine's audience. His early training, like that of so many of his leading contemporaries, had been in rhetorical argument. And the dominant conception of philosophy in late Roman culture was a product of the rhetorical tradition. Augustine might have challenged the presuppositions of pagan philosophy; but his method was very much that of the Ciceronian rhetorician.

His view of social and political order, however, marked a decisive departure from pagan conceptions of public life. The crucial dimension in his thought is the significance he attaches to sin. What we see throughout the *City of God* is a double perspective on human affairs, the one putting its trust in (a necessarily fallible) reason, the other taking account of men's limitations in their fallen condition. Augustine identifies pagan philosophy with the former view. Despite its manifest achievements, it is precluded by its initial premises from gaining a proper understanding of the limited competence of reason.

On the question of order and peace within and between communities, for example, the pagan view is hampered by an inability to see evil, disorder, and chaos as other than unnecessary, irrational, or simply inexplicable. For Augustine, however, everything in creation has a positive significance. And though it is axiomatic for him that evil itself is a mere privation, with no substantive identity of its own, he nevertheless insists that practices which seem to be evil on a superficial view actually perform a positive role in an ordered cosmos. Even war, villainy, and domestic strife are treated as attempts to impose some sort of order on human affairs (XIX. 12). The peace and order established by such practices cannot, of course, be accepted at face value; but, in the context of men's sinfulness, peace on any terms is to be valued as a necessary condition for the continuance of human societies.

Augustine's theory of political institutions is a direct corollary of his conception of sin. What men have sacrificed through sin is a harmonious enjoyment of themselves and their fellows in which obedience is owed only to God. After the Fall, however, the basic passions (pride, lust, envy, greed, fear) set men apart from one another, making each individual a potential enemy of every other. And because the root cause of their wretchedness is the corruption of their own natures, they cannot look to their own resources for a remedy. Men are saved, in the last resort, only by God's providential ordering of human affairs. Among men's cardinal sins is a lust for domination which aggravates relations between both individuals and communities. But the very fact that men are basely motivated to dominate one another at least ensures that certain sorts of ordered relations emerge in human affairs. Slavery, for example, which is a wholly unnatural institution, is a direct consequence of men's refusal to accept God's natural order. If they cannot bring themselves to obey God's natural law, they are obliged to endure the discipline of slavery as a punishment for their transgressions (XIX. 15). And though slaves might naturally resent the authority which their masters have taken upon themselves, they should nevertheless accept that order of some kind is a necessary condition for the enjoyment of any way of life.

Nor is slavery unique among social institutions. Order at the most basic level is established through relations of command and obedience. The smooth functioning of a household, for example, will depend upon a hierarchy of command stemming from the husband and extending through the wife to children and servants. It does not follow, of course, that in the exercise of his position the head of the household should indulge his 'lust for domination'. Indeed, having accepted the necessity for domestic peace, relations within the family can be construed as an 'ordered harmony about giving and obeying orders among those who live in the same house', with those in authority assuming a 'dutiful concern for the interests' of their dependants (XIX. 14, p. 874). It remains the case, however, that the need to impose order within the family only arises because men's natures require discipline and correction.

Coercion, indeed, is (for Augustine) an ineradicable feature of social life. Its exercise is absolutely essential if order is to be sustained in society. And though it would be wrong for a good man to delight in the infliction of punishment for its own sake, it is certainly not a service to an individual or society to allow error and sin to go uncorrected. If peace in the household or city is a desirable end, then coercive measures must be employed to restrain unruly passions.

Nor is it simply that punishment is justified in utilitarian terms. The correction of a wrongdoer is a moral obligation incumbent upon anyone in authority. From the household to the city, a system of ordered relations should prevail. Just as the wise parent should chastise a wayward child, so rulers in the city should strive to impose standards of conduct upon their subjects. Augustine, in fact, sees no qualitative distinction between rule in the city and rule in the family—'the ordered harmony of those who live

together in a house in the matter of giving and obeying orders'
contributing 'to the ordered harmony concerning authority and
obedience obtaining among the citizens' (XIX. 16, p. 876). And in
other writings he was perfectly prepared to use the need to punish
sinfulness as a justification for the employment of secular power
in defence of religious orthodoxy.[4]

An ordered peace is thus the objective of social and political
institutions in the earthly city; but it does not follow that the
terms on which that peace is arranged would satisfy the requirements of the Heavenly City. In his account of social order
Augustine retains the dualistic conception that pervades the whole
of the *City of God*. His crucial distinction is between the elect and
the reprobate, with the former able to take advantage of the institutional arrangements which sustain fallen men without losing
sight of the limited significance of social and political goals. What
is pursued in the 'earthly city' is, in fact, an 'earthly peace', limited
to a 'harmonious agreement of citizens concerning the giving and
obeying of orders' which establishes 'a kind of compromise
between human wills about the things relevant to mortal life'
(XIX. 17, p. 877). While the Heavenly City, by contrast, 'which
lives on the basis of faith', treats earthly peace as a temporary con-
venience, essential for the daily management of mortal life but
without intrinsic significance (XIX. 17, p. 877). What both cities
share, however, is a need to live together; and hence pilgrims
should 'not hesitate to obey the laws of the earthly city by which
those things which are designed for the support of this mortal life
are regulated' (XIX. 17, p. 877). The only exception Augustine
allows is in the case of laws prescribing religious practices contrary to the tenets of Christianity. But even in the face of persecution, Christians are enjoined to limit their response to a passive
dissent which leaves the secular order intact.

Augustine is still left with a problem in his characterization of
justice in the earthly city. Earlier in his argument he had reported
Cicero's definition of a commonwealth as 'an association united

---

[4] In his writings against the Donatist schism and the rebellion of the Circumcellions,
Augustine specifically set aside his earlier reservations about confounding the spiritual
mission of the Church through association with the secular power of the civil authorities.
He now felt able to justify coercion both as an incentive to right thinking among waverers
('compel them to come in') and as a defence of civil order.

by a common sense of right and a community of interest' (II. 21, p. 73). The implication of Cicero's insistence on 'a common sense of right' as a criterion distinguishing a 'people' from a 'multitude' was 'that a state cannot be maintained without justice' (XIX. 21, p. 881). Yet what sense could there be in describing a commonwealth as just which laboured under a fundamental misconception about the relations between its citizens and God? According to this definition, not only would it have to be denied that the Roman state was just, it could not actually be classed as any sort of community. Indeed, on the strictest interpretation of Cicero's position, justice would be identified with the pilgrimage of the Heavenly City on earth. And though Augustine had no wish to weaken his characterization of true justice, he was nevertheless unhappy with a view which could not discriminate between the different modes of political arrangement within the earthly city.

His solution to the dilemma was to introduce a dual standard of justice. While true justice (and, with it, true virtue) could not be attained without the support of true religion (XIX. 25), it remained possible for the more limited objectives of social and political communities to be achieved despite a manifest wrongheadedness on matters of faith and doctrine. Instead of insisting on moral and political rectitude as a constitutive requirement for the existence of a community, Augustine is content to argue that a human gathering may be regarded as a people whenever an 'association of a multitude of rational beings' is 'united by a common agreement on the objects of their love' (XIX. 24, p. 890). Precisely what the 'objects of their love' might be is left unspecified (though Augustine is clear that the quality of a community's 'loves' is the relevant criterion to appeal to in any appraisal of its worth). His crucial point, however, is that a community's righteousness is not a necessary condition for the attainment of a minimal standard of social and political order. It is common objectives which make a polity viable, not the quality of those objectives. No matter what form a social consensus might take, it will necessarily involve a degree of harmony and peace. And without peace, social life of any kind becomes problematic.

What emerges from Augustine's account of civic life, then, is an absolute insistence on the need to sustain the established relations of authority within a community. From the family to the highest offices of state, a chain of command and obedience structures the dealings of individuals with one another.[5] Authority, of course, may be abused; and Augustine has rich passages on the misery which the lust for domination has wrought in human history. In the last resort, however, he cannot trust the political judgement of fallen men. Our corrupted inclinations have rendered each one of us potential enemies. And while we continue to turn our backs upon the natural harmony which obedience to God would restore, we must endure coercive institutions as both a punishment for our sins and as the necessary means for the further enjoyment of social life.

The peace of the earthly city is thus a poor thing in itself. Yet it does serve a wider purpose. The final triumph of the Heavenly City depends upon the maintenance of a framework for the pursuit of social and political ends. God's pilgrims, embattled with the evil before them, are bent upon the creation of institutions which are parasitic upon a wider legal order. They therefore have an interest in preserving temporal peace, despite reservations about the terms on which that peace is established (XIX. 26).

In the final analysis, though, Augustine is concerned with the meagre benefits of civil society only in relation to his larger vision of the perfect peace and tranquility which awaits the elect. The passions which disfigure social life—envy, fear, greed, lust—will no longer prevail in the Heavenly City; and hence coercive institutions will be redundant. The precarious peace of the earthly city will give place to untrammelled enjoyment, leaving individuals wholly at ease both with themselves and with one another (XIX. 27). But all this is dependent upon absolute obedience to God. Men lack the intellectual and emotional resources to create a situation of this kind for themselves. All they can do is to trust in God's grace, while exploiting the moral criteria implicit in their vision for a richer understanding of the possibilities of human life.

Yet there remains in the *City of God* a theory of *de facto* authority which stands independently of Augustine's theological arguments. It is, to be sure, a more sombre position than the one

---

[5] Augustine extends his theory of authority even to the Church. In his anti-Donatist writings he was concerned to counter the contention that the authority of a bishop depended upon the moral and spiritual purity of his character. For Augustine, it was not the man, but the office, which conferred authority. In both the secular and spiritual spheres, the social means to desirable ends are all-important. Institutional procedures serve as a necessary corrective to the impotence and frailty of individual judgement and will.

he actually defends, with no hope for a final transcendence of suffering and strife. The emphasis is upon the endemic problems which give human life the character of a struggle. But it would be wrong to give the impression that we are dealing here with a gloomy argument. Given the plight that men find themselves in, it is something of a miracle to Augustine that communities are enabled to flourish. And though he is wont to attribute the continuance of social life to God's providence, he is clear that men supply the means for their preservation. Despite their mistaken notions, men continue to be ingenious and resourceful creatures. What has led them astray is their inability to understand their own natures. Self-knowledge, for Augustine, is a matter of grasping the limitations of human nature. And nowhere is this limitation more evident than in the political sphere. Men can contrive a set of institutional arrangements to satisfy their immediate needs; but tampering with social and political devices will not transform their natures. Redemption is not to be had through politics. In the economy of human culture, the state stands as a significant but limited contrivance, valuable as a means to certain ends but without intrinsic worth.

Bibliographical Note

The most convenient modern translation of *The City of God* is by Henry Bettenson in the David Knowles edition (Harmondsworth, 1972). Reference in the text is to this edition (reissued in 1984 with a new introduction by John O'Meara).

The Latin text is available, with parallel English translation, in the Loeb Classical Library edition edited by George E. McCracken *et al.* (7 vols.; London and Cambridge, Mass., 1957–72). Of earlier English translations, the most widely used is probably the Marcus Dods (2 vols.; Edinburgh, 1872). There is an abridged translation by J. W. C. Wand (London, 1963). R. H. Barrow, *Introduction to St. Augustine: The City of God* (London, 1950), is a translation of selections from Augustine's text, including most of book XIX, together with detailed commentary. Students interested principally in Augustine's influence on early modern political thought might do better to use the classic John Healey translation (London, 1610) which has been reissued in modern editions edited by Ernest Barker (London, 1931) and R. V. G. Tasker (London, 1945).

The student coming to Augustine for the first time should begin with
Henry Chadwick, *Augustine* (Oxford, 1986). The definitive biography is
Peter Brown, *Augustine of Hippo: A Biography* (London, 1967), though the
earlier work by John J. O'Meara, *The Young Augustine: The Growth of St.
Augustine's Mind up to his Conversion* (London, 1954), is still worth consult-
ing.

On the historical background see A. Momigliano, ed., *The Conflict
between Paganism and Christianity in the Fourth Century* (Oxford, 1963), especially the editor's seminal essay 'Pagan and Christian Historiography in
the Fourth Century A.D.'; E. R. Dodds, *Pagan and Christian in an Age of
Anxiety* (Cambridge, 1965); C. N. Cochrane, *Christianity and Classical
Culture* (Oxford, 1940); and Peter Brown, *Religion and Society in the Age of
Saint Augustine* (London, 1972).

On Augustine's use of his sources see Harald Hagendahl, *Augustine and the
Latin Classics* (Stockholm, 1967). Augustine's debt to Cicero on a detailed
issue is dealt with in Neal Wood, '*Populares* and *Circumcelliones*: The
Vocabulary of "Fallen Man" in Cicero and St. Augustine', *History of Political
Thought*, 7 (1986). Far and away Augustine's most important source, however, was the Bible. Students with only a cursory knowledge of the text
should read (at least) the Pauline Letters.

The surest guide to Augustine's intellectual biography is his own *Confessions*, ed. R. S. Pine-Coffin (Harmondsworth, 1961). But the importance
of the *Confessions* extends far beyond the development of his mind. Students
intimidated by Augustine's technical theological discussions can grasp the
rudiments of his doctrine of grace from the *Confessions*.

The best detailed study of the gamut of Augustine's thought is still
Étienne Gilson, *Introduction à l'étude de Saint Augustin* (Paris, 1943, 2nd edn.).
On a specific theological issue which students of political theory should not
neglect see G. R. Evans, *Augustine on Evil* (Cambridge, 1982).

Augustine's wider views on history and society are also crucial for an
understanding of his political thought. See R. A. Markus, *Saeculum: History
and Society in the Thought of St. Augustine* (Cambridge, 1970); and G. L.
Keyes, *Christian Faith and the Interpretation of History: A Study of St.
Augustine's Philosophy of History* (Lincoln, Nebr., 1966).

More specifically on Augustine's political thought, the most comprehens-
ive account is Herbert A. Deane, *The Political and Social Ideas of St. Augustine*
(New York, 1963). Rex Martin, 'The Two Cities in Augustine's Political
Philosophy', *Journal of the History of Ideas*, 33 (1972), considers the central
distinction in the *City of God*. Of older studies, students will still profit from
J. N. Figgis, *The Political Aspects of S. Augustine's 'City of God'* (London,
1921); Norman H. Baynes, *The Political Ideas of St. Augustine's 'De Civitate
Dei'* (The Historical Association, pamphlet no. 104, London, 1936); and
Ernest Barker, 'St. Augustine's Theory of Society', originally published as

the introduction to the English translations of Augustine of 1931 and 1945 and now reissued in his *Essays on Government* (London, 1951, 2nd edn.).

The *Revue des études augustiniennes* is an indispensable source for bibliography. See also Terry L. Miethe, *Augustinian Bibliography, 1970–1980* (Westport, Conn., 1982).

4

Niccolò Machiavelli:
The Prince and the *Discourses*

PETER SAVIGEAR

NICCOLÒ MACHIAVELLI came to the writing of politics from within an established tradition, that of the Renaissance humanists. His significance lies in his departure from that tradition. He presented his political ideas in a number of different works and it may come as a surprise to those unfamiliar with his writing that he left no single, coherently argued political text. He was no Plato or Thomas Hobbes. Much of Machiavelli's reputation was based on a short book *The Prince*, but this work alone does not convey the depth of his many insights into government and the nature of political institutions. At least one other longer work by him needs to be read in conjunction with *The Prince*, and the most appropriate is the *Discourses on the First Decade of Titus Livy*, which is his commentary on the origins and development of the institutions of the Roman Republic. These two very different works complement each other and the description which follows will concentrate upon them.

The subject-matter of *The Prince* and the *Discourses* is the relationship between rulers and ruled. The former is primarily concerned with the qualities needed by rulers, especially single rulers, in their handling of people and institutions, while in the *Discourses* Machiavelli comments on the development of republican constitutions and the safeguarding of public liberties in such regimes. Neither of these themes is presented in a logical and direct manner, and the works abound in anecdotes and aphorisms drawn from contemporary and ancient history. Even Machiavelli's commentary on Livy's history of Rome in the *Discourses* follows the original text in the loosest of ways.

Machiavelli believed that his special knowledge of politics enabled him to present something original, 'to enter upon a new way' (*Dis.*, bk. I, Preface)[1] in the study of the subject. He seemed

---

[1] See Bibliography for comment on translations.

to think that his originality lay in the application of historical knowledge to political action, yet his special place among the theorists of the body politic rests, as we shall see, on his separation of the study of politics from other disciplines, notably history and religion, and his according it a distinctive status.

The Context of *The Prince* and the *Discourses*

Machiavelli, who was born in 1469 and died in 1527, was both a writer of history and politics and an experienced Florentine diplomat and administrator. His political career was hampered by the fortunes of a city-state troubled by civil disturbance and by the wars in the Italian peninsula which followed the French invasion of 1494. His writing, on the other hand, brought him great renown, although many of the more famous of his works (including *The Prince* and the *Discourses*) were not published in his lifetime.

Machiavelli grew up immersed in the teaching and principles of a humane education, with its stress on the classical authors and disciplines as opposed to those of medieval Christianity. The flowering intellectual life of Renaissance Italy turned to the work of the 'ancients' in the matter of knowledge as well as in the arts. Above all, in the study of history, especially the ancient history of Greeks and Romans, the humanist tradition was influential, and Machiavelli worked from within this world.[2] Humanist thinkers from the late fifteenth century to the seventeenth century regarded the successful conduct of past rulers as models for those of later times because the principles of human reason and action were fundamentally the same. The world of classical civilization was therefore a source of relevant examples of political conduct, and the description of that conduct for later generations was the purpose of historical study and writing. Machiavelli was as insistent upon the didactic nature of history as any of the humanist authors. Not only are his works full of examples, but he emphasized the need for 'a proper appreciation of history' (*Dis.*, bk. I,

---

[2] The humanist tradition as it emerged in the Renaissance looked back to the classical authors, especially those of republican Rome like Cicero and Polybius. Their sympathies lay with the successful and orderly rulers of those times and their works were devoted to the description and explanation of those models. See Benedetto Croce, *History: Its Theory and Practice*, trans. D. Ainslie (New York, 1960).

Preface). Indeed it sometimes seems as though he were adding nothing to the humanist arguments of his time; he wrote that his *Discourses* 'will comprise what I have arrived at by comparing ancient with modern events, and think necessary for the better understanding of them, so that those who read what I have to say may the more easily draw those practical lessons which one should seek to obtain from the study of history'.[3]

Nevertheless Machiavelli took a new step, beyond the point reached by his humanist contemporaries. He shifted the emphasis away from the imitation of specific policies and actions to an assessment of why those commendable actions had been so successful. He demanded a deeper analysis of the nature of political events and circumstances, and a study directed towards the explanation of policies and not merely their imitation. Above all, Machiavelli sought the principles upon which rule had been established and urged their study and application, both of which had been neglected by his contemporaries. 'In setting up states, in maintaining governments, in ruling kingdoms, in organising armies and managing war, in executing laws among subjects, in expanding an empire, not a single prince or republic now resorts to the examples of the ancients' (*Dis.*, bk. I, Preface). The details of history were therefore of less significance than the principles of political action they illustrated. The accuracy of the bewildering array of classical and more recent examples and anecdotes that Machiavelli provided was not his major interest, and it should not be that of the modern reader. His concern was not with historical accuracy. He was not obsessed by the need to imitate the example of past rulers, but adjusted his focus on to the logic that he discerned in public affairs.

The New Way of Politics: Accommodating Evil

Machiavelli's most prescient perception was that the place of evil in politics required a new analysis and was not merely to be condemned. It was for this reason that he acquired a reputation as the advocate of any self-seeking act and of the rejection of moral considerations. The proposition that the end justified the means became associated with his name and the adjective 'machiavellian'

---

[3] Cf. *The Prince*, ch. 14, 'the prudent prince reads histories . . .'.

has been used to describe any devious, immoral, and unscrupulous act or the practice of duplicity. However, this is a misleading description of Machiavelli's theories and leaves out of account the single, all-important purpose that was his passionate concern, the creation of a stable world, based on the autonomous state, in which people might live in security. This central element in his theory was based on a pessimism about human nature, although he did not develop a systematic theory of human nature as Hobbes did. Machiavelli did not advocate evil and he never ceased to point out the essential wickedness of mankind, but he thought this wickedness had to be brought within the bounds of a valid doctrine of politics, and not merely shunned.

Given men's propensity for violence and selfishness, it became a puzzle for Machiavelli to explain how things might be arranged better in order to achieve a sound constitution for the state and thereby a secure life for its citizens. In seeking this order he discovered that the bases of moral judgement in the public and private realms were different. What was condemned in one arena might be acceptable in the other. He placed the need to acknowledge evil in the context of the need for public order, and therefore only political ends justified any means: 'For when the safety of one's country wholly depends on the decision to be taken, no attention should be paid either to justice or injustice, to kindness or cruelty, or to its being praiseworthy or ignominious. On the contrary, every other consideration being set aside, that alternative should be wholeheartedly adopted which will save the life and preserve the freedom of one's country' (*Dis.*, bk. III, ch. 41). An analysis of Machiavelli's writing appropriately centres on his argument about evil.

The criteria by which private conduct is judged are said by Machiavelli to be distinct from those applied to the state. The world of the private conscience had no direct connection with that of politics. Moreover, what became individuals in their private lives was inappropriate in public affairs. The qualities that command respect in the former are twisted and distorted in politics. In *The Prince* Machiavelli warns against the confusion of the two moral worlds, a necessary warning because the single ruler could most readily make the error of supposing that identical moral criteria applied in his private and his public life. It was for this reason that Machiavelli took time to explain 'those things for which men and especially princes are praised or censured' (*Pr.*, ch. 15), and to explore the political consequences of 'liberality and stinginess' (*Pr.*, ch. 16), and 'cruelty and mercy: is it better to be loved than feared, or the reverse?' (ch. 17). His caution is sharp— 'Hence, a prince, in order to hold his position, must acquire the power to be not good, and understand when to use it and when not to use it' (*Pr.*, ch. 15). Qualities that are intrinsically good but are mislocated in politics, may bring ruinous results, he warns. Such were generosity and mercy. In the case of the former, if employed in a wise and appropriate manner 'it is not recognised'. If generosity is to be publicly recognized, then the ruler must distort it, turn it into excess, in short become lavish and bring ruin (*Pr.*, ch. 16). His conclusion is stark: 'nothing uses itself up as fast as does liberality; as you practice it, you lose the power to practice it, and grow either poor and despised or, to escape poverty, grasping and hated' (*Pr.*, ch. 15).

And so it was that Machiavelli found that many good men, of high moral standards in their private lives, failed in public life. Even so great a man as Scipio faced a rebellious army, 'an action that resulted from nothing else than his too great mercy' (*Pr.*, ch. 17). On the other hand, there had been men of despicable private character who had nevertheless managed to create a secure and sound public order. Such was Severus. He was 'very cruel and grasping', yet the actions of this man 'were great and noteworthy in a new prince' (*Pr.*, ch. 19).[4] Thus Machiavelli believed the enjoyment of true goodness in the individual was a consequence of life in a secure and well-ordered state. He had no doubt that there was goodness and evil, but their application and assessment in public life were of a special nature. Evil might be a necessary element in the securing of the institutions of the state, although this in no way altered the essential nature of evil. In his chapter devoted to 'Men who gain a princedom through wicked deeds' he explains this, and leaves the reader in no doubt that the political achievement of the Sicilian ruler Agathocles could not remove the stigma of 'his outrageous cruelty and inhumanity' (*Pr.*, ch. 8).

Machiavelli drew a clear distinction between the lives of the rulers and those of the subjects; two moral worlds lived side by side in his writings. He focused on the public realm and the working of institutions in the state, and in doing this, what he writes of

---

[4] Cf. *Discourses* bk. I, ch. 10.

the private world is often obscure. His gloomy view of human inclinations and habits, constantly stressed in all his writing, may make it unlikely that a fine, flourishing world of private goodness could exist, but Machiavelli's intention was to explain how the opportunity for private conscience might be encouraged through the sound ordering of the state, allowing the citizens to display their goodness in the security of a stable public realm. It was for this reason that he admired the political world of the Roman Republic. However his admiration was all the greater precisely because public qualities had been pre-eminent.

Conversely, Machiavelli condemned Christianity because this religion had diverted mankind from truly political considerations and produced a confusion of public and private qualities. He criticized the Christian obsession with individual moral quality and the internal concern with goodness at the expense of the secular, public good. His review of the different kinds of principality and constitution included a chapter on 'Ecclesiastical princedoms' (*Pr.*, ch. 11). In these principalities he saw a conjunction of religious and political institutions which could 'keep their prince in his position' (*Pr.*, ch. 11) by their harmony and strength. His comments on the Papacy show admiration for the successful *temporal* power of the Church, not its moral worth. But the crucial contrast for Machiavelli was between the more usual Christian moral emphasis on individual conscience and the religious institutions of the Roman Republic. His thought was essentially secular. Heaven and hell were not effective political instruments, and action stemmed not only from divine prescription, from the providential, but also from human thought and decision. This brought a new dimension to Machiavelli's political thought; he sought to define the limits of human free choice and the extent of necessity.

Much of Machiavelli's attitude to religion was shared by humanist thinkers of the Renaissance. Where Machiavelli differed was in his association of political and religious institutions, the harnessing of religion to politics. Above all, the religious life of the Romans of the Republic served political ends, in contrast to the condition of Italy when he wrote. He lamented that 'it is the Church that has kept, and keeps, Italy divided' (*Dis.*, bk. 1, ch. 12). Thus he was not opposed to religion itself. On the contrary, he accused the Church of Rome of destroying religious devotion in Italy by its example, and, still worse, of fostering such political divisions that Italy remained weak (*Dis.*, bk. 1, ch. 12). Religion might be used to bind people together and strengthen the political community, as had been the case in Rome. 'Numa, finding the people ferocious and desiring to reduce them to civic obedience by means of the arts of peace, turned to religion as the instrument necessary above all others for the maintenance of a civilised state' (*Dis.*, bk. 1, ch. 11). A secular religion could thus contribute to the struggle for the creation, preservation, and extension of the state.

The State, the Army, and Institutions

It was this, the ordering of public institutions in the state, that formed the kernel of political activity in Machiavelli's eyes, the building of secure institutions and a stable rule over people; 'so let a prince set about the task of conquering and maintaining his state' (*Pr.*, ch. 18). But this 'thing' the state possessed special attributes in the writings of Machiavelli, some of which were shared with the state as described by his contemporaries, and some of which were peculiar to Machiavelli.

The state was essentially a passive object, something that required constant attention and nurture. A particular skill was needed in order that rulers might preserve their states. Others called this skill 'reason of state', although the phrase was not used by Machiavelli. Few close contemporaries expressed the matter more concisely than Giovanni Botero, albeit an opponent and critic of Machiavelli's theories: 'state is a stable rule over a people and reason of state is the knowledge of the means by which such a dominion may be founded, preserved, and extended . . . it is concerned most nearly with preservation, and more nearly with extension, than with foundation'.[5] Therefore the essential truth for the ruler was the need to retain his rule, the preservation of the state, for rule and state were equivalent.[6]

Machiavelli shared with several of his contemporaries the view that politics was a creative activity. The state, as it emerged in Italy, Burgundy, France, and elsewhere in Renaissance Europe, was not an organic, natural event but 'the outcome of reflection and calculation'.[7] It was an artificial creation, shaped by human

[5] Giovanni Botero, *Ragion di stato.*

[6] J. H. Hexter 'Il principe e lo stato', *Studies in the Renaissance*, 4 (1957), pp. 113–38.

[7] Jacob Burckhardt, *The Civilisation of the Renaissance in Italy*, pt. I, 'The State as a Work of Art'.

minds and actions to produce an administration, armies with defined structure and organization, laws, and the apparatus of government. Where Machiavelli departed from the more usual view of Renaissance writers on the state, was in his stress on instability as a perpetual element in politics. The state was never still but in a condition of flux. Daily adjustment and attention were necessary for effective government. His theory of the state rested on this belief in the need for constant vigilance in the public world. The work of the ruler required great assiduity, especially when new provinces had been conquered, and he had much advice for new rulers on subjects like the dangers of conspiracy (*Pr.*, ch. 3). For this reason also Machiavelli concentrated a great deal of attention on the way in which states had survived through dynamic change, as had Rome. Institutions carefully preserved were the key to this survival. 'Hence those [states] are better constituted and have a longer life whose institutions make frequent renovations possible' (*Dis.*, bk. III, ch. 1).

What then was required in order to sustain the state? Machiavelli gave priority to military organization. 'The principal foundations of all states, the new as well as the old and the mixed [i.e. constitutional as opposed to autocratic], are good laws and good armies. And because there cannot be good laws where armies are not good, and where there are good armies, there must be good laws, I shall omit talking of laws and shall speak of armies' (*Pr.*, ch.12). He spent three chapters of *The Prince* discussing military organization, a subject that he developed in other writings, notably his work on *The Art of War*, and in his administrative experience as secretary to the committee that established a militia in Florence in 1506. Just as religion was a necessary element in binding together any community, so he believed that a citizen army was essential to the state. Rulers could not depend on mercenaries or other troops. His advice to the rulers of Florence was that the city-state should 'provide herself with her own armies, because there cannot be more faithful or truer or better soldiers' (*Pr.*, ch. 26). The military therefore were an element in the creation of stable government, although for Machiavelli they were never the preferred sole rulers of the state.[8] Princes were urged to pay special attention to arms, to 'war and its laws and discipline'

---

[8] N. Wood, 'Introduction', *The Art of War* (New York, 1965), p. lxxviii.

(*Pr.*, ch. 14). However this would be hard, and perhaps more easily achieved in republics, the political form which Machiavelli preferred. Soundly organized citizen armies, defending their community, were a necessary condition for stable government, yet they were not a sufficient condition. The search for those sufficient conditions was not easy.

What of constitutional structures? In Machiavelli's view no single constitutional form could guarantee the security of the state. The flux of politics prevented any such straightforward solution. Yet the constitution of the state moulded the people who were its inhabitants; there was a connection between laws and organization and the quality of the people. He was no advocate of simple tyranny, but presented a complicated interwoven picture of institutions and constitutional forms, adjusting to the demands of political life. In the opening chapters of the *Discourses* Machiavelli rejects any preference for democracy or aristocracy over other forms. All were 'far from satisfactory' (*Dis.*, bk. I, ch. 2). He concluded that 'the prudent legislators, aware of their defects, refrained from adopting as such any one of these forms, and chose instead one that shared in them all, since they thought such a government would be stronger and more stable' (*Dis.*, bk. I, ch. 2).

Machiavelli constantly asserted that institutions had to be adaptable in order to survive the infinite flux of politics, and that a republic was 'better able to adapt itself to diverse circumstances owing to the diversity found among its citizens than a prince can do' (*Dis.*, bk. III, ch. 9). In republics there was less conformity. Only through constant adaptation to changing circumstances could the state survive, as had the Roman Republic. The *Discourses* were a paean, praising the capacity of that republic to adapt itself to such differing circumstances. In Rome there had been a blended constitution in which all the different segments of the population were in a balanced relationship. In a rather loose manner Machiavelli wrote of the 'people' and the 'nobles' or richer classes. He specifically commented on the historical relationship between the Roman *plebs* and the nobility. The stability of a state depended on the adjustment of the relations between such components of the state. While he used these terms in a general manner, the essence of his argument was precise, that these differing elements had to be reconciled and that such a reconciliation of tensions had to be achieved through political institutions. Thus, in a typical generalization, he insists that 'before everything else he [the prince] tries to win the people's support' (*Pr.*, ch. 9). In an instructive and extended example, Machiavelli shows how social tensions, between the populace and the nobility in Rome, led to the development of new institutions, in this case the popular tribunes.

He returned again and again to this theme. Internal conflict could be contained through the development of institutions through which such tension could be kept within bounds and turned to the maintenance of liberties; 'it was friction between the plebs and the senate that brought this perfection about' (*Dis.*, bk. 1, ch. 2). Thus in Rome the privileged were not humiliated and destroyed by popular forces, nor did they refuse to share political power through the creation of new institutions. The fact of constantly changing circumstances and latent conflict moved Machiavelli to see political development, through institutional changes, coming from potentially damaging conflict: 'in every republic there are two different dispositions, that of the populace and that of the upper class and all legislation favourable to liberty is brought about by the clash between them' (*Dis.*, bk. 1, ch. 4). But here too no abiding proposition could be made, only a restatement of Machiavelli's demand for adaptation to circumstances. 'I cannot give a final judgement without knowing the details about those states where princes must make such decisions' (*Pr.*, ch. 20).

Machiavelli was certain that the integrity and support of the body of citizens, as opposed to factions and corrupt and partial groups gathered around rival politicians, were necessary to principalities and republics alike. He feared the rule of faction and reiterated his view that 'the people's friendship is essential to a prince. Otherwise in adverse times he has no resource' (*Pr.*, ch. 9). Machiavelli warned particularly against the 'corruption' of institutions and of the citizens. Once this decline had occurred, with the loss of respect for the common good and the added risks to the independence of the state, then a change was difficult to bring about. Corruption, the disposition of the people for violence and faction, prevented a return to autonomous institutions and the liberty of the citizens so ardently desired by Machiavelli. Even 'good legislation is of no avail' (*Dis.*, bk. 1, ch. 17) as a remedy once corruption has set in, he cautioned. The remedy which he indicated was the initiative of a strong ruler, in effect a dictatorship, and his *Discourses*, as well as his other writings, are full of such advocacy. Failing a powerful statesman of that kind, only good Fortune might permit the recovery from corruption.[9] Happier circumstances were those where the people were not corrupt, as had been the case with the citizens of Rome.

Small communities, unable by their size to constitute a state, he tells us, cannot survive and are 'not strong enough to resist the onslaught of an invader' (*Dis.*, bk. I, ch. I), and a measure of power alone assured security. The type of constitution could facilitate the conjunction of power and security. In both *The Prince* and the *Discourses* Machiavelli placed great emphasis on the kind of institutions found in different states. He grasped a special truth, that the constitution of the state affected the mind and nature of the inhabitants. Just as the mentality of slaves was characterized by the structure of the institutions of slavery—he pointed to the officials of the Turkish Empire of his day (*Pr.*, ch. 4)—so the subjects of republics and kingdoms developed different qualities. While legislation might not serve as a remedy against corruption, the structure of the constitution itself could be expected to stand as a bulwark against decay. As a direct result of their institutions, republics were more resilient in the defence of their freedom than were principalities with less experience of independent institutions. 'It is not the well-being of individuals that makes cities great, but the well-being of the community; and it is beyond question that it is only in republics that the common good is looked to properly in that all that promotes it is carried out' (*Dis.*, bk. II, ch. 2). Nevertheless Machiavelli's caution remained important; there were no universal prescriptions for stable government and the slavish imitation of history was futile.

The historical lesson to be learned by statesmen was that force of circumstance needed a full understanding. Machiavelli was no determinist. The impact of his 'advice' to politicians was to introduce a further dynamic factor, the relationship between free will and circumstance. Only an appreciation of the conditions that exist can show the scope for free will and decision. Thus the basis of political action was the rigorous study of particular conditions and of what was necessary and inescapable. The starting-point

---

[9] See Quentin Skinner, *Machiavelli* (Oxford, 1981), pp. 65 ff.

was the need to grasp the realities as they existed: 'Many have fancied for themselves republics and principalities that have never been seen or known to exist in reality. For there is such a difference between how men live and how they ought to live that he who abandons what is done for what ought to be done learns his destruction rather than his preservation' (*Pr.*, ch. 15). The sensitive understanding of circumstances was the first principle of statesmen, of reason of state. The experience of the soldier was to be recommended. 'A wise prince, then, never withdraws his thought from training for war; in peace he trains himself for it more than in time of war. He does this in two ways, the first with his actions, the second with his mind' (*Pr.*, ch. 14). Detailed examination of the terrain was the vital knowledge needed by soldiers. Rulers needed the habit of precise and accurate observation.

Moreover a clear understanding of the existing conditions explained the many variations in the past conduct of statesmen. The different policies that had been successfully adopted and the apparently contradictory results of similar actions could only be explained by an exact study of the particular situation. Greatness had been achieved by such different characters as Hannibal and Scipio (*Dis.*, bk. III, ch. 21). Thus it was that Machiavelli admitted that princes could be humbled by necessity, a term which reached the dignity of a principle in his political writing. 'I believe also that a prince succeeds who adapts his way of proceeding to the nature of the times. . . . Likewise, we find two men with two differing temperaments equally successful, one being cautious and the other imperious. This results from nothing else than the nature of the times, which is harmonious or not with their procedure' (*Pr.*, ch. 25). Machiavelli's pages are filled with exhortations to pay close attention to the details of the times, and examples of successfully doing so as well as those of failure. The method for the ruler is not to weigh the importance of precedent, but to develop the sensitive perception of circumstance, almost an intuitive and unreflective perception of the connection between how the world is and how it might be changed.

The Struggle with Circumstance: Fortune, *Virtù*, Necessity

Machiavelli's acute awareness of particular circumstances moved him to consider the pressure of what he called Fortune. The

introduction of Fortune into his arguments was not merely a device
to explain away what he could not otherwise analyse. The wheel of
Fortune became an important concept for his political theory.

The political world was never still and rulers needed to be sensitive to these vagaries. Particular circumstances affected even
Machiavelli's well-known principle that human affairs knew no
progress, only a kind of cyclical movement. He noted 'the cycle
through which all commonwealths pass', namely monarchy, aristocracy, democracy, anarchy, and back to monarchy (*Dis.*, bk. 1,
ch. 2). He observed the twists of politics; 'what usually happens is
that, while in a state of commotion in which it lacks both counsel
and strength, a state becomes subject to a neighbouring and better
organized state. Were it not so, a commonwealth might go on for
ever passing through these governmental transitions' (*Dis.*, bk. 1,
ch. 2). At times Machiavelli appeared more convinced of the continuity between past and present, at others, sceptical of the role of
circumstance and necessity, but 'one never finds any issue that is
clear cut and not open to question' (*Dis.*, bk. 1, ch. 6).

In chapter 25 of *The Prince* he gave his most graphic and elo-
quent account of 'Fortune's power in human affairs and how she
can be forestalled'. Fortune was more than a set of particular circumstances, and its impact was itself variable. This variation was
in direct proportion to the ability of the statesmen. No ruler,
whatever the condition of his armies and the institutions of his
state, could expect to reverse the forces of inevitable circumstances (i.e. necessity) nor to overtake the direction in which
Fortune had pushed events. However, the clearer the understanding of this direction, the greater the scope for mastery of one's
Fortune. In a famous passage, Machiavelli explains the dilemma
by portraying Fortune as a river whose flow cannot be reversed,
but against the force of whose waters there is room for the building of dykes and embankments. Fortune 'shows her power where
strength and wisdom do not prepare to resist her, and directs her
fury where she knows that no dykes and embankments are ready
to hold her' (*Pr.*, ch. 25). Where chance is not taken, there remains
a greater scope for the inexorable pressure of events to dominate
the individual and the ruler. Thus Fortune is neither good nor
bad. Only the keen-eyed ruler, aware of those points at which
Fortune could be tamed or deflected, could hope to determine the
path of events. Such moments were perhaps rare. Machiavelli's

political science therefore consisted of the full and true understanding of the relationship between what he called Fortune,
necessity (*necessità*), and *virtù*. The free choice of those responsible
for the affairs of state, whether republics or principalities, had to
take this interplay into account. The science of politics focused on
the quality that he believed to be essential for rulers and people
alike, the quality he called *virtù*.

A problem arises over the translation of this word *virtù*. There
is no satisfactory equivalent in English. 'Virtue' cannot be
accepted as a translation on account of the moral overtone. Other
English translators have used a range of words for *virtù*, from
prowess and ability to strength of character, qualities, and talent.
On occasion the word has been ignored and not translated at all,[10]
despite the emphasis given to the concept by Machiavelli and its
crucial place in his argument. The usual translations, such as
'prowess', suffer from a failure to convey the subtle sense of both
the individual's brilliance in possessing *virtù* and the philosophical
understanding contained in the Italian word. The word required
is a substantive conveying the impact of the cognate Italian word
which has an English equivalent, *virtuoso*. Yet 'virtuosity' lacks
the seriousness of the Machiavellian *virtù*, and on this concept he
placed great weight in his evaluation of political experience and in
grappling with the relationship between Fortune, necessity, and
the individual will.

Virtù could be found in individuals and in the people as a
whole. *The Prince* naturally enough contains many examples of
the former; the *Discourses* are principally a tribute to the *virtù* of
the Romans of the early Republic. In contrast, Machiavelli
lamented the deficiency in *virtù*, especially military *virtù*, of contemporary Italy (*Pr.*, ch. 26). The 'great virtù' of Rome, however,
'was maintained for so many centuries' (*Dis.*, bk. 1, ch. 1). The
attribute of *virtù* was therefore not a moral one but rather a political and military attribute primarily concerned with the relationship between free will, Fortune, and necessities. Thus it was a
practical matter, the discernment of the relationship between
these elements, with no necessary good or evil colouring. *Virtù*
was a special discipline, with its own rules, judged by essentially

---

[10] See for example G. Bull, *The Prince* (Harmondsworth, 1961), ch. 8, p. 63, where the
sentence beginning 'So whoever studies that man's actions . . .' omits all reference to the
word *virtù* in the original Italian.

political criteria and not by moral precepts drawn from the individual conscience or from Christianity. Politics, based on *virtù* in rulers and ruled, was no mere branch of theology or ethics, but a self-contained activity, recognized by the application of *virtù* or its lack.

The heart of the matter came with the juxtaposition of *virtù* and Fortune. In effect, these forces operated in inverse ratio in their influence upon human political affairs. In chapter 6 of *The Prince* Machiavelli wrote of rulers who had come to power through their own ability—*virtù*—and those who came to rule through Fortune, where they had not had the opportunity to impose themselves on events. One or other of these forces and their combined effect was responsible for the success of the prince. Among such successful rulers—he selects a curious cluster of names in this chapter, Moses, Cyrus, Romulus, and Theseus—he found a common element: 'on inspecting their actions and their lives, we see that they had from Fortune nothing more than opportunity, which gave them matter into which they could introduce whatever form they chose; and without opportunity, their strength of will (*virtù*) would have been wasted, and without such strength (*virtù*) the opportunity would have been useless' (*Pr.*, ch. 6). What Machiavelli is indicating here is that the *virtù* of these men was so great that Fortune was limited in its sway over events and actions to the expression of necessities, factors which were inescapable. Thus without the opportunity (he uses the word *occasione*), great *virtù* would have had no relevance, no chance to grasp events and create effective rule. Similarly, without the *virtù* of these leaders, the occasion itself would have been missed and Fortune taken a greater hand. Therefore he can point to the two different ways of becoming a prince—'either through strength and wisdom or through Fortune' (*Pr.*, ch. 7).[11] Princely *virtù* was again not a moral quality, but a political one, engendered by the force of political circumstances. 'Necessity engenders *virtù*', Machiavelli asserts in the *Discourses* (bk. II, ch. 12). This permitted him to draw a distinction between the free and untrammelled operation of human choice, and the application of *virtù* for which the human spirit was thrown against the force of circumstance. 'Men work either of necessity or by choice, and . . .

---

[11] The word *virtù* is here translated by the phrase 'strength and wisdom'.

there is found to be greater virtue (*virtù*) where choice has less to say to it' (*Dis.*, bk. I, ch. I). *Virtù* could therefore never be considered apart from Fortune and necessity. These were locked in a changing but inextricable embrace.

The pressure of events acted as the stimulus which gave rise to *virtù*. Without such pressures and the resulting *virtù*, chaos might follow for 'when they [men] are too free to choose and can do just as they please, confusion and disorder become everywhere rampant' (*Dis.*, bk. I, ch. 3). Machiavelli thus found his most admired political attribute where there was room for decision and choice but not an excessive room. Wide freedom of choice did not engender *virtù*. The great and praiseworthy political actions were produced by the conjunction of *virtù* and necessity: 'We have in other discourses shown how useful a part necessity plays in human affairs, and to what glorious deeds it may lead men. As some moral philosophers in their writings have remarked, neither of the two most noble instruments to which man's nobility is due, his hands and his tongue, would have attained such perfection in their work or have carried man's works to the height which one can see they have reached, if they had not been driven to it by necessity' (*Dis.*, bk. III, ch. 12). The ability to see what decision was necessary and to take it thus became itself a free and creative act. The state, rule, was composed of the skill and ability to take such decisions, and this was what Machiavelli advocated. Many times he praises decisions taken because they were necessary, and the free act of seeing that they were necessary was a manifestation of *virtù*. For example it is this response to the circumstances that Machiavelli had in mind when he advised that 'a prudent conqueror makes a list of all the harmful deeds he must do, and does them all at once, so that he need not repeat them every day, because, not repeating them, he makes men feel secure' (*Pr.*, ch. 8).[12] Thus it was that the tide of Fortune might be deflected and stable rule established.

Machiavelli then turned to the content of *virtù*, the actual definition of this attribute so closely related to destiny and indispensable for political stability. The key was without doubt the capacity to adapt to the circumstances that engendered *virtù*. On this subject Machiavelli thought that he had something new to

---

[12] Cf. 'to frustrate any of your enemy's designs, it is best to do of your own volition what he endeavours to force you to do' *The Art of War*, ed. N. Wood, 1965, p. 121.

say. 'Now it remains to examine the wise prince's methods and conduct in dealing with subjects or with allies. And because I know that many have written about this, I fear that, when I too write about it, I shall be thought conceited, since in discussing this material I depart very far from the methods of the others' (*Pr.*, ch. 15). The essence of his advice came in an extended metaphor in which the ruler was compared to animals, in particular the lion and the fox. In chapter 18 of *The Prince* he urged the constant modulation of the principal qualities of these animals, adapting and adjusting strength and cunning as the needs of the circumstances required. *Virtù* was present when the character of the rulers flexed with the demands of the times, and in so doing, his Fortune would remain constant (*Pr.*, ch. 25). In this way rulers held Fortune at bay and mastered their world.

This flexibility of character might require a ruler to learn how to be evil—'essere non buono'—and to make use of this appearance if necessary (*Pr.*, ch. 15). Indeed the relationship between evil and political *virtù* was based on expediency, and this naturally meant that rulers of evil or despicable character in their personal lives could also demonstrate *virtù*, as had Severus.[13] It was prudence that characterized *virtù* and not its moral worth. The prudent is never far from Machiavelli's descriptions of successful rule. Prudence accompanied foresight and intuitive grasp of political conditions. He linked 'early recognition' to prudence and admired the Romans who 'seeing their troubles far ahead, always provided against them' (*Pr.*, ch. 3). Even evil actions, judged by the conventional moral standards, should be applied with prudence and then success might follow (*Dis.*, bk. III, ch. 6).

In his praise of rulers and his description of *virtù* in politics, Machiavelli admired an opportunity appropriately used. The ability to see and use the opportunities characterized the ruler possessed of *virtù*. In his account of the life and conduct of Cesare Borgia, it was this ability to seize the moment and the chance that was praised: 'such a chance came to him well and he used it better' (*Pr.*, ch. 7). Both Hannibal and Scipio, about both of whom Machiavelli had much to say in *The Prince* and in the *Discourses*, were commended for their efficiency. No single action universally assured of success or imbued with *virtù*, but it was the

---

[13] See above, p. 100.

manner in which actions were carried out that conveyed this political mastery: 'I conclude, therefore, that it does not matter much in what way a general behaves, provided his efficiency be so great that it flavours the way in which he behaves, whether it be in this way or that' (*Dis.*, bk. III, ch. 21). The measured and sensitive application of prudence, efficiency, and flexibility thus formed the basis of political *virtù*. Only the folly of individual arrogance could undermine such a combination of qualities, as had been the case with the tyrannical Roman ruler Appius, noted for his fickle character (*Dis.*, bk. I, ch. 41), or the frustration coming from totally adverse Fortune. Great *virtù* did not automatically guarantee political success. It was the *mis*fortune of one of his great heroes, Castruccio Castracani, that deprived him of yet greater renown despite the outstanding political *virtù* of this ruler of the tiny city-state of Lucca. He 'would, without doubt, have exceeded Philip of Macedon and Scipio, if he had had Macedonia or Rome as his native country instead of Lucca'—Machiavelli was prone to exaggeration but the point is clear. Fortune could not be totally controlled whatever the degree of *virtù*.[14]

However, if *virtù* was remarkable in rulers, it was even more so in the population. Machiavelli admired and desired a public spirit endowed with *virtù*, and distinguished this from the mob or mere rabble. He found a cohesion and 'goodness and respect for religion' among the people of the Roman Republic and among the Germans of his day (*Dis.*, bk. I, ch. 55). Respect for the laws and the common good (he employs the phrase *bene commune* in this context, *Dis.*, bk. II, ch. 2) formed the basis of such public *virtù* and allowed the transformation of the masses into an ordered community like that of the Romans. It was indeed the discipline of the laws which lay at the heart of this change.[15] We have seen how military organization contributed to the creation of *virtù* among peoples, and similarly, social or class tensions stimulated a people towards *virtù* in their understanding of and reaction to public events.[16] What emerged was Machiavelli's stress on the need to associate princely *virtù* and that of the people. The prince

---

[14] This is the final sentence of *The Life of Castruccio Castracani of Lucca*, trans. A. Gilbert in *Machiavelli: The Chief Works and Others*, 1965.

[15] See *Dis.*, bk. I, ch. 58. The title of this chapter is also significant: 'The masses are more knowing and more constant than is a prince'.

[16] See above, pp. 103, 105.

could not succeed against the force of the people. Thus it was that 'if princes are superior to populaces in drawing up laws, codes of civic life, statutes and new institutions, the populace is so superior in sustaining what has been instituted, that it indubitably adds to the glory of those who have instituted them' (*Dis.*, bk. I, ch. 58). He concluded that 'government by the populace is better than government by princes' (*Dis.*, bk. I, ch. 58). The best safeguard against corruption was the mixed constitution, combining elements of the republic and the principality. However Machiavelli feared corruption, and where the people's *virtù* had decayed only a great prince could rescue the state. His position had to be strong to enforce obedience 'until such time as the material [i.e. the people] has become good' (*Dis.*, bk. I, ch. 17), for here was a cycle that Machiavelli believed was irreversible. 'When I reflect that it is in this way that events pursue their course it seems to me that the world has always been in the same condition, and that in it there has been just as much good as there is evil, but that this evil and this good has varied from province to province' (*Dis.*, bk. II, Preface). And so it was with public *virtù*. This had passed, so to speak, from Assyria to Media and on to Rome. From the Romans it passed to the Goths.[17] The question therefore arose whether *virtù* had returned to the peoples and rulers of Machiavelli's Italy.

Machiavelli's Patriotism

Machiavelli was a patriot. He wished to see Italy with a sound government and secure administration not divided and exposed to invasion, as had occurred in his lifetime with the major invasion by King Charles VII of France in 1494. This had led to other ills, notably the extensive use of mercenaries. For this reason he concluded *The Prince* with his 'Exhortation to grasp Italy and set her free from the barbarians', and reiterated the same theme throughout the *Discourses*, contrasting contemporary Italian misfortunes with Roman greatness and *virtù*. Yet he was optimistic. There existed 'great *virtù*' in parts. This might require a thorough reorganization of the institutions. But the extent of Italian *virtù* was still limited: 'it is necessary to have, besides laws, a superior force, such as appertains to a monarch, who has such absolute and

[17] Cf. *Pr.*, ch. 13.

overwhelming power that he can restrain excesses due to ambition and the corrupt practices of the powerful' (*Dis.*, bk. 1, ch. 55). Machiavelli regretted the divisions within Tuscany, preventing further progress towards Italian unity based on the leadership of Florence. It was here that the reorganization of Italian institutions might begin. However 'a wise man, familiar with ancient forms of civic government, should easily be able to introduce there a civic constitution. But, so great has been Tuscany's misfortune that up to the present she has come across nobody with the requisite ability and knowledge' (*Dis.*, bk. 1, ch. 55). The crux therefore was leadership.

Nevertheless Machiavelli was positive. There had been the fine example of Cesare Borgia, much praised in *The Prince* and a ruler of whose administration Machiavelli had personal experience. But Cesare had died in 1507, respected by Machiavelli and presented as a model for others. 'I for my part cannot censure him. On the contrary, I think I am right in bringing him forward in this way as worthy of imitation by all those who through Fortune and by means of another's forces attain a ruler's position' (*Pr.*, ch. 7). However, there remained Lorenzo de' Medici, to whom *The Prince* was dedicated. The princes of Italy had been responsible for the tragic political conditions that Machiavelli experienced—they 'may not blame Fortune but their own laziness' (*Pr.*, ch. 24). Therefore only a strong ruler could grasp the moment, relying upon the latent qualities of the people, for 'I cannot express with what love he will be received in all the provinces that have suffered from these alien floods, with what thirst for vengeance, with what firm loyalty, with what gratitude, with what tears. What gates will be shut against him? What peoples will refuse him obedience? What envy will oppose him? What Italian will refuse him homage?' (*Pr.*, ch. 26). These flowery lines express the confidence that Machiavelli retained in the *virtù* of the Italians and their rejection of the 'floods' of invasion and barbarity that had recently affected them. This confidence in the people not only emphasized his fundamental commitment to constitutional, popular government, but also gave him the opportunity to return to a favourite theme, the need for a citizen army.

The potential redeemer, as Machiavelli calls him, had to raise a citizen militia, 'to prepare such armies in order with Italian might (*virtù*) to defend herself against foreigners' (*Pr.*, ch. 26). Thus

Machiavelli appealed to his patron and to his contemporaries that they take the opportunity that was offered, and in so doing he implied an awareness of nationalism, although his primary concern was for the creation and preservation of stable government and an end to invasion and division which had plagued the Italian peninsula. Since his death in 1527, shortly after the restored republican regime in Florence had rejected his services in their administration, and also after the devastating sack of Rome by the foreign armies of the Holy Roman Emperor Charles V, commentators have debated the issue of his patriotism and his selfish pleading for reinstatement in the Florentine administration. These matters have never been definitively resolved and remain obscure, as awkward for his readers as the confused history, the innumerable examples that he quotes, and the sweeping generalizations and summaries.

Conclusion

None of Machiavelli's theory seems at all scientific or systematic, yet Machiavelli produced an original, almost dialectical analysis of the relationship between the world as he found it and the extent to which it might be changed. In the political and public realm there was no stable, universal moral order, true for all, but a condition of constant flux because 'inherent in everything is its own peculiar malady' (*Dis.*, bk. III, ch. 11). In this profound phrase Machiavelli touched the heart of his contribution to political theory, his search for an understanding of how statesmen might grapple with such a 'malady', a search in which private morality played no relevant part. This understanding required an assessment of how to deal with the complexities of the relationship between people, the higher classes—call them nobles or the rich—and the ruler or rulers. But his probing into the world of politics did not stop with the domestic order. He possessed an acute sense of the logic which pervaded inter-state relations as well as that between the domestic forces of the state. Internal disorder might give rise to new institutions, as had occurred with the Romans at the time of the creation of the tribunes of the people, but the fate of Italy in Machiavelli's lifetime was more usual and more to be feared, that is, internal disorder opening the way to foreign invasion. Ambition and 'the natural hatred which neigh-bouring princes and neighbouring republics have for one another' (*Dis.*, bk. III, ch. 12), the impulse to domination, might bring a kind of stability, making 'it difficult for one to seize the other' (*Dis.*, bk. III, ch. 12). This prescient appreciation of the balance of power went with his rejection of neutrality[18] and his praise of the Roman Republic which had turned external threat into a cause for internal reorganization: 'It was Rome's neighbours who in their desire to crush her, caused her to set up institutions which not only enabled her to defend herself but also to attack them with greater force, counsel and authority' (*Dis.*, bk. I, ch. 34). Politics therefore became the ceaseless adjustment to the demands of necessity and the pressures of Fortune, internal and external.

Machiavelli's life and his reading of history had taught him how fragile the political world was. In striving single-mindedly to show how a stable state or rule might be created and preserved under which people might enjoy their private lives in security, he reopened Aristotle's search for a political science with its own discipline and logic.

Bibliographical Note

There are serious difficulties in prescribing a suitable English edition and translation of Machiavelli's works. There have been a great number, notably of *The Prince*, but problems face the English editor. Early Italian editions frequently have no paragraphing and, for the *Discourses*, have no chapter headings. Greater problems arise over the translation of key words, e.g. *virtù*, *citta*, *ordine*, *bene commune*. Some editions readily available are loosely translated and inconsistent in this important respect of finding the appropriate word. For this reason no single edition has been recommended to the exclusion of others. The quotations in the chapter taken from *The Prince* come from A. Gilbert, *Machiavelli: The Chief Works and Others* (3 vols.; Durham, NC, 1965). This is also the source of the texts edited by J. Plamenatz, *Machiavelli: The Prince, Selections from the Discourses and Other Writings* (London, 1972). However the edition and translation by G. Bull, *The Prince* (Harmondsworth, 1961), is a freer work and needs great care when referring to key words. There is another important annotated edition of the *Discourses*

---

[18] See *Dis.*, bk. II, ch. 1, where he warns against ignoring a conflict until 'the conflagration is at their doors'.

on the First Decade of Titus Livy, by L. Walker (2 vols.; London, 1950). This was used by Bernard Crick for his commentary on the *Discourses* (Harmondsworth, 1970), and this has been used for the quotations in the above chapter. The introduction to the older edition of *The Prince* by L. Burd (Oxford, 1891), remains a splendidly written critical piece.

The most useful and accessible secondary work on Machiavelli in English, being critical and based on many years of study, as well as reasonably priced, is Quentin Skinner, *Machiavelli* (Oxford, 1981), in the Past Masters series. This also has a brief but good critical bibliography. In addition to the many useful introductory essays to the critical editions mentioned above, a number of substantial works cover Machiavelli's thought, its origins, and the context. The two most relevant to the study of *The Prince* and the *Discourses* are J. Pocock, *The Machiavellian Moment* (Princeton, 1975), and J. H. Whitfield, *Discourses on Machiavelli* (Cambridge, 1969). Some earlier studies are still valuable for analysis of Machiavelli's ideas, their explanation and origins. These include S. Anglo, *Machiavelli: A Dissection* (London, 1969), F. Chabod, *Machiavelli and the Renaissance* (London, 1965), F. Gilbert, *Machiavelli and Guicciardini* (Princeton, 1965) (this book compares Machiavelli's ideas and presuppositions with those of the important contemporary historian Guicciardini), H. Butterfield, *The Statecraft of Machiavelli* (London, 1955), and Leo Strauss, *Thoughts on Machiavelli* (Glencoe, 1958), a work critical of the moral implications of Machiavelli's theories.

The complicated nature of the vocabulary used by Machiavelli has produced a large number of detailed studies of the terms and concepts. The more significant include I. Hannaford, 'Machiavelli's Concept of *Virtu* in *The Prince* and *The Discourses* Reconsidered', *Political Studies* (1972), pp. 185–9, R. Price, 'The Senses of *Virtu* in Machiavelli', *European Studies Review* (1973), pp. 315–45, R. Orr, 'The Time Motif in Machiavelli', *Political Studies* (1969), pp. 145–59, and N. Wood, 'Machiavelli's Concept of *Virtu* Reconsidered' *Political Studies* (1967), pp. 159–72. A number of aspects of Machiavelli's thought are covered in essays by different scholars in a volume edited by A. Parek, *The Political Calculus: Essays on Machiavelli's Philosophy* (Toronto, 1972). I. Berlin has an essay entitled 'The Originality of Machiavelli', in *Against the Current* (London, 1979).

The best work on the intellectual and historical background of Machiavelli's ideas is Quentin Skinner, *The Foundations of Modern Political Thought* (Cambridge, 1978), but the Renaissance world of thought is also covered by H. Baron, *The Crisis of the Early Italian Renaissance* (Princeton, 1966). Two major authorities have approached and explored this period of politics and thought, J. Burckhardt, *The Civilisation of the Renaissance in Italy*, English translation (London, 1960), and B. Croce, *History: Its Theory and Practice*, trans. D. Ainslie (New York, 1960), and his *History as the Story of Liberty*, trans. S. Sprigge (London, 1941). The Renaissance environment is the subject of Guy Mattingly, *Renaissance Diplomacy* (London, 1961) and J. R. Hale, *Machiavelli and Renaissance Italy* (London, 1961). Two additional works on Machiavelli deserve a mention, G. Prezzolini, *Machiavelli* (London, 1968), and J. H. Whitfield, *Machiavelli* (Oxford, 1947). Two great books that have taken the impact of Machiavelli's idea further in its effect on later ideas, are E. Cassirer, *The Myth of the State* (London, 1946), and F. Meinecke, *Machiavellism: The Doctrine of Raison d'Etat and its Place in Modern History* (London, 1957).

Thomas Hobbes: *Leviathan*

MURRAY FORSYTH

THOMAS HOBBES'S political philosophy, which comes to full fruition in *Leviathan*, marks a shift in the axis of political reasoning. Hobbes rejected as inadequate the fundamental assumption of ancient classical theorizing that in the *polis* or republic man found his natural fulfilment, and that civil freedom was to be defined as the privilege of the citizen who participated in rule. For him the classical thinkers, and in particular Aristotle, did little more than describe and recommend the regimes in which they themselves lived. At the same time, and with equal vehemence, Hobbes rejected the idea, common to so much medieval theorizing, that the body politic was the lower, temporal power, subordinate by its very nature to the higher, spiritual one. He rejected the theological relativization of politics. With extraordinary boldness he claimed that in his writings he was not merely reforming or correcting the political philosophy of the past, but founding political philosophy itself. The claim may have been extravagant but it was by no means hollow. *Leviathan*, like Plato's *Republic*, is a work of inauguration. It inaugurates the modern theory of the state.

Doubtless many of the ideas contained in Hobbes's masterpiece can be detected in earlier writings. The harsh realism with which Machiavelli contrasted the necessities of politics with the maxims of morality is echoed in *Leviathan*. Hobbes's concept of sovereignty is foreshadowed in Bodin's *Six Books of the Commonwealth* with which he was familiar. Continuities such as these do not, however, alter the fundamental nature of the break that Hobbes effected, a break that has its root in the fact that he was not content to advance new ideas, but to weld them together and to ground them in first principles. With Bodin, the concept of sovereignty falls, as it were, from the heavens. With Hobbes it emerges at the end of a logical demonstration. It is the internal logic of *Leviathan* that gives it its remarkable self-subsistent, timeless quality, separating it both from its forerunners and from other contemporary writings, and marking it out as a classic among classics.

Leviathan, to borrow some words which Diderot used to describe another of Hobbes's works, is 'a book to read and to annotate all one's life'.[1] The boldness, tenacity, and sheer scope of Hobbes's reasoning makes the text a field for almost endless exploration. The purpose of the discussion that follows is not to forestall such exploration, but rather to assist it by elucidating a few of the key features of Hobbes's argument.

The Context of *Leviathan*

How is the radicalism of *Leviathan* to be explained? First of all, it is helpful to recall that the book is but one product—albeit a major one—of a general movement to establish philosophy itself on fresh foundations that developed in Europe during the seventeenth century. Well before that time the ecclesiastical and theological tutelage of the human mind that had characterized the medieval period had been loosened. The rediscovery of classical antiquity by the humanists, scientific discoveries such as those of Copernicus, and above all the religious rebellion initiated by Luther had profoundly shaken the old order. It was not, however, until the seventeenth century that a properly philosophical stock-taking of these vast changes took place, and a succession of thinkers began to reflect systematically on what the human mind, having broken loose from its long tutelage, was capable of doing. What was it possible to know? How did the mind arrive at certain knowledge? What *was* science or—for the two terms were at that time still interchangeable—philosophy? These were the radical, almost naïve questions that stood at the heart of the seventeenth-century philosophical renaissance, and Bacon, Descartes, and Hobbes—with Galileo acting as a powerful stimulus in the background—were its main progenitors. The common goal of their enquiries may be summed up as the discovery of a *method* of attaining knowledge.

Hobbes thus was not, and did not see himself, as a thinker

---

[1] Diderot was referring to Hobbes's treatise on *Human Nature*. See G. C. Robertson, *Hobbes* (Edinburgh, 1901), p. 227 n.

concerned exclusively with political philosophy. He saw himself
in much broader terms, as someone engaged alongside a select
band of contemporaries in mapping out afresh the logic and scope
of philosophy or science as such. His aim was to give methodo-
logical unity and direction to all the different branches of philosophical enquiry, to show how they sprang from a common root,
and to show how they were linked each to the other. Hobbes was
what has come to be known as a 'system builder', and this feature
of his thought is perhaps conveyed most immediately by the diagram in chapter 9 of *Leviathan* in which he maps out the entire
terrain of scientific or philosophical knowledge.

As this diagram shows, political or civil philosophy was seen by
Hobbes as one of the two main branches into which science
divided, the other being natural philosophy. Man he considered
to be the object of both the main forms of philosophizing. As a
special kind of animal he came within the orbit of natural philosophy, or, more precisely, of physics. As part of the fabric of a
body politic he came within the orbit of civil philosophy. In
Leviathan Hobbes began with an assessment of man as a special
kind of animal and from there proceeded to deduce his role in the
making of the body politic. The book moves across the boundary
line from natural philosophy into civil philosophy.

Hobbes was unusual amongst the leaders of the seventeenth-
century philosophical renaissance in plunging as deeply into civil
philosophy as he did into natural philosophy. *Leviathan* was not
the beginning but the culmination of his efforts in the former
field. It was first published in 1651 when Hobbes was sixty-three,
and it had been preceded by *The Elements of Law*, which he had
written, but not published, in 1640, and by *De Cive*, which had
been published in 1642.[2]

Leviathan then represents the ripened thoughts of a self-
consciously pioneering spirit who was seeking to found philosophy anew, and for whom civil philosophy was but one segment
of an overarching system of knowledge. This, however, only

[2] The *Elements of Law* was published in the form of two separate treatises, *Human Nature*
and *De Corpore Politico*, in 1650. It was not published as a single text until 1889, and it has
recently been republished (see bibliographical note). A second edition of *De Cive* was published in 1647, and an English translation of it appeared in 1651. A Latin version of
Leviathan was published in 1668. Hobbes's account of the English Civil War entitled
Behemoth, which in some respects can be seen as the counterpart of *Leviathan*, appeared in
print in the year of his death, 1679.

explains the radicalism of the book in part. *Leviathan* was also the response to a radically disturbed, abnormal political situation. Hobbes, in other words, did not engage in civil philosophy solely because he wished to round off his philosophical system. He was driven to it with equal urgency by a profound contemporary problem, the problem of war and peace, or more exactly of civil war and civil peace. This is the second intellectual impulse behind the book, and it is precisely the employment of a radically new method of thinking to resolve a radical political issue that gives the book its unique relish.

The second impulse behind the book is revealed most vividly in a passage from one of Hobbes's other works in which he asked himself what was the use of moral and civil philosophy (and for him it was axiomatic that all philosophy had a use). He replied that moral and civil philosophy were to be estimated

not so much by the commodities we have by knowing these sciences, as by the calamities we receive from not knowing them. Now all such calamities as may be avoided by human industry, arise from war, but chiefly from civil war, for from this proceed slaughter, solitude, and the want of all things. But the cause of war is not that men are willing to have it; for the will has nothing for object but good, at least that which seemeth good. Nor is it from this, that men know not that the effects of war are evil; for who is there that thinks not poverty and loss of life to be great evils? The cause therefore, of civil war is, that men know not the causes neither of war nor peace, there being but few in the world that have learned those duties which unite and keep in peace, that is to say, that have learned the rules of civil life sufficiently. Now the knowledge of these rules is moral philosophy. But why have they not learned them, unless for this reason, that none hitherto have taught them in a clear and exact method?[3]

At the end of this passage the two great motive forces behind the writing of *Leviathan* can be seen converging: only through 'clear and exact' thinking will the problem of civil war be overcome. It remains only to add that the civil wars with which Hobbes was concerned, the wars which had plagued Europe from the middle of the sixteenth century onwards and which broke out in Hobbes's own native land in 1642, were distinctive. The struggles were not only concerned with the political rights of estates,

---

[3] Hobbes, *Elements of Philosophy: The First Section, Concerning Body*, in *English Works*, ed. Molesworth (London, 1839), vol. i, p. 8.

parliaments, and kings, they were also concerned with heaven and hell, damnation and salvation. They were *religious* civil wars, the outcome of the Reformation, and as such they were peculiarly bitter, like the ideological struggles of the twentieth century. Hobbes himself always thought religious factors were primarily responsible for them. As he wrote in *Leviathan*:

> The most frequent pretext of sedition, and civil war, in Christian common-wealths, hath a long time proceeded from a difficulty, not yet sufficiently resolved, of obeying at once both God and man, then when their command-ments are one contrary to the other (ch. 43).

It is little wonder therefore that his systematic attempt to lead men out of the delusive slaughter of civil war should also be, in very large measure, a systematic attempt to lead them out of the delusions of religion.

Hobbes however never believed that religion was the sole cause of the civil wars of his time. Contributing to the incipient anarchy were the fallacious political theories that men had imbibed from the classical teachers of antiquity, and above all the idea that the freedom of the citizen of a body politic was the freedom to par-ticipate in ruling, or as Hobbes expressed it, the equation of one's 'private inheritance, and birth-right', with 'the right of the public' (ch. 21). It is scarcely surprising therefore that he should have had contempt for Aristotle, and little wonder too that, in an age of endemic instability of government, he should have had little patience with the idea that the body politic was a 'natural' pheno-menon.

The Method of *Leviathan*

To those who approach the book for the first time, *Leviathan* presents some of the forbidding qualities of the armour-plated creature described in the book of Job after whom it was named. (See chapter 29 for Hobbes's justification of the title.) Hobbes did not believe that philosophical writing should be ornamented or diverting. He makes few efforts to charm the reader. After a brief but illuminating Introduction, he plunges into an account of the origins of man's knowledge and, from that moment, the argu-ment drives remorselessly on its way, almost defying the reader to accept it *en bloc* or not at all.

The initial shock of encounter can be eased by grasping the method which Hobbes was applying in his exposition, the method on which he placed such great importance. Much has been written about it, and Hobbes has been from time to time categorized as a rationalist, a mechanist, a nominalist, a naturalist, a materialist, and so on. It is probably best at the outset to ignore these pigeon-holes, and to try to get inside Hobbes's own frame of reference. What did he think could be known philosophically, and how did one achieve such knowledge? His definition of philosophy in one of the later chapters of *Leviathan* provides a useful starting-point:

By Philosophy is understood the knowledge acquired by reasoning, from the manner of generation of any thing, to the properties: or from the properties, to some possible way of generation of the same; to the end to be able to produce, as far as matter, and human force permit, such effects, as human life requireth (ch. 46).

Philosophy was thus a specific form of ratiocination. Hobbes equated it with the disciplined use of 'natural reason', marking it off sharply from supernatural revelation. Philosophy was confined to understanding the things of this world, which Hobbes defined as 'bodies', or entities, whether animate or inanimate, which were self-subsistent, that is to say, existed 'without us' and occupied some particular space or 'place'. Such bodies *were* reality.

For the *universe*, being the aggregate of all bodies, there is no real part that is not also body; nor any thing properly a *body*, that is not also part of that aggregate of all *bodies*, the universe (ch. 34).

Throughout *Leviathan* and throughout all his philosophical work Hobbes strove to purge reality of all those occult qualities and metaphysical or spirit substances by which theologians and clergymen had—in his view—not only confused men's understanding of the world, but weaned them from their allegiance to the civil power. This is the polemical edge of his constant and sometimes crude insistence on the sole reality of the corporeal.

Motion in and between bodies produced all the rich variety of sensuous qualities that 'appeared' in the mind of man. Some bodies were 'natural' or made by 'nature', which in turn was made by God. They were the subject of natural philosophy. Others were 'artificial' and made out of nature by man. The 'body politic', the subject of civil philosophy, was an artificial body, with the distinctive characteristic of being made by man out of man. Once again the pivotal position that man occupied in Hobbes's scheme of things is evident. On the one hand, he was a part of nature or a created being, and on the other, he was a creator or artificer, a being with a God-like power *vis-à-vis* nature. The Introduction of *Leviathan* makes his dual status particularly clear. For this reason it is necessary to be very careful in defining the 'naturalist' component in Hobbes's political philosophy. Clearly he believed (as we shall see again in a moment) that civil philosophy must proceed from 'nature'. This had to be the starting-point. Civil philosophy had to break its *mésalliance* with theology and root itself instead in the workings of the physical universe. But this did not mean that civil philosophy was reducible to or equatable with natural philosophy, or that man himself was but a natural mechanism.

The task of philosophy, Hobbes argued, was to understand bodies by understanding how they were 'produced' or 'generated', whether by nature in the case of natural bodies, or by man in the case of artificial ones. It followed that there could be no philosophical knowledge of God, who was not produced, and who also did not occupy a determinate 'place' in the universe, but was 'infinite'. The 'nature of God is incomprehensible; that is to say, we understand nothing of *what he is*, but only *that he is*' (ch. 34). This was Hobbes's consistent position. Philosophy was thus radically distinct from theology, and faith was not knowledge—though Hobbes was always insistent that what was believed through faith could not be at variance with the conclusions of philosophical reasoning.

As a disciplined search for how things are produced, philosophy was not the same as empirical fact-grubbing. It was not the register of how things appear over time, or 'history'. Nor was it the register of natural phenomena. A good memory for facts and much experience of facts might make a man 'prudent', but prudence was not philosophical knowledge. How then did philosophy proceed? For Hobbes the two great levers of enquiry were analysis and synthesis, or, as he sometimes expressed it, resolution and composition. He was not the discoverer of this route to knowledge, glimpses of which can be obtained in both Plato's *Republic* and Aristotle's *Politics*, but he established it at the centre of his logic in a way that was unprecedented. Using analysis the mind took apart the bodies that pressed themselves on to the senses, beginning with their 'appearances' or 'effects' or 'properties' and then working back to what caused or conditioned these. This decomposition was not a literal physical dissection but a conceptual one. It was carried out with the aid of hypotheses, by which Hobbes did not mean more or less arbitrary assumptions made 'for the sake of argument', but postulates, suppositions, factors deliberately distinguished as the grounds or conditions of what was apparent or, to put it differently, as implicit in what was apparent. Using hypotheses the mind could move progressively from what was immediately known to what was unknown. The search was for what was *logically* prior. The ultimate goal was to uncover and define the first 'principle' or 'cause' of the body under examination and hence the logical sequence of its production. 'If this is so, that is so, and if that is so, this follows . . .' Such was the 'conditional' or 'consequential' language of analysis. It was concerned essentially with establishing necessary relationships.

Analysis was hence the logic of discovery or 'invention' and not the sterile logic of verbal disputation that dominated medieval scholastic philosophy. It did not focus on words but on things, using words as instruments to stake out the different stages in the production of a thing. 'Let this be called x, and that be called y . . .' For Hobbes such definitions were an absolutely vital part of philosophical method and they can be found in abundance in *Leviathan*. Note also that analysis did not involve the accumulation of examples. It could proceed with only one, and by conceptually multiplying a single case, could move on to the study of interrelationships. The task of analysis was not to generalize from *many* things, but to uncover the universal core of *a* thing, by stripping away all that was contingent and subjective and particular about it. Hobbes wrote explicitly that 'the method of attaining to the universal knowledge of things, is purely *analytical*.'[4] This sentence incidentally shows that treatment of Hobbes as a 'nominalist' can be profoundly misleading if it is taken to imply that he thought that there could be no 'universal' knowledge.

Synthesis or composition moved in the opposite direction to

---

[4] Hobbes, *Elements of Philosophy*, i, p. 69.

analysis. It 'constructed' things in their logical or necessary sequence, starting from first principles. It proceeded a priori, while
analysis proceeded a posteriori, but the two were complementary
procedures in Hobbes's view and not (as so many people assume
today) opposed to one another. The 'method of philosophy . . . is
partly analytical, and partly synthetical; namely, that which proceeds from sense to the invention of principles, analytical; and the
rest synthetical.'[5]

Hobbes did not only argue that analysis and synthesis (albeit
employed in differing proportions according to the different subjects under consideration) provided the method of philosophical
enquiry, he also argued that there was a logical order in which the
various branches of philosophy followed on from one another.
Natural philosophy 'preceded' civil philosophy. More precisely,
the logical sequence of science ran from 'first philosophy' (or the
study of quantity and motion indeterminate) to geometry, and
from there to physics, and from the physics of man (or men considered as a species of animal) to civil philosophy. This seems to
have been what Hobbes meant when he implied that the proper
approach to civil philosophy was 'synthetical'.[6] He seems to have
meant that once one had a scientific understanding of the 'natural'
properties of man, one could proceed to 'construct' the body
politic in a purely a priori manner. On the other hand, he also
argued that it was quite possible to understand the body politic in
an a posteriori manner, beginning with the properties of a body
politic, decomposing these into their component elements, i.e.
men, and then analysing man himself in order to get at the first
principle of the whole body. He further argued that it was quite
possible for any person, by rigorous self-analysis, to get at the first
principles of the state, without a special knowledge of geometry
and physics. (See again the Introduction to Leviathan, where he
quite clearly indicates that individual self-analysis when it is properly conducted can lead to the 'universal' knowledge of man that
is necessary in order to understand the body politic.)

Whichever path of enquiry was taken, a priori or a posteriori,
one thing was certain: the method of *demonstrating* or *teaching* the
results of any philosophical enquiry was, for Hobbes, always synthetical, it was always a priori. Hence the method of Leviathan, at

---

[5] Hobbes, *Elements of Philosophy*, pp. 74–5.
[6] Ibid., pp. 73–4.

least throughout the first two parts, 'Of Man' and 'Of Common-wealth' respectively, is synthetical. These two parts form one continuous sequence of 'natural reasoning', from which all super-natural or theological arguments have been banished and which leads from a consideration of the universal natural qualities of man considered separately from other men, to a consideration of men interacting with one another, to the logical construction or formation of a body politic, and from there to an extrapolation of the logical consequences of such a constructed body. It is a logical deduction of what the state is universally, that is when stripped of all contingent and subjective factors.

What then of the other two parts of the book? In the third part, which is entitled 'Of a Christian Commonwealth', Hobbes does not abandon 'natural reason' but he does not rely on it alone. He applies it to the revealed word of God in the Bible, to demon-strate what is meant there by the 'kingdom of God'; what is the nature of ecclesiastical power; what is the basic core of the Chris-tian faith; and hence what tenets it is necessary for a state to up-hold for it to be deemed a Christian one. Needless to say, the argument that Hobbes constructs out of scripture complements the argument that he constructs using natural reason alone.

In the fourth and last part of the book, 'Of the Kingdom of Darkness', Hobbes assembles together and castigates afresh the opponents that he has attacked throughout the earlier parts. He describes them as 'a confederacy of deceivers, that to obtain dominion over men in the present world, endeavour by dark and erroneous doctrines, to extinguish in them the light, both of nature, and of the gospel; and so to disprepare them for the king-dom of God to come' (ch. 44; the original is italicized). Erroneous and irrational theological doctrines propagated by a power-hungry clergy (both Roman Catholic and Protestant) form the main target of his attack, but he also takes the opportunity to ridi-cule Aristotle's metaphysical, ethical, and political doctrines. This fourth part of the book reminds us again how intensely polemical and problem-orientated Hobbes's logical construction of the state is. It is not something done as a purely academic exercise. It is a campaign against irrationalism. Hobbes brings his book to an end with a brief 'Review, and Conclusion'.

Such then is the method and the overall outline of *Leviathan*. The discussion will now concentrate on the more purely philosophical parts of the book, namely the first and second, and identify the main stages in the unfolding of Hobbes's argument.

Hobbes's Conception of Man

The account of man that is given in the opening chapters of *Leviathan* is crucial to an understanding of the later, more explicitly political argument. The account is remarkable for its lack of any religious or moral presuppositions. Man is approached as one physical being amongst others. He is seen as a kind of animal, and the question which Hobbes seems to be posing and answering throughout these early chapters is simply this: what kind? What distinguishes man from other animals? In answering this question Hobbes looks first at man's cognitive or conceptual power (ch. 1–5) and then at his motive or passionate power (ch. 6 onward).

At first he treats man in isolation from his fellow men. As we have seen, the analytical method could be practised using only one example. Then, with no warning to the reader, he assumes a multiplicity of men and deduces the relationships that develop between them, given their particular make-up. This move from singular to plural starts in chapter 8, and becomes fully evident in chapters 10 and 11 where men are portrayed seeking power over and through one another and esteeming one another in this light. The long chapter on religion that intrudes at this point (ch. 12) testifies to the great importance that Hobbes attributed to it as a factor affecting power relations between men.

What then, according to Hobbes, distinguishes man from other animals? At first sight, it seems there is little. Consider his account of the passionate side of man's nature in chapter 6. The passions push man towards those things that appear to afford him pleasure or delight (desires) and away from those things that appear to afford him molestation or displeasure (aversions). He does not move naturally, that is, by some innate characteristic, towards what is good and away from what is evil. On the contrary, he calls 'good' that which he is drawn towards, and he calls 'evil' that from which he retreats, and he strives continuously to obtain the one and to repel the other. Moreover the desires and aversions of different men rarely coincide, and even the passions of a particular man change over time.

Man thus does not have a static 'essence' or 'being'. He is not inherently 'good' or 'evil'. He is essentially activity, assertion, dynamism. He is modern, Faustian. His natural faculties are the means to obtain some future apparent good, and through them he acquires instrumental means—riches, friends, and so on—to extend his original ones (ch. 10). The dynamism is thus one of 'power'. 'I put for a general inclination of all mankind', wrote Hobbes, 'a perpetual and restless desire of power after power, that ceaseth only in death' (ch. 11). Obviously power here must not be crudely equated with 'power over others', but more generally, with the means to acquire, and the actual acqusition of those things that men at different times desire. To be continuously successful at acquiring such things, Hobbes called 'felicity'. 'I mean the felicity of this life. For there is no such thing as per-petual tranquillity of mind, while we live here; for life itself is motion . . .' (ch. 6).

Man, however, is not always driven directly and immediately by passion. He is capable of 'deliberation', that is, of weighing up the advantages and disadvantages of competing appetites and aversions, and the action decided upon at the end of such delibera-tion Hobbes defined as the 'will'. His conception of the latter was subtle and idiosyncratic. It rested on a sharp distinction between a 'voluntary agent' and his 'will'. It is worth pausing to examine his argument.

A voluntary action is one taken by a being who is able either to will to do or to will not to do something, a being who is 'free' in this sense. But the 'freedom to choose' that any voluntary agent had logically to possess did not, in Hobbes's view, alter the fact that the concrete choice of a particular course of action, made by such an agent—or 'willing' itself—is always necessitated or caused by something that is not the will. To think of the will as 'causing' the will was absurd. To think of the will as 'uncaused' was equally absurd. Moreover, the concrete choice marks by its very nature the end of the 'freedom to choose' possessed by the voluntary agent while he is deliberating. The freedom of a voluntary agent hence does not exclude the necessitation of his will.

Conversely, Hobbes thought that while the will is always necessitated, it is not, and could not logically be said to be, com-pelled. A 'compelled will' is a contradiction in terms. However it is quite possible for a voluntary agent to be compelled, by which Hobbes meant 'to be subject to extreme fear or terror', and this compulsion might well be the cause of his will. Willing by a person subject to extreme fear—always supposing that some choice, however, constricted, could still be said to have existed before he willed—is hence a genuine form of willing.

This explanation of Hobbes's concept of the will—based on chapters 6 and 21 of *Leviathan*, but taking into account also his elaboration of the subject in his dispute with Bishop Bramhall[7]— is necessary in order to understand Hobbes's later argument that the establishment of the body politic logically takes place under compulsion, that is when man is subject to extreme fear, and yet is also an act of will. It also helps to explain his statement that the sovereign power in the body politic must be able to 'form the wills' of his subjects by the 'terror' of his power.

In none of the faculties of man so far described did Hobbes see any qualitative distinction between him and the other animals. They too were driven by desire and aversion; they too could deliberate; and therefore they too could will. But wait. There was one passion that Hobbes expressly singled out as distinguishing man from other living creatures: the desire to know why and how, or curiosity. Other animals were overwhelmed by immediate physical desires and appetites; man alone delighted in something that went beyond such desires. Hobbes called curiosity 'a lust of the mind, that by a perseverance of delight in the continual and indefatigable generation of knowledge, exceedeth the short vehemence of any carnal pleasure' (ch. 6; see also the discussion of curiosity in ch. 3).

Here then was the seed of what distinguished man from other animals, and Hobbes's account of man's cognitive faculties (with which *Leviathan* begins) shows how this seed comes to fruition. Man, he argues, does not have any inborn cognitive faculty that marks him off from other animals. Like them his thoughts originate in the data of the senses; like them he can remember the impressions of the outside world communicated by the senses; like them he can act on the basis of his remembered experience of the outside world, or in other words, he can act 'prudently'. Unlike them, however, he has a drive, a passion to know the causes of things, that can outweigh the desire for immediate sensual gratification. In other words, he does not necessarily see

---

[7] See particularly his debate with Bishop Bramhall on the question of liberty, necessity, and chance which is to be found in vol. v of the *English Works*.

things purely in relation to his own immediate wants; he can also stand back and detach them from such wants. He can and does seek to see them as they are objectively, in themselves.

The passion of curiosity shares the universal quality of human passion; it is a branch of the desire for power. It is a means to power. But if it is different because it is an indirect means, an 'ascetic' means. It holds back man's immediate animal instincts and permits a 'disinterested' standpoint. More than this: by looking at things in a disinterested way, by seeking to understand them for what they are and in their own terms, man comes to have a power over them that qualitatively exceeds that of any other animal. Human 'arts' have their root in this capacity.

Although Hobbes does not make it absolutely clear in *Leviathan*, it is evident from his other writings that he held the passion of curiosity responsible for the 'invention' of speech.[8] This discovery was crucial because it enabled man's memory to be raised to a level qualitatively different from that of other animals. Through the use of words memory was able to become that very process of reasoning, or of analysis and synthesis, that has been described earlier. As Hobbes expresses it in *Leviathan*, man's mind was enabled to add and subtract, not merely in numbers, but in relation 'to all manner of things that can be added together and taken one out of another' (ch. 5).

Hobbes thus argued that man's distinctive passion of curiosity drove him to develop a cognitive capacity—in the form of reasoning—that qualitatively surpassed that of any other animal. Man was not born rational, but he was able to become a reasoning being. Reason was not essentially a contemplative faculty—as in the Platonic tradition. It was a practical activity directed towards ovecoming and mastering the things of this world, by penetrating beyond the immediate data of the senses.

How did Hobbes envisage the relationship between the rational and the passionate sides of man's nature? In man's pursuit of natural science he believed that there was little or no conflict between the two—and this was doubtless one of the reasons why he wanted to base civil philosophy on natural science. It was 'neutral ground'. But in the dealings of men with one another reason and passion conflicted. Passion drove towards the

[8] Hobbes, *The Elements of Law*, ed. F. Tönnies (London, 1969), p. 46.

particular, private interest; reason pointed to what was universally necessary.

Sometimes Hobbes's words suggest that in human interaction reason was but the weapon or instrument of the passions. It was a technique for achieving one's particular desires. But at the same time he castigated those who 'clamour and demand right reason for judge', and 'yet seek no more, but that things will be determined, by no other man's reason but their own'. Such men betrayed their want of right reason 'by the claim they lay to it' (ch. 5). Reason seems to have become a thing debased when it was no more than a technique for getting one's own way.

Hobbes's main theme seems to have been rather that while reason was the nobler faculty in man, passion was the stronger. In chapter 19 he wrote explicitly that 'the passions of men are commonly more potent than their reason'. The passions, it must be recalled, were for him the motive power of all voluntary action; each man willed his own good or apparent good. It followed that reason, if it was to shape or mould actions had at least to concur with one or more of the passions. To state that something was rational *in abstracto* was for Hobbes not enough to persuade men to do it. The rational had also to be aligned with a particular interest if it was to stand a chance of realization. As Hobbes wrote at the start of his first work of political philosophy, he wanted 'to put such principles down for a foundation, as passion not mistrusting, may not seek to displace'.[9] He did not want to sketch another ideal ought-to-be after the manner of Plato; he wanted to show that what ought to be was simultaneously in accord with certain basic desires.

This determination to demonstrate the convergence of reason and passion can be traced throughout Hobbes's construction of the state. The passion on which he placed greatest reliance as the 'motor' for the realization of the rational was a negative one, an aversion—fear.

The State of Nature; the Right of Nature; the Law of Nature

The most dramatic image in *Leviathan* is that of the state of nature, which appears abruptly in chapter 13. From the earlier

---

[9] Hobbes, *Elements of Law*, p. xv.

discussion of Hobbes's method it will be plain that the 'natural condition of mankind' which is described in this chapter is not an historical fact but a logical postulate developed in accordance with his method of analysis and synthesis. It can be seen either as a logical consequence of the definition of man as a passionate and rational being that precedes it in *Leviathan* or as a logical presupposition of the state of 'civil society' that follows it. In either case it is an abstraction, isolation, and localization of those factors which Hobbes argues are logically the 'cause' of the formation of the body politic. The state can only be conceived as overcoming something anterior to it, something that empirically can only be glimpsed here and there, but which it is the task of the political theorist to draw out and present in its unadulterated form.

The lineaments of the Hobbesian state of nature are well known. It is a 'condition which is called war; and such a war, as is of every man, against every man'. In the constant flux and reflux or warring atoms no civilized existence is possible. There is no industry, no cultivation, no arts or sciences, no society. Moreover, the

notions of right and wrong, justice and injustice have there no place. Where there is no common power, there is no law: where no law, no injustice. Force, and fraud, are in war the two cardinal virtues . . . It is consequent also to the same condition, that there be no propriety, no dominion, no *mine* and *thine* distinct; but only that to be every man's, that he can get; and for so long, as he can keep it.

It is, Hobbes adds, akin to the manner of life that men degenerate into in the course of civil war, and the parallel with his definition of civil war, which was cited earlier, is plain.

What precisely does Hobbes mean when he says that 'nature' has placed man in this terrible condition? It must be said that the logical deduction by which he establishes the state of nature is not a very convincing one. He calls it an 'inference, made from the passions', and he seems to mean by this that the reasoning capacity of man, the very capacity which, as we have seen, raises him above all other animals, has been deliberately left out of account or, perhaps more accurately, is not yet considered as having applied itself to the problem posed by human interaction. The 'inference' itself is peculiar. Not passion, but the fact that men are roughly equal in their bodily and mental capacities—'setting aside the arts grounded upon words'—stands at the start of the deduction. This, together with *amour propre*, which gives each man the conceit that he is the equal of any other, makes them each confident that they can attain the objects of their desires, and ready to use force in order to do so. This acquisitive competition in turn creates distrust ('diffidence') so that each man attempts to secure himself against the aggression of others by taking pre-emptive defensive measures. Some men also take a positive delight in conquest, regardless of their needs, and this drives even moderate men to be aggressive. Finally, all men seek to be esteemed by others as highly as they esteem themselves, and this factor—the desire for glory—can lead to armed struggles.

The weakness of this 'inference' is that it lacks logical necessity. Why should rough *de facto* equality not lead to peace as well as to war? Do defensive measures not lessen the possibility of attack? And does not Hobbes himself state that the desire for glory only accounts for war on occasion?

There is thus a certain contingency about Hobbes's state of nature which is at variance with his systematic philosophical method. This is all the more puzzling because later on in *Leviathan* (at the end of chapter 15) he deduces the state of nature in a more direct manner from his general proposition that men's passions drive them to define 'good' and 'evil' each in his own 'private', different, and inconstant way. If a number of men are placed in close proximity to one another, then these private definitions will lead to 'disputes, controversies, and at last war'. The state of nature here becomes a generalized picture of a world in which men are guided solely by their own ideas of what is 'good' and 'evil' and refuse to make any acknowledgement of a 'common good' or a 'common evil'. It is a simpler and more credible argument than that given in chapter 13.

In whichever way it is deduced, the state of nature reveals man in contradiction with himself. As each man seeks ardently for his own felicity, the very basis of felicity—life itself—is destroyed. And so, Hobbes argues, certain passions that helped to drive man into the state of nature—fear of death and a desire for the conveniences of life—combine to drive him out of it. Most important of all, experience of the state of nature drives man to bring into play his most noble capacity—his capacity for reasoning—to resolve the contradiction posed by his confrontation with his fellow men. In reaction against a 'common evil', a 'common good' comes to be defined. The way to civil society is thus not natural, but rather a 'disciplining' of nature. The contrast with Aristotle is plain.

Using his reason man uncovers the laws of human coexistence, the so-called laws of nature, which Hobbes proceeds to describe in chapters 14 and 15. Before he does so, however, he briefly defines man's 'right of nature'. This right plays a far more important role in his argument than his short account of it might suggest. It breaks in unannounced and yet it is one of Hobbes's most original, fascinating, and puzzling notions.

What is the right of nature? Hobbes defines it as 'the liberty each man hath, to use his own power, as he will himself, for the preservation of his own nature; that is to say, of his own life; and consequently, of doing any thing, which in his own judgment, and reason, he shall conceive ·to be the aptest means thereunto' (ch. 14). Liberty as here defined is not the same as liberty in what Hobbes calls its 'proper signification' (ch. 14: see also ch. 21 where the duality of definition reappears). Liberty in the latter sense means simply the absence of external impediments to motion, whether such motion be human, animal, or inanimate. Liberty as a 'right of nature', however, inheres in each man as such. It expresses indeed a new and important kind of human equality, different from the rough *de facto* equality that Hobbes had described in chapter 13. It is a freedom to act according to one's own judgement and reason, hence, a freedom not to be subjected to the judgement and reason of others, or a right to resist. Does it inhere in animals as well as man? In *De Cive* Hobbes had indicated that he thought it did (ch. 9). In *Leviathan* he keeps silent on this matter. He appears to consider it as a specifically human right.

Yet this freedom to determine oneself he defines solely in relation to the extreme situation, to self-preservation. It is the right to do everything that a man considers could conduce to such preservation, and this includes, according to Hobbes's scattered observations, the right to judge when danger threatens; the right to decide which measures are necessary to repel danger; and the right to use any measure including force in order to do so. The right of nature is indeed strikingly similar to the right of sovereignty which is later invested in the ruler of the Hobbesian commonwealth.

Although Hobbes does not directly discuss the right of nature in chapter 13 on the state of nature (it is only referred to obliquely), he clearly considered that this right was equally responsible, with the passions, for creating such a state. The right of nature, so to speak, legitimized the state of nature; it gave each person a right of war against all others, while the passions provided the matter of war.

This interpretation is confirmed when we turn to the laws of nature, for it is plain that these laws, discovered by reason, direct man to restrain both his original right and his belligerent passions. The laws are perhaps best defined as the necessary, objective forms of behaviour that are required of beings that are at once free, equal, and passionate, if they are to coexist. Hobbes considered them to be as universal and immutable *vis-à-vis* men as Galileo's laws were *vis-à-vis* matter. The science of them, Hobbes wrote, 'is the true and only moral philosophy. For moral philosophy is nothing but the science of what is *good* and *evil*, in the conversation and society of mankind' (ch. 15). These last words hammer home their significance: originally man's conception of 'good' and 'evil' was purely subjective, the reflex of his passions; but reason, prompted by the painful encounter with other men, enables him to recognize a good that transcends subjectivity. This good is precisely the placing of oneself in the position of the other person and of modifying one's own behaviour accordingly; it is the idea of a 'common good'. (This idea is made particularly clear in Hobbes's summarization of the laws of nature for men of 'the meanest capacity' at the end of chapter 15.) Hence with the laws of nature a second layer of morality has appeared in Hobbes's scheme, a layer not natural in the sense of being the spontaneous product of the passions, but in the sense of being a discovery of man's natural reason, prompted by certain passions.

The status of the laws of nature, as Hobbes himself acknowledged, is a peculiar one, and much scholarly debate has raged around it. They were not for him properly speaking laws, that is to say, the commands of a superior person. Only when they were regarded as being contained in the injunctions of the Bible, the word of God, did they take on this guise. (See the end of chapter 15.) But for Hobbes the laws of nature did not apply solely to Christians, any more than they applied solely to men of science or philosophers. They were accessible to all who used their naturally developed capacity for reasoning. They were 'dictates' in the sense that truth discovered imposes itself on the mind, and is not the arbitrary product of our will.

The dictates of the laws of nature were 'categorical' because, plainly, if they were not observed at all, then man was doomed to self-destruction. But they were not categorical in the sense of abolishing man's natural right to judge when his existence was endangered and to take measures to preserve it. The laws restrained and corralled this natural right; they obliged man 'to endeavour peace, as far as he has hope of obtaining it' (ch. 14). But they did not oblige him to act regardless of circumstances, or of situations, or of the consequences to himself of his action. Men, even when endeavouring to follow the rules of reason, remained 'judges of the justness of their own fears' (ch. 14). Hobbes's laws of nature must therefore not be equated with Kant's categorical moral imperative. They were more like the rules that sovereign states 'naturally' follow without abandoning their sovereignty. Indeed later on in *Leviathan* (at the end of chapter 30) Hobbes equates them with the 'law of nations'.

Hobbes indicated the equivocal character of the laws of nature by saying that they

oblige *in foro interno*; that is to say, they bind to a desire they should take place: but *in foro externo*; that is, to the putting them in act, not always. For he that should be modest, and tractable, and perform all he promises, in such time, and place, where no man else should do so, should but make himself a prey to others, and procure his own certain ruin, contrary to the ground of all laws of nature, which tend to nature's preservation (ch 15).

This leads directly on to a consideration of the content of the laws of nature. They did not merely tell men to seek peace where it could be found, but told them how to find it. First and foremost, they enjoined men to enter into mutual agreements to restrain their original 'right to all things', or in other words, to make contracts, covenants, and pacts. Such contracts or covenants, once made, created obligations of a more intense kind than that of the laws of nature in general. This is because they involved the internal or voluntary acceptance by the contractors of an external restraint on their natural right of self-determination. In this act of self-limitation can be seen the kernel of Hobbes's concept of political obligation, although of course when the state came to be formed the obligation became far more intense because the 'external restraint' was then far stronger than simply the 'other partner to a contract'.

The laws of nature also enjoined men to perform covenants once they were made, and Hobbes wrote that in this injunction lay 'the fountain and original of justice'. However he proceeded to argue that until there was a power established that was capable of compelling men equally to the performance of covenants, that is, until a common power or state had come into existence, justice could not be properly said to have come into existence. To understand this paradox, that the laws of nature enjoin something that nevertheless cannot be fully implemented without something more than the laws of nature, it is helpful to recall that in an order, such as the international order, which is based *entirely* on contracts, it is implicit and taken for granted that the partners to the contracts remain the judges of their validity. Should the contractors or treaty makers judge that circumstances have altered, or that their partners have failed, or are failing, to carry out their side of the bargain, then the contract may rightfully be renounced. In such a situation contracts are made and have a function, but are not, by the very nature of things, completely binding. It is precisely this kind of precarious order that Hobbes seems to envisage when he introduces the laws of nature into the original state of nature.

The remaining laws of nature (Hobbes lists nineteen in chapters 14 and 15, and adds a twentieth in his conclusion to the book) enjoin man to restrain unilaterally those passions that tend to war; to recognize his fellow men as equals; and to observe certain forms of procedure, based on the idea of equality, which facilitate the peaceful settlement of disputes.

The scholarly arguments which have circled around Hobbes's laws of nature should not be allowed to obscure the fact that his definition of them marked an epoch-making breakthrough. Gone was the idea that the laws of nature were those laws which were common to man and beast; gone was the idea that they were the result of some past agreement by all men, or all nations, or most men, or the most civilized, to respect certain values; gone was the idea that natural law was deduced from God's commands or eternal wisdom, to which man had some kind of direct access; gone finally was the idea that natural law summed up the 'natural inclinations' of man which were self-evidently 'good'. The new and fruitful idea that Hobbes launched was that natural law embodied the rationally deduced forms of behaviour that were required of beings who were free and equal (or what others were to call 'moral beings' as distinct from 'natural beings') if they were to coexist with one another. This fundamental idea was to be developed further by Pufendorf, Kant, and Fichte.

The Creation of the State

The laws of nature modify and temper the state of nature but they do not eradicate it. Why not? The answer has already been suggested by the brief description that has been given of them. The laws rely for their implementation on the self-same free, equal, and passionate beings whose conduct they regulate. They are not transcendent, but immanent in the reason of particular men. More specifically, the laws of nature do not remove, but presuppose the sovereign right of each individual to decide how to preserve himself. Each person remains the judge of 'the justness of his own fears'. In addition, covenants and pacts that take the form purely of agreements to respect one another's rights are not strong enough to hold in check the passions of the contractors. As Hobbes repeatedly emphasizes, a form of words, however reasonable, is not in itself enough for this purpose. Passions can only be checked by reason *and* a more powerful passion. There must be a force behind the agreements that makes the pain of breaking them outweigh the pain of keeping them. Fear again is the key.

If it is argued that at least the common endeavour for peace has some external or objective existence, namely in the reality of the 'other person' with whom one may have made a contract, and who may take action against one if one fails to carry it out, Hobbes replies that the power of those men that one might offend by breaking contracts or covenants in the state of nature has 'not place enough, to keep men to their promises; because in the condition of mere nature, the inequality of power is not discerned, but by the event of battle' (ch. 15). For this and the other reasons that have been outlined, war and the fear of violent death are not abolished by the laws of nature. Even after their discovery 'every man will, and may lawfully rely on his own strength and art for caution against all other men' (ch. 17).

Something more is patently needed if the ground of man's search for 'felicity' is to be secured, and this something more is an act of union by which the common endeavour for peace is given a distinct 'place' through personification, and is also given real power *vis-à-vis* individuals. This is way, at the end of his exposition of the laws of nature, Hobbes turns to the subject of 'persons, authors, and things personated', and introduces the two vital concepts of representation and authorization which prepare the way for his account of the 'generation' of the state (ch. 16).

The foundation of the body politic can only be a contract or covenant, for as Hobbes states succinctly in chapter 21, there is 'no obligation on any man, which ariseth not from some act of his own; for all men equally are by nature free'. But it is a covenant that goes far further then than any normal one: it is a constituent covenant between a multiplicity of men that creates a 'real unity' into which the contractors are incorporated (ch. 17). On the one hand, it creates a common representative, some one man or assembly of men that will make present or give visible and distinct 'place' to the common will of those who covenant together. Representation for Hobbes means essentially personification. On the other, it is a covenant of authorization in which all the participants 'own' or identify themselves with whatever the representative person shall do for the sake of their common peace and safety. In this act of authorization man's original right to do anything he judges apt for his own preservation is 'given up', though Hobbes will not allow it to be extinguished completely. There is always a small residuum—the right to save oneself from death, wounds, or imprisonment—that continues to be possessed by man in the civil state. But note that the act of authorization is more than a negative act of renunciation; it is also expressive of a positive willingness to place men's powers at the disposal of the representative person in the carrying out of the tasks that have been entrusted to him. It gives the representative the resources to inspire a fear or terror that can outweigh the anarchic passions of the contractors.

As a result of this creative act an artificial man or 'Leviathan' comes into existence, and this artificial man is the body politic, with the sovereign, or the person representative of the whole, as its 'soul'. The rights, powers, and, it must be added, the duties of the sovereign are immense. It is significant that, at the core of the rights that define sovereignty, Hobbes places one that is in effect the original natural right of man writ large. The sovereign, Hobbes writes, has the right 'to be judge both of the means of peace and defence, and also of the hindrances, and disturbances of the same; and to do whatsoever he shall think necessary to be done, both beforehand, for the preserving of peace and security, by prevention of discord at home and hostility from abroad; and where peace and security are lost, for the recovery of the same' (ch. 18). Freedom as sovereignty was what natural man had to give up; freedom as sovereignty is what the artificial man or body politic has to receive if it is to be genuinely a 'state'. A state without sovereignty—whether that sovereignty be invested in a single physical person, as in a monarchy, or in a corporate or collective 'person', as in an aristocracy or democracy—cannot perform its essential task.

The remaining attributes of sovereignty that Hobbes lists in chapter 18 are essentially the powers that are necessarily implied by the need to expunge all possibility of war from within the body politic, and to hold off the enemy without. It is not possible here to examine them in detail, but it is important to note (because it is not immediately apparent from the discussion in this chapter, and is only demonstrated in detail in the third part of the book) that for Hobbes the sovereign necessarily possesses the right to be the ultimate arbiter of what religious doctrines will be taught to the citizens, and what public form of worship they will observe. There cannot be two powers—church and state—coexisting within the body politic. 'There is . . . no other government in this life, neither of state, nor religion, but temporal' (ch. 39).

Through the creation of the sovereign power, and through the positive laws that the sovereign enacts, with punishments attached, the natural laws of reason lose their conditional character and become peremptory. 'When a commonwealth is once settled, then are they [the laws of nature] actually laws, and not before; as being then the commands of the commonwealth; and therefore also civil laws' (ch. 26). Men are now compelled to keep their obligation to perform such contracts and covenants as they agree to, and this being the heart of justice, the latter now becomes a reality. The uncertainty of possession is simultaneously transformed into the security of property. To this extent Hobbes's state may be called the actualization of right and reason, and indeed the rule of reason.

Yet the liberal side of Hobbes's construction must not be over-stressed. Hobbes's emphasis throughout *Leviathan* is on the dangers of freedom and on the absolute necessity of man renouncing his original liberty, rather than on the enlargement of man's liberty that results from the formation of the state. Securing peace rather than securing liberty is his governing preoccupation. This is made abundantly clear by his readiness to envisage two alternative forms in which the body politic (described in essence in chapter 17) may come into existence. In the first of these, the 'commonwealth by institution', the lineaments of the nationally constituted representative state of modern times are perceptible. The 'people' is expressly acknowledged to be the original foundation of the state (ch. 18). They decide by majority on the form of representation. But in the second the 'commonwealth by acquisition', there is no suggestion of the 'people' creating a body to represent them, but only of submission by individuals, singly or together, to a man who holds their life in his power (ch. 20). The profound gulf between the two forms of 'Leviathan' was later defined with exemplary precision by Rousseau, who may well have been thinking of Hobbes's exposition:

There will always be a great difference between subduing a multitude and ruling a society. If one man successively enslaved many separate individuals, no matter how numerous, he and they would never bear the aspect of anything but a master and his slaves, not at all that of a people and their ruler; an aggregation, perhaps, but certainly not an association, for they would neither have a common good nor be a body politic.[10]

With Rousseau's crisp reminder of the limits of Hobbes's liberalism, this discussion of some of the leading themes in *Leviathan* may fittingly conclude. The strength and weakness of the book would seem to be its rootedness in the extreme situation. Its logic runs from the freedom of the individual to preserve himself from subjugation and destruction to the freedom of the state to preserve itself from subjugation and destruction. All the middle ground of politics, where bargains and compromises are struck, seems to be swallowed up in an immense either-or: either the state is sovereign and thus truly a state, or it is not. Yet this focusing on the extreme situation is also the great strength of the book, for the extreme situation is not an invention of Hobbes, it is a reality that

---

[10] Rousseau, *The Social Contract* ed. M. Cranston (Harmondsworth, 1968), p. 58.

from time to time thrusts its way awkwardly through the more civilized give and take of normal politics. No political theory which ignores it can be complete.

In pursuing the logic of the extreme situation Hobbes broke the old moulds of theorizing. He showed that the state was not a mere datum, nor the invention of wicked men or (to use the modern idiom) of wicked classes of men, nor the unfortunate penalty for man's inherent sinfulness. Man creates the state; it is the act by which he cures the evil of insecurity that inexorably accompanies his spontaneous interaction as a free and passionate being with his fellow men. Political obligation is not natural, but artificial. It is the self-restriction and self-subordination of beings who originally possess absolute freedom. Finally, the state itself is not a web of contracts between individuals or groups to further their own particular ends, it is a 'real unity', the creation of a visible, powerful representation of the common, rational, human endeavour for peace.

Bibliographical Note

The Clarendon Press, Oxford, is currently engaged in producing a new collected edition of Hobbes's philosphical works. So far only *De Cive*—in both the Latin and English versions—has appeared, edited by Howard Warrender (1983). The Molesworth edition of Hobbes's works (London, 1839–45) thus remains the standard one. It was reprinted by Scientia, Aalen in 1961–2.

Leviathan has remained in print continuously in the post-war period and there are now several paperback editions available. The compression of the text into small, paperback format has its drawbacks. Legibility is not always good, and the useful side-headings are sometimes omitted. For this reason the older hardback versions may still be recommended, and in particular the edition originally published by Basil Blackwell (Oxford) in 1946, with a valuable introduction by Michael Oakeshott. This is the text that has been cited in the present chapter.

Two works by Hobbes which are of great relevance to *Leviathan* have been republished: *The Elements of Law*, in which he first set out his political philosophy, and *Behemoth*, in which he examined the causes and course of the English Civil War. Both books have been reprinted (London, 1969) in the form in which they were originally edited by F. Tönnies, with new introductions by M. M. Goldsmith.

An anthology of Hobbes's writings entitled *Body, Man, and Citizen* (ed.

R. S. Peters, New York, 1962) provides useful access to his ideas on philosophical method. For the details of Hobbes's life the new biography by
A. A. Rogow (New York and London, 1986) may be consulted.

The scale and scope of the secondary work on Hobbes's political philosophy is indicated by Charles H. Hinnant's *Thomas Hobbes: A Reference
Guide*, published by G. K. Hall and Co., Boston, Mass. (1980). This provides
a year by year list of books and articles about Hobbes (and new editions of
his works) that have been published between 1679 and 1976, with brief notes
on the entries. The inclusion of works in languages other than English makes
this a particularly valuable catalogue.

Those seeking a clear and balanced introduction to Hobbes's philosophical method may turn to J. W. N. Watkins's study of *Hobbes' System of Ideas*
(London, 1965; 2nd edn., 1973). The essays included in *Hobbes Studies*, edited
by K. C. Brown (Oxford, 1965), provide an excellent introduction to the
main controversies that have developed around Hobbes's political ideas since
the war, in particular the debates over the so-called 'Taylor–Warrender'
thesis about Hobbes's concept of obligation, and over Hobbes's alleged
'bourgeois' perspective. Another symposium, *Hobbes and Rousseau: A Collection of Critical Essays*, edited by M. Cranston and R. S. Peters (New York,
1972), indicates some of the interpretative themes that have developed most
recently.

Leo Strauss's provocative study *The Political Philosophy of Hobbes, its Basis
and Genesis* (Oxford, 1936; reprinted Chicago, 1952), was chiefly responsible
for initiating the modern debate. Subsequent landmarks include A. E.
Taylor, 'The Ethical Doctrine of Hobbes', in *Philosophy*, 13 (1939), pp. 406–
24; Oakeshott's introduction to his edition of *Leviathan*, mentioned earlier;
Howard Warrender, *The Political Philosophy of Hobbes: His Theory of Obligation* (Oxford, 1957; 2nd edn., 1970); C. B. Macpherson, *The Political Theory
of Possessive Individualism: Hobbes to Locke* (Oxford, 1964); F. C. Hood, *The
Divine Politics of Thomas Hobbes: An Interpretation of* Leviathan (Oxford,
1964); F. S. McNeilly, *The Anatomy of* Leviathan (London, 1968); David P.
Gauthier, *The Logic of* Leviathan: *The Moral and Political Philosophy of
Thomas Hobbes* (Oxford, 1969); Thomas A. Spragens, *The Politics of Motion:
The World of Thomas Hobbes* (London, 1973); and W. von Leyden, *Hobbes
and Locke: The Politics of Freedom and Obligation* (London, 1981). This is but a
brief indication of the wealth of secondary literature that has appeared.

6

John Locke:
The Second Treatise of Government

CHRISTOPHER HUGHES

To read for the first time a book which successive generations have accounted a classic, is an experience to be mentally recorded. With what expectations does one open the *Second Treatise of Government*? These must be pitched high, for it was written by a great philosopher, and published at the height of his powers, at a decisive moment in English history. It is held to be a parent of the American Rebellion, and thereby among the ancestors of the French Revolution.

If the expectation is that it will only be a textbook of majority rule, human rights, and the modern democratic package generally, then there is room for disappointment with Locke's book. It is also an exploration of the difficulties and inconsistencies of this set of ideas by a thinker evidently leaning passionately towards them. When we expect a clear denunciation, for example of slavery, Locke's argument is subtle and not immediately convincing. If in some passages he bases government upon consent, in others (e.g. s. 75)[1] he voids consent of its natural meaning.

Was Locke timid, blind, foolish? We remind ourselves how historically recent is universal adult franchise, and further, how short of perfection are its results and how precarious its tenure, how ambiguous is the inner legality of some governments it produces, and how cluttered with reservations are our declarations of the rights of man. In general, indeed, the results of the twentieth-century democratic package are encouraging, but the verdict of history is still unexpectedly inconclusive. With renewed interest we turn to Locke's text.

The interpretation here followed treats the *Second Treatise* in this spirit, as a text given sense and logical coherence by history.

---

[1] All references are to sections from the edition by Peter Laslett, *John Locke*, Two Treatises of Government (Cambridge, 1960).

However insubstantial Locke's expressed appeal to history, anthropology, and comparative government may at first sight appear, his endeavour is to make sense of the world which confronts our eyes, not chopping it down, or not excessively, to fit in with his arguments from first principles, his ideology. The reader whose native language is English will assuredly come to Locke before he comes to Hegel, but when he does so come, he will observe how similar the structure of the *Philosophy of Right* is to the *Second Treatise*. In claiming Locke as in some measure a historicist, we claim him for the great organizing principle of thought of the last century. This makes Locke closer to Rousseau and Burke than he is to Hobbes, and in style as well as content. The *Treatise* is full of apparent contradictions, because it is an argument, a dialectic, not a geometrical proof: his statement that man is free legitimates and explains the statement that he is under government (i.e. not free). Locke seeks to find a level, a structure of society, which reconciles the two assertions.

The train of Locke's main argument as ordinarily understood runs: sections 4–8, 25–51, 87–9, 95–9 (and, one might think 'or', Locke's own summary in sections 123–32). The discussion of property could be regarded as an excursus, but here I treat it as the central jewel, the remainder being the setting, and the wrappings (with Locke even the wrapping cannot be discarded). But here again some of it may be taken as involving an unconnected or even a contradictory line of thought. After all, in or around 1689 Locke published works on five other important topics, each of which seems to exhibit a different tendency, on the theory of knowledge, on education, on economics, on religion, and on toleration. Even the *First Treatise of Government* seems inconsistent with the *Second*.

Locke's style is in general that of conversation, pioneering this style in printed English for serious discourse. On rare occasion it rises into eloquence, even with a touch of poetry, but it also sinks, as does ordinary conversation, into windings, obscurities, and repetitions which, to make matters worse, are not quite repetitions. At times he loses the reader's attention, but even here the general effect is of a striving for extreme and embarrassing intellectual honesty, not, as with Hobbes, to conceal the weak point of the argument. It is in some ways reminiscent of Aristotle's *Politics*, and not only in style. Locke inherited from his early years as an undergraduate and junior teacher at Oxford a coloration of Aristotelianism mediated through religious writing of the century which ended in 1660, represented in the *Second Treatise* by quotations from Hooker. The papal encyclicals, notably *Rerum Novarum* (1891) (which a century ago founded the Christian Democracy that is the normal political ideology of Western continental Europe) read in their economic and political–moral aspects unexpectedly like the Locke of the *Second Treatise*, especially on property, and on nature. This set of ideas is not derived from Locke, but it shares a common source in the Christian Aristotelianism of the Middle Ages. This is unexpected in that Locke's own brand of Christianity grew from a background which might loosely be called puritanism and ripened into what looks from the outside to be deism or indifference, but the readership he was trying to convert was the world of the High Anglican gentry, who would have been brought up on Hooker.

It was the Locke of the *Essay concerning Human Understanding* which guided the two stages of the European and American Enlightenment of the eighteenth century and provided the backbone of the more powerful trend of liberalism, and the harder trend of conservatism, in the nineteenth century in English-speaking countries. It still typifies what is most English in the English-language philosophical tradition. *Some Thoughts concerning Education* is still an influential book, to different effect, in its sphere. The *Letters on Toleration* have spent themselves, beneficial in their generation, and Locke's ideas on religion have been absorbed into the body of tolerant indifference. The present book, Locke on government, nature, property, and consent, is a disturbing work, and is unexpectedly once again a message usable by the younger generation of today.

The *Second Treatise*

This companion to the text is constructed on the basis that the *Second Treatise* is built up on a theory of *successive* stages of society. It is 'generative' in method; the nature of a thing is how it comes about. There is, first, natural society, that is to say, half a dozen stages of natural society (it is here simplified to three), then civil society, and then political society. So to the enquiry 'What is Locke's theory of freedom?', the reply is 'Freedom in natural society is . . . so and so, freedom in political society, on the other hand . . .' The same applies to equality and property. In Locke's words (s. 22, my own punctuation and spelling, and explanatory additions in square brackets):

The *natural* liberty of man is to be free from any superior, . . . the liberty of man *in society* is to be under no other legislative power but that established by consent, . . . but freedom of man *under government* is to have [i] a standing rule to live by [ii] common to everyone of that society and [iii] made by the legislative power erected in it.

Secondly, it is to be recognized that the content of these key concepts survives from the earliest into the latest stages of nature and society. The laws of nature as between God and Adam continue to apply, modified and fulfilled, in later stages of nature, in family life, in modern economic life, and in the state properly speaking. The laws of animal society survive alike in school, family, and politics. But the tendency of natural law theories such as Locke's is to imply that the earlier moralities in some way prevail against the later ones. Locke anchors, for example, a natural right of property against the state, because property is more fundamental and earlier than the state, but his sense of history prevents him from pressing the 'natural' claim against manifestly unequal property. History also confirms, surprisingly, that the early freedom of nature is enhanced by political liberty (see e.g. s. 60) and given a new sphere of action and rationality by it.

Thirdly, my canon of interpretation is to accept as many as possible of Locke's verbal contradictions into his theory, as being contradictions present in real life, explanatory of the movement of history. The *Second Treatise* is a revelation of wisdom, not a demonstration of geometrical logic. Locke's spiritual biography, which is that of his society and age, started (perhaps after republicanism in childhood) with a youthful enthusiasm for the Restoration of Charles II, and then (as a client of a Whig patron) changed to a position which brought him under suspicion of sedition or even treason, and finally, with the successful Revolution of 1688, brought him back into the centre as a supporter of the new regime. This life story is built into the *Second Treatise*, which is thereby given the force of Locke's whole personality, and not just of his momentary stopping place in 1689 in his voyage across the political spectrum. Nevertheless, some carelessness there is, and this Locke acknowledges (Preface to the *Two Treatises*, and s. 52) while lambasting Filmer for the same qualities. Locke here shows the reader samples of his thought over a period of twenty years, and the very artlessness is effective in a book whose role was to introduce pluralism and tolerance into politics and, eventually, into nearly every sphere of life.

Locke's Preface and First Chapter

The Preface to the *Two Treatises* (which is not included in some editions of the *Second Treatise*) is to be read at the beginning with some caution. It is an afterthought, and should be read again at the end, together with Laslett's commentary. The first chapter of the *Second Treatise* is also an afterthought: it is Laslett's contention that the (unreadable) *First Treatise* was designed to come second, and the order was reversed, and he draws attention to the changed reference in section 54. This first chapter provides a link, and the last two sections contain a somewhat incautious key definition; maintaining that the state properly so-called is different in kind from patriarchal or Hobbesian relationships. Some of the tendency of the book is against this, for example when he writes that 'to understand political power right we must derive it from its original' (s. 4): the state *includes* a patriarchal element and grew insensibly out of it (chapter VI—apparently lifted out from the *First Treatise*), the logic of natural society survives into the state (e.g. property rights), and crime and slavery are situations where natural society is re-enacted. Locke here is superadding the special, unique, obligation of the citizen to his own state, political obligation, to the ordinary obligation everywhere of a man to the powers that be, the obligation of the Englishman abroad to French or Dutch law, for example: he reverts to this problem frequently (e.g. ss. 9, 14, 118, 122, 145).

The First State of Nature

In chapter II, sections 4–10, and also in sections 25–7, Locke presents the state of nature as a sort of tableau vivant. The curtain rises, on a darkened stage two allegorical figures are revealed, Freedom and Equality, dressed alike. As our eyes become accustomed, we see two huge characters God and Nature were already present in the background, who are accompanied (or were they already present there?) by Reason and Law. Then Property enters, a normal human being. She, or he, is to hog the limelight, wearing successive disguises reminiscent of those worn by other characters, of Reason, etc. It is evident that the action we are to witness is already half-way through its course, and the drama lies in conjecturing what has already happened.

Locke, in some ways, goes too far in personifying abstract qualities, nature, reason, where it is not appropriate, and scarcely further in personifying God, where it belongs. The idea of freedom may or may not have come earlier to our civilization than equality, but which of them is logically prior? There is at least some overlap; if all are equal, all are free from one another. What is the relationship of reason to God? If we know God by reason, then in some sense reason is prior, the form of our cognition of God. But He created us reasonable and, in virtue of that, gave man sovereignty over nature. Are these two concepts used just as a device to enlist sympathy from the monarchical Right (God) and the republican Left (reason)? There seems also an overlap between reason and nature. Did God or reason or nature make us (a) free and (b) equal? Many patterns can be created by arranging and rearranging these concepts. We must also remember two absent friends Truth and Justice, whose presence might have led to more traditional, authoritative conclusions (a polity not ruled by majority decision for example).

As for God, He is too large a figure to be allocated a minor role, confined to the Big Bang, the creation of man. Are we thereafter left 'to get on with it'? We know Him by reason, but also by revelation, the big book, the Bible. The God of Christianity is a person with a will, a rational mind, in charge of the destiny of the universe, but with a care for each individual soul which thereby has a certain god-like status, equally god-like in all men. In politics the presence of God excludes all lesser concepts, leading, on the one hand, into republicanism, but on the other hand, into authoritarianism, into the sovereignty of those whom He has appointed, kings for example. Revelation is as ambiguous as reason. But Locke does not quite think of God as having lost interest in mankind at a rather early stage; He is also prepared to intervene on request in a battle or rebellion; this is the appeal to Heaven (which will be considered later on, along with some kindred concepts). Apart from this, reason, law, and nature take over for practical purposes.

Reason, nature, God, law, it is best to regard them as one package. The taste left in the mouth by Locke is of reason as the name for this package. In using the style of the creation myth of the Old Testament to express a highly abstract argument (in section 6, which is too long to quote in full, and too intricate to quote by excerpt), Locke is doing something the Christian is encouraged to do. But he does it to different effect, i.e. to apply abstract principles to concrete political practice.

The creation of man manifestly takes place in time. Here the generative method is appropriate, first one man, then wife, children, brothers, servants, each situation giving rise to concrete moral relationships. Applied to these the Big Words change their nature and come down to earth. Sin becomes crime. Nature becomes a boundless wood in Virginia or Carolina containing beasts of prey. Nature later becomes an object of property. Adam and Eve merge imperceptibly into English settlers taking possession of land for colonization in North America. For many purposes the modern reader can substitute words such as 'the course of history' for God. Locke henceforth uses the Old Testament as one source among others of anthropological information about early society.

But between men, there are also abstract principles of organization, freedom, equality, law. These are closely related to one another. One can visualize them as at the points of a triangle, each concept analysable in terms of the other two (ss. 4–8). The name of the triangle itself is society, at first thought of as all mankind, and then as separate societies following the same evolution and not yet significantly in competition with each other.

The values implied in the creation myth are regarded as still applicable. They are summoned to deal with a new factor, the conflict between reason as the will of particular men, and reason as a general principle. Man is not a good judge in his own cause when in competition with another man. Reason makes provision for this concrete situation by an agreement between the two to set up a third as arbitrator. And thus (s. 8) in the very first 'state of nature one man comes by a power over another'. Logically, the sanctity of contract itself cannot depend for its validity on contract, so Locke belatedly places it in, or prior to, the very first state of nature. As Rousseau knew, all theories of social contract get into this difficulty—contract itself has to be made morally prior to the compact of society.[2]

The Second State of Nature

We are now from section 11 onwards in the second state of nature.

Equality is freedom, but it is also an organizing idea; society is the living together of men who see each other as equals (s. 5). Looking forward to Kant (as well as backwards to Hooker), we can see the whole moral law as included in equality, and it is indeed an element in Christianity and other religions—but these are also *revealed* religions, and Kant never got airborne without *positive* law. Hobbes uses the antisocial potentialities of equality, physical equality, and freedom to necessitate positive law, unfreedom, inequality, and Locke himself (s. 21) takes this idea aboard, in order to get mankind out of a state of nature which is all too desirable.

Freedom involves political equality in that it is negatived by inequality, but it is not defined entirely negatively (section 57 is the extreme assertion of positive freedom and law in the *Second Treatise*), it is not the passive state of not depending on the will of another, but the activity of the will when not controlled, when disposing for example of one's own possessions or person. It appears simultaneously with property.

The concept of property introduces already a second 'natural state of nature'. Property in the first state of nature is imperfect in the absence of a judge. In the second state of nature there are already third-party judges. Reason and even God (s. 8) are still around in their old form, but the law of nature has undergone a sea change, it has become a criminal law exercisable by any third party and a civil law (s. 10) perhaps visualized as being exercised by a magistrate on the demand of the injured party, in the interest of mankind as a whole.

Chapter III is concerned with the false or artificial state of nature, the Hobbesian state of war. This is an important topic, for this situation can occur at any stage of development when the

---

[2] Jean-Jacques Rousseau, *The Social Contract*, Bk. II, ch. 7. (Harmondsworth, 1968).

natural balance of society breaks down. Locke's main treatment of it comes in chapter XVI and later, so I am postponing discussion of it, and taking it together with slavery (ch. IV) and the appeal to Heaven (ss. 21, 87, etc.). For the moment it is enough to observe that without unreason and crime there would be no inducement to mankind to move out of the early state of nature. This state is depicted as so happy, almost as the peaceable kingdom of Isaiah, that it would seem unreasonable of mankind to leave it. The *Second Treatise* has even been read in this manner, as it were in reverse, with the initial state of intelligent anarchy placed as the conclusion. In Edmund Burke's *Vindication of Natural Society* (1756) this suggestion was worked out fully: Burke belatedly assured readers that this was meant as a youthful spoof, but if so it was a perilous one. It has been said that the *Vindication* was taken seriously in Germany and elsewhere on the Continent, and may be one source of the sentimental idealization of nature that became a commonplace in cultured society after the mid-eighteenth century; it is present in Rousseau, even if on occasion criticized by him. There are also later passages in the *Second Treatise* (ss. 110–11) which anticipate the sentimental idealization of nature of the eighteenth century and there is an indirect connection through the medium of Shaftesbury's *Characteristicks* (1711): the Third Earl of Shaftesbury was for a time Locke's pupil, and his works once enjoyed an extravagant reputation on the Continent, but are now read too little. Another connection is made through Locke's own *Thoughts concerning Education*, a book which advocates a certain open-air naturalness.

The state of nature is not presented only as a sort of supposed historical period or as an ideal, and we are today interested in it as an argument in metaphysics that certain moral ideas are logically prior to others. If we assume that a morality is possible, then that morality must be like this. We are also tempted to interpret the state of nature as an assertion that certain ideas, such as the nature of goodness, are inborn in man. Here we land ourselves into difficulties.

In the *Essay concerning Human Understanding*, Locke's most influential book, there is a long diatribe against 'innate ideas', but on the face of it the contention of Locke's happy 'state of nature' is that social morality is innate in man. This is too large a topic to discuss here. It would seem that there is indeed contradiction between these two books sent to the press in the same year—the *Treatises* were assuredly by Locke, but were during his lifetime published anonymously. References to 'Locke' in eighteenth-century works on political matters are often to this 'other' Locke, more universally studied.

Property

(Chapter v, and sections 36, 73, 88, 94, 123–4, 128–42, 180, 222, but consult Laslett's Index for a complete list of references.)

If there were no more to Locke than a statement that society is natural but government is artificial, and ought to be conducted in the interests of the governed, some would say the *Second Treatise* could be consigned to the same oblivion as the *First*, along with many vapid and optimistic writers. But the intrusion of property ensures Locke's immortality.

Chapter v, the third state of nature, starts with an assertion that the world and all it contains was given by God to *all* mankind *in common*. *Private* property is therefore secondary (which is historically quite plausible). This original commonality is not necessary to Locke's whole argument, and seems to detract from it, and God's gift could have been derived more usefully from nature or reason. This may be a quirk or a false trail in a book formed over a period of years and not much revised, or it may be a belated desire to adhere to a standpoint adopted in section 29 of the *First Treatise*, but it has a larger significance. The idea of community, even the community of mankind, occurs repeatedly. Locke has the popular repute of being an extreme individualist, but he often and needlessly makes large concessions to collectivism and in section 87 (his own summary of this chapter) reiterates this grant, more ambiguously, and goes on to describe in very explicit terms the social pact as a grant by each man separately of his own power to the *community*, and to those holding authority from the *community* (see s. 120). Taking all the references together, his individualism is tempered by very large concessions to collectivism, inviting an interpretation in which this socialism is the rule, not the exception. (See Laslett's references under 'Communism' in his index, and the work by Kendall.[3])

---

[3] Willmoore Kendall, *John Locke and the Doctrine of Majority Rule* (Urbana, 1965).

Locke sometimes uses the word property in a restricted sense (reflecting the normal usage, land and goods), and sometimes in a wider sense, 'life, liberty and estate' in which one 'owns' all that one 'is'. One's property is the whole of one's social personality. One is what one has: in property the external world, or portions of it, become *a part* of oneself (s. 26, the fruit or venison which nourishes the wild Indian becomes 'his, and so his, i.e. a part of him'), one's personality, one's freedom, one's life.

We may distinguish also the objects of property. In the innermost circle Locke speaks of property in one's own body (s. 27) which implies a *se ipse*, a oneself, which 'owns' one's body. In the next concentric circle are the things the body grasps or treads on, or the deer the Indian kills in the forest, which are thereby made a part of oneself: this joining is called labour, the labour of my hands etc. (s. 27 again). This labour is itself a commodity which can be bought and sold (s. 40). Beyond this still, there is what one might call 'capital', for example, land to be used to produce a crop, where labour has cleared the forest and reduced it to cultivation (s. 43), or the horse man has tamed or the tools he has made (so we might say: Locke is thinking mostly of land, but we today would think of machinery and factories).

Having once broached the idea of capital (e.g. labour invested in making land fertile) Locke becomes enthusiastic about it, as a justification of private accumulation, containing in itself a justification of government: government makes capital secure ('government has no other end but the preservation of property', s. 94, and six later places). Capital invested in the soil of Virginia can increase the value tenfold, nay 100, nay 1,000 (ss. 37, 40, 43). Of Locke's perceptions this is the most obvious, the most innovative, the most fertile. Apply Lockian-style government to an isle off the China coast or to Manhattan, and skyscrapers will shoot out of the rock.

Next (or perhaps it is prior to property in the form of industrial capital) there is property in gold. In money, we would say, or in oil shares, or in Bank of England stock. But this lies in the future, it lies just over an invisible frontier between natural society and civil society: for as to money, and suchlike (s. 184) 'these are none of Nature's goods, they have but a phantastical imaginary value: nature has put no such upon them'. It is the use of gold by weight as a unit of account, by common consent of all mankind, that is within nature; coined gold belongs to particular societies. In Locke's day and later in some countries the currency of foreign princes circulated by weight and fineness, unless prohibited by express legislation.

Finally, though not certainly, there is voluntary servitude, wage labour (scattered references, a grotesquely unfeeling one in section 28, also section 85, where it is distinguished from slavery). This idea is to be cumulated with the alienability of labour (the possibility of selling it), with the idea of capital (stored labour as value), and with the idea of gold as a primitive money which can be stored up. The three together legitimate an oppressive society, and pass outside the frontier of the rules governing the state of nature to an extent which to modern readers seems excessive. But it also, one presumes, is outside the absolute sanctity attached to property as a right that precludes taxation, though Locke does not revert to such speculations when he comes to consider government in detail. It is probable that Locke assumes that freehold in land, or a freehold tenure of office, is the qualification for participation in political life and enjoyment of the right to rebellion. Servants, i.e. wage labourers, and apprentices, making up one half or more of the male heads of household, could be left out of account (except perhaps as beneficiaries of a trusteeship). Historically, they have mostly been, perhaps still are, largely left out of account: the expression 'the people' has a felicitous ambiguity in political usage, the objects of power often, but seldom as the owners of power. It is going too far, but not much too far, to attribute to Locke the perception that the exclusion of the propertyless from the doctrine of consent is the chief object of government.

On the brink of leaving natural society for civil and political society, one can look back on the method Locke followed in his interpretation of the economic and social history of mankind (e.g. in ss. 100–32). In part, his method is that disturbing mixed mode, a priori (or armchair) history. But there is no a priori science of history; one cannot construct a history from first principles and then draw conclusions from it wherewith to bind the future and construct a new morality. One can perhaps generalize from real history, and that hope is the justification for studying history. Locke does, indeed, make highly intelligent use of what evidence is to hand, the Old Testament (s. 109), for example, and the large literature on the then newly discovered lands in North (e.g. 3, 49, 108) and South America. The superstructure of speculation built upon Locke by others (e.g. Adam Smith) throughout the eighteenth century is impressive and solid, even if his own foundations are a somewhat unsystematic and too-gentlemanly reading of the books on his own shelves. Miraculously, he may have got things right, just as, unexpectedly, his rambling philosophizing is part of the basis of a Western civilization that has changed the face of the world—the skyscrapers are really there as a physical fact. Are his conclusions vitiated if his history and anthropology are wrong? Leaving this question unanswered—it haunts us with Machiavelli and Rousseau, and the lack of even a speculative history disappoints us with Hobbes—one can draw support from the manifest self-consistency of the partly fictional society sketched by Locke; this sort of economy requires this sort of constitutional structure, this attitude to religion, this doctrine of property and capital, this style of discourse. It coheres as a construct, it convinces, just as *Macbeth* does. It is freedom which produces wealth, converts the forests of New England into factories, and not into Christian cathedrals nor into pyramids like the Egypt which inspired Plato.

Civil Society

The distinction between civil and political society, i.e. between economic society, the world of buying and selling, and the state, can be attributed to Locke, although it was on occasion abandoned by him. The thing itself was happening in England in Locke's lifetime, had already happened in Amsterdam, is incipient in urban life almost everywhere (or at least in the West), and was to be fully released after the American and French Revolutions. Civil society, *bürgerliche Gesellschaft*, bourgeois society, the social and economic market-place, was to obtain a life of its own, the success story of economic society left to itself by government, infinitely fruitful (ss. 219, 222). Such a society depends, however, on the controlled use of violence to maintain the institution of property. This use of physical coercion, including war, is allocated to the government, kings, the executive. Against this violence, the law-abiding citizen is 'fenced' (s. 93, line 16). Midway between civil and political structures, and linking them, are the courts of law (regarded as principally within the civil society sphere) and the elected legislature. Political party (referred to by Locke, s. 158, but only in the old, unprofitable, way as a distortion of representation, not as the life and condition of it) lies just beyond the curtain bounding Locke's prescience. The distinction between legislature and the executive in political society tempts one to assert the paramountcy of parliament over the executive, and of the civil over the official, military, and ecclesiastical. But Locke is too wise to go as far as this, or rather, in his usual mode, he contrives both to go farther and not as far.

Interpreted as a tract printed (but not written) in defence of the Revolution of 1688—a legitimate but not an easy interpretation— one expects Locke to understand the event in terms of English civil society rebelling against government and recreating government in a new form to its own liking (ch. xix). As usual, the text disappoints such an expectation, not as wrong, but as too crude.

The idea of civil society, dependent on government principally for the maintenance of property as an institution, and ideally the master of government and the source of its legitimacy, receives its name from Locke and its inspiration. The doubt is whether the distinction of civil from political society was actually fully present in his mind, or is contained in the text of the *Second Treatise* (e.g. s. 89). To say it is not there in express words, taking into account repetitions and denials, is defensible. In the case of the other, connected, idea capital, Locke does not give it a name nor does the thing in any way go back to his authority, but he makes a new use of it. To civil society he does give a name, and confers his authority upon it, but it escapes the grasp when reading the text. It is a crucial idea of Western civilization which came to fruition in the nineteenth century (by way of the eighteenth-century Scottish Enlightenment).

There is also a good reason why it is not consistently there on the page of Locke. Civil society develops into government, and creates government by an act of will, but having created it, is changed and perfected. It needs government. It even needs a single man with a will-to-power (ch. xiv, especially s. 165) to give it rationality and direction (comparable to Rousseau's lawgiver and Machiavelli's Romulus, etc.), and it needs the struggle to free itself from this master and to give itself another sovereign. In intuiting this, by timidity and muddle, by humanity, Locke remains greater than the idea he fathered. Sections 87–9 are at the centre of this concept. They need to be expanded rather than summarized, and can with advantage be read and read again, together with sections 95 and 96. For the purpose of my argument I would have preferred chapter VII to be entitled 'Of Civil Society' leaving chapter VIII as 'Of the Beginning of Political Societies'.

Political Society

Political society, then, is erected by economic society as a deliberate act. Is this the social contract? The contractual element in the *Second Treatise* is (more or less) confined to three sections just quoted as needing to be expanded rather than summarized. On the day of revolution, the community being already present, every one of its members, all private judgement being excluded, consents, and thus the community comes to be Umpire (legislator, constitution maker) 'by settled standing rules . . . the same to all parties, and by men having Authority from the community for the execution of those rules' (s. 87). For the moment, civil society is identical with political society, it is a moment of exaltation and Locke becomes a visionary, quickly side-tracking himself, then recovering his inspiration in sections 95–9, breathless and, at first reading (and twentieth reading), confused, a creative outburst reminiscent of Rousseau.

As for government, it has no other end than the protection of property. This allots government its place as the servant of civil society. What requires protection, as Adam Smith points out (*Wealth of Nations*, v. i. 2), is grossly unequal property, and to perform this task in a political society where all heads of family are equal, looks miraculous. But history tells us it can be done, and economics teaches us that it is desirable, inequality is the condition of investment of capital. Yet whatever consent means, it carries some implications of sovereignty welling up from below.

Consent

Property is natural. But government is artificial. The conflict is reconciled by a theory of consent, a concept which is on the surface of things a simple one. When more closely examined this simplicity evades the enquirer, and is difficult to recapture, although it is there.

It is usually understood that Locke argues that consent is the only lawful title to government, indeed, that this is virtually the whole of his argument, and Locke on occasion (e.g. in the meandering second sentence of his Preface to the *Treatises*) says just this. 'But stop!' the reader exclaims, 'How can consent be a basis to *government*?' Taken on the same plane, government, the smack of firm government, excludes consent. There may be individual consent to government in general, and general consent to government decisions in particular (e.g. where to site an airport), but there will not always be an individual's consent to particular decisions to his own disadvantage (e.g. to pay quite that amount of tax) or when government is acting as government in its repressive aspect. Taken on a different plane, in one sense all government is by someone's consent, if only by the consent of the emperor's Praetorian Guard, as Hume pointed out. And, in effect, Locke's usage of the word ranges all the way from the natural meaning of 'explicit agreement' to the meaning almost voided of any content ('a tacit and scarce avoidable consent', ss. 74–5).

The most deliberate discussion of consent is in sections 119–22 (other references include sections 15, 22, 95–9, 104, 112, 117, 171). Here Locke recurs to the distinction in section 2, between obligation to one's own government as a full citizen, and that to a foreign government, for example to the French government when in France on holiday. In the latter case, merely being within the frontiers, by will or necessity, obliges me to obey all the laws and perhaps, beyond that, to a general courtesy and non-interference. Analogous, but not the same, is the position of the subject of a government which is arbitrary, unlawful, or despotic. Both situations imply a certain measure of consent, which is another way of describing, from a different standpoint, the degree of obligation. A small child to his father, an oarsman in a galley, a slave to his master, a servant to his employer (s. 2), have obligations to this extent willingly to obey, and this can be called consent. But in the ideal situation, that of a citizen of a free country, owning property and the right to vote, there is a positive obligation on both sides binding citizen and office holder. This obligation is freedom itself (in the sense of sections 22 and 57), and is equality. Consent is a sort of enthusiastic identity of purpose (as in marriage, s. 82, perhaps the idea of love is appropriate, although foreign to Locke's world of concepts). All this is in addition to the minimal consent due to government as government, derived from rationality.

Contract and Majority Rule

The logic of Locke's theory of contract or, rather, consent as a continuation of a contract, would seem to imply two contracts, a contract of society and a contract of government. Society is a metaphor drawn from law, *societas*, a partnership, but Locke's society seems to go beyond this into another legal metaphor, a joint-stock company or corporation. Like marriage, a corporation is formed by contract, but once formed it changes its nature: a corporation has a personality of its own, different from that of its individual shareholders, it is a person in its own right. It appoints the members of the governing body under its own seal, but its constitution is already set up by the articles of incorporation, the contract. Subordinate corporations such as the East India Company also required the royal charter, but this does not fit Locke's metaphor (unless God is brought again out of semi-retirement). The word Locke most often uses for the corporate body is 'community' but this clue might lead to a false trail in German theories of corporation.

On other occasions, later on, Locke tries out another metaphor, specifically from English law perhaps (the law of trusteeship was being developed in his day by Chancery, but Locke shows no particular understanding of it). Through the device of trustees, the substance of corporate personality can be obtained (for example, by a club) without permission of the state, but the metaphor cannot be pushed too far—those who are the beneficiaries of a trust, those who set up a trust, and the trustees, are three distinct legal persons. Even if we hold Locke to contract we are in difficulties enough, because contract, bargain and sale, implies a third party, the enforcer of the bargain that has been struck. Another word 'covenant' (like an English deed under seal) is available, a one-sided undertaking of obligation, but this would lead to a too Hobbesian conclusion, though Locke on occasions allows an oath. Hobbes is probably right, in the eyes of a liberal, when he insists that obligation to the sovereign derives from the obligation to fellow citizens, and this can be extrapolated to the case of a democratic sovereign, the community as sovereign, which a modern reading of Hobbes requires.

Meanwhile in the midst of this flurry comes the transition from unanimity to majority rule (ss. 95–9, and also s. 132). This is a passage made the more difficult to follow in that there exists virtually no political philosophy of majority decision. One would be happier if there were two decisions, the first that the majority should prevail and be accounted as the decision of the whole, and the second, the decision on the actual issue. Unanimity is unanimity, and nothing follows, for there is no minority to be bound and even the tyrant has a vote. But to appeal to the majority is to appeal to Heaven, not to reason. Locke has two defences available, one is that action requires decision and decision requires a procedure, and given the alternatives of majority decision and minority decision it is impossible to will anything except majority decision. Locke plays with this, but for conviction he would need also to appeal to history. History, into which Locke here declines to enter, records rather early some majority elections (e.g. of the Pope by Cardinals), but with the proviso that the person elected by majority represents the choice of the whole; majority decisions on disputed *issues* occur historically somewhat later, at first with the same proviso. The English jury, and indeed, the British Parliamentary election and Cabinets, retain the early ambiguity of majority and unanimity: closed doors keep secrets, acclamations intimidate. It is true that majority rule 'works', but this has no moral consequences; dictatorship may work, divine right monarchy worked from the dawn of records down to 1918. In his use of history, examples of which accumulate as the *Treatise* proceeds, Locke, like Machiavelli, is interested in learning about 'necessity': he usually stops well short of legitimizing rule through an accident of history.

The Critique of the English Constitution

This (in chapters XI–XIV and later) would seem to be the proper province of the historian of institutions, but has some importance for us as illustration, and doubtless had a disproportionate influence on Declaration of Independence in 1776 and the USA Constitution (1789).

As to the constitution of the ideal commonwealth, Locke is ambiguous; the principal passage is in section 132, the Form of Government. Although a constitution under that name occurs in sections 153–4, Locke seems really to be thinking of an unwritten constitution (s. 141).

The separation of powers in these chapters anticipates Montesquieu, but the judicial power is assumed to be included in the latest stage of natural society (in civil as opposed to political society). Distinction is made between the legislative power and the executive, both of which are, properly and logically, called supreme (s. 151), as is the people or community (who are supreme over the legislature as such and in some circumstances: see especially sections 140, 154, and chapter XIX). With the executive can be included the control of foreign relations, the federative power (ss. 146–8, 153).

Only the legislature is distinctly conceived, as a body of persons meeting occasionally (ss. 135, 143, 153, 160), usually visualized as the House of Commons only, sometimes as including the Crown. Ministers as controllers of the House receive no attention (but only as servants of the king). A standing army is not visualized. County government, and the Church, are ignored in this context. The dicussion is abstract, perfunctory, and already in Locke's day was old-fashioned, but then, much discussion today of the House of Commons losing power to the executive, etc. visualizes the England of two centuries ago.

Sovereignty

The absence of the word sovereignty in the *Second Treatise* (except in one passage referring to the First Treatise, where the word abounds) draws comment, though less exclusive terms such as the 'supreme power' abound. The *Treatise* is, after all, on civil government, not about 'the state', and the theme is of pluralism, of a variety of powers supreme in their sphere, the individual, the family, society, the community, Parliament, the king (the executive power when acting within the legislative power), the judges. In such a society, interest groups would, we may speculate, flourish. But in chapters XIII and XIV Locke comes close to the inner nature of the state, the power of acting *illegally* (s. 160) for the common good, a power active in the same world as the right of rebellion. Society properly speaking can operate with a judicial power, and a legislature acting in conjunction with it to amend the law and provide a rational policy. But it is the power lawfully to act unlawfully which fascinates citizens, and characterizes a dynamic, progressive civilization, Machiavelli's Prince who can establish a new order—'he that will look into the history of England will find that Prerogative was largest in the hands of our wisest and best princes' (s. 165). This is a dangerous perception, quickly buried; prerogative is the medicine of the constitution, not its daily bread, and for our last four centuries it has been God-like statesmen, not kings, who have flashed across the sky of civilized peoples. These two chapters, which look forward to Carl Schmitt, are outside the accepted picture of Locke, one of the many surprises which make the text more worth while to read than expected.

Slavery, Rebellion, War, Tyranny

(Chapter III—War, chapter XVI—Conquest, and then until the end of the book, scattered references throughout.)

Parallel to Locke's sober idealism about the possibility of constitutional rule, arising from and leading to morality, and prosperity, is the shadow of non-moral government, based on force and arbitrariness. Even in natural society, there is the fact of actual crime, the wolf in man, taken for granted by Locke in his argument from common sense. The metaphor implies there is no morality about the relationship of citizen to criminal nor, more disconcertingly, of the criminal towards society; he is outside the society, does not consent to it. Analogous to crime is defeat in war. The conqueror, at least in a just war, has a power of life and death over those captured under arms (ss. 178–9), and therefore can enslave the prisoners of war—the practice of Locke's age (in war between Christian powers) was more enlightened than he asserts. This leads to the problem of slavery in law-regulated society (ch. IV and s. 172; see Laslett's Index) such as the American colonies. These perhaps are considered as first-generation slaves purchased from some African conqueror 'in just war', or their under-age children. He treats the relationship as non-moral on both sides, a continuation of war. Analogous again to this is the relationship in political society between the community of citizens and an unjust ruler. The community can rebel, coded by Locke as 'appeal to Heaven' (ss. 8, 19–21, 87, 94, 125, 168, 176, 240–3; see also chs. XVIII–XIX). This extreme case affects the whole of Locke's theory 'of politics'. Politics, after all, is the method of regulating the situation where both sides are in the right, a 'just' ideological war played out as a sort of chess game (the reader may imagine), as when appealing to a majority in the legislature after discussion. But when these understandings are breached by the ruler himself, the appeal must be to physical rebellion. This seems to be the right of the community under natural law—there are perhaps no enforceable human rights inhering in the individual in Locke's commonwealth, no individual right or duty to rebel, but a collective one, a right of minorities, or majorities where there is no representative government, perhaps sparked off or initiated by some daring citizen. Citizenship, to reverse the way of looking at society, is confined to those with the effective power to rebel. For an individual, the remedy is self-exile, which was easier in Locke's day for a person of property than it was before or after.

But though there may be a right to start a war, there is not a right to win it. It is not clear whether the appeal to Heaven is the appeal to force or to history, or whether God does, or should, intervene. It is rashly assumed that Locke has English history in mind, but he may have been more pressingly under the influence of the Dutch provinces, and he might have spared a thought for the Huguenots in France, or Monmouth's Rebellion. The appeal to Heaven is the most striking example of Locke perceiving an inconvenient truth but unable to make it intelligible.

The same might be said of an entire vein that runs through the *Second Treatise*, war, slavery, rebellion, tyranny. At every stage of the unfolding theme moving from the first state of nature to political society, there lurks evil, an evil on the left as well as on the right: there is licence to be feared (s. 6), as well as a corrupted traditional monarchy. Locke's contemporaries would have Hobbes's fearful choice in mind, whether to prefer Leviathan, or to leave mankind as wolves to each other. Just as Locke, after all, finds a place for Filmerism at the edge of his scheme of things, so he finds a place for Hobbes.

Locke escapes from Hobbes's cycle of ideas by the means of

self-consciousness. In seeing himself as man, a man sees others as equal, and derives from this a will towards society (but requires a limitation of his subjectiveness through arbitration of a third party). The potentially competitive state of nature is instantly overlaid by a social state of nature, but this can break down. Indeed, in two instances it almost necessarily breaks down. In the international relations of sovereign to sovereign, there is a potentiality of regular, lawful, war, perhaps followed by conquest. In normal relations of travel and commerce there is the case of a foreigner in a strange society, or in relations with foreign subjects. There is the act of rebellion, and there is slavery. Within society, there is crime, highway robbery for example (ss. 8, 11, 19, 182, 186, 202, 207, 228, 232–3, 243). It would have been easy for Locke to have worked with an Augustinian doctrine of the inborn sinfulness of man, but for once he perceives the possible dangerous implications of such an argument, it would lead to a different political theory and another role for religion and the Church. Locke uses the idea of crime, implying deliberate outward breach of a law rather than sin. But the idea of inborn sinfulness is also present in the distrust of absolute princes: Locke is less optimistic concerning man than one expects.

To make an ideology, there is at least a strong temptation to regard one's opponents as oppressors and as beasts, to put the judges in the dock as exercising force, and to excuse the terrorists as acting in self-preservation. A more dispassionate observer might see the capacity to act as 'tygers' to be inherent in man as man, including himself. In this mood, Locke sees, for example, that no man judges truly in his own case, and argues that the tyrant is a man as bad and as good as any other. The greatness of the achievements of the Revolution of 1688 was, in the judgement of posterity, to allow the Tories to contend in parliamentary elections and, in the course of time, to obtain a majority there. No doubt during the elections Whigs called the Tory rural clergy lyons, tygers, and wolves, as Locke does in his more turgid passages (ss. 11, 16, 93, 137, 172, 181–2, 228). But Locke is on solid ground if he condemns cruelty in man, the suppression of the Monmouth rebellion, or the persecution of the Huguenots in France (to both of which there is no explicit allusion), and the rule of the Turks over their Grecian subjects (s. 192). Here his emotion and revulsion are entirely in place.

Conclusion

There is no agreement on a single answer to the question, how is a young person of university age to read Locke? It is necessary for a citizen to speculate on the modern equivalents of the concepts Locke discusses in the *Second Treatise*; these windmills are also with us today, to tilt against, and to grind our corn and gunpowder. It is possible to reflect on these without reading Locke, and to read Locke and reflect on other things. The language of discourse, however, is facilitated if we agree on which books to use in this manner, and also if we choose the same books as our ancestors chose, books which have themselves formed our civilization and laws. The case that this book is a profitable one to study can only be made by actually doing so, by mulling over the concepts, and seeing whether a new perception comes from doing so. The student of moral and political philosophy is here in much the same situation as the young citizen. For myself, this book is one of those that has, as it were, been carried in my knapsack throughout my life, and I have found it is one which stands up to the treatment of being read and reread, with enjoyment, exasperation, and some profit—along with several dozen other dog-eared books of varied character.

Bibliographical Note

The text used here is that of Peter Laslett, cited below, and references are to sections of the *Second Treatise* in that edition.

Laslett's Introduction also provides an example of the historical approach associated with Cambridge studies of Locke's political works. The reader might suppose that such an approach would find its whole being and end within the enclosed garden of history: but such is not the case. Nevertheless, he might be advised at this stage to choose a different approach, such as Geraint Parry's book, reading the text of the *Second Treatise* again, and also looking up quotations in their context.

After this, the student might select a particular topic, such as Property, and read a book such as Macpherson's (or Tully, or Ryan) again looking up the references in the text. He would now be in a position to think for himself, adopting his own interpretation.

The names of the authors cited in the booklist are also a guide to a first selection of articles to be read in learned journals. Scholarly writing on

Locke is increasing exponentially—the total of bibliographic entries during the years 1970–80 was ten times that between 1900 and 1940. This means that the latest studies may be taken as building on their predecessors and the most recent may thereby be the best. The explosion of interest in England's great philosopher is overdue, and welcome. The absolute size of this literature is still not large, and the field for original contributions remains wide open.

Booklist:

Ashcraft, Richard, *Revolutionary Politics and Locke's* Two Treatises of Government (Princeton, 1986)

Ashcraft, Richard, *Locke's Two Treatises of Government* (London, 1987)

Cox, Richard H., *Locke on War and Peace* (Oxford, 1960)

Cranston, Maurice, *John Locke: A Biography* (London, 1957)

Dunn, John, *The Political Thought of John Locke: An Historical Account of the Argument of the* Two Treatises of Government (Cambridge, 1969)

Gough, J. W., *John Locke's Political Philosophy* (Oxford, 1950)

Kendall, Willmoore, *John Locke and the Doctrine of Majority Rule* (Urbana, Ill., 1965)

Laslett, Peter, *John Locke,* Two Treatises of Government: *A Critical Edition with an Introduction and Apparatus Criticus* (Cambridge, 1960)

Leyden, Wolfgang von, *Hobbes and Locke: The Politics of Freedom and Obligation* (London, 1981)

Macpherson, C. B., *The Political Theory of Possessive Individualism* (Oxford, 1972)

Parry, Geraint, *John Locke* (London, 1978)

Polin, Raymond, *La Politique morale de John Locke* (Paris, 1960)

Ryan, Alan, *Property and Political Theory* (Oxford, 1984)

Seliger, Martin, *The Liberal Politics of John Locke* (London, 1968)

Steinberg, Jules, *Locke, Rousseau, and the Idea of Consent* (Westport, Conn., 1978)

Tully, James, *A Discourse on Property: John Locke and his Adversaries* (Cambridge, 1980)

Yolton, John, *John Locke: An Introduction* (Oxford, 1985)

7

Jean-Jacques Rousseau: *The Social Contract*

MAURICE KEENS-SOPER

ROUSSEAU'S single attempt at the full exposition of his political thinking was published in 1762 and immediately banned in France. In his birthplace, Geneva, the *Social Contract* was condemned as subversive of religion and government and publicly burned by the official hangman. It was not until after the outbreak of the French Revolution in 1789 that the book became well known. Since then it has become Rousseau's most famous work and one of the most widely acclaimed treatises on politics.

The Setting of the *Social Contract*

At the time of the *Social Contract*'s appearance Rousseau was at the height of his powers. His name was known throughout the cosmopolitan culture of mid-eighteenth-century Europe. Success had not however come until, at the age of thirty-seven, he abandoned a long-developed love of the countryside for the literary *salons* of Paris. There he became associated with the *philosophes*, whose boundless belief in the progressive power of reason to enlighten and better mankind is to be found in the extensive volumes of the great *Encyclopaedia*. Rousseau contributed articles—mostly on music—to this monument of the Enlightenment which is, in effect, the ground-plan of the modern world. But what secured Rousseau's early reputation was an essay which scandalized the *philosophes* by directly challenging their beliefs. In the *Discourse on the Arts and Sciences* (1749) Rousseau found and invented himself as a man, a moralist, and the author of a new literary style. He did so by denouncing and denying the claim that moral progress accompanies that of science and the arts. 'Oh virtue! Sublime science of simple souls,' Rousseau concludes the *Discourse,*

Are so many difficulties and preparations needed to know you? Are not your principles engraved in all hearts, and is it not enough to learn your laws to commune with oneself and listen to the voice of one's conscience in the silence of the passions?

Rousseau's thinking and imaginative energy stem from this insight. If such it be. His conviction that goodness and happiness are to be united in ordered simplicity permeates all that he wrote. He presents it as a new ethic and uses it as a weapon to judge and condemn the servile values of city-centred cosmopolitan life. His determination to voice and shape the implications of his insight into the natural—but socially subverted—goodness of man has transcended his own life. Rousseau's voice has become part of our self-interrogation into the content of modernity, our enquiry into what we are and how we should live in 'an age of reason'.

The writings which originally made him famous consider these questions by reference to individual men, largely detached from political life. In the *New Héloïse* (1761) Rousseau makes the triumph of moral virtue over romantic feelings attractive to a handful of intimates, and in *Émile*, which appeared the same year as his treatise on politics, Rousseau envisages an education in moral independence designed to fit a man to withstand the influences of social life. The distinctive mark of the *Social Contract* is that it considers how men are to live together as moral but also as political beings.

The *Social Contract* is a shortish book and the Foreword gives the misleading impression that it was salvaged from a more comprehensive work whose intended scale defeated the author's talents and which, out of modesty, he abandoned. It is true that some eighteen years before the publication of the *Social Contract* when he was a man of thirty-one working in Venice as secretary to the French Ambassador, Rousseau envisaged a work on politics which he refers to as the *Institutions politiques*. In Venice he was struck by the pervasive influence of politics in all aspects of life, and the conviction that good or bad political arrangements make a world of difference to the way men are, was one he never subsequently doubted. Despite the self-deprecatory tone of the Foreword, the *Social Contract* is more than a fragment extracted from a larger work which never saw the light of day. It is a book in which Rousseau worked with hardened passion to give exactness and force to his political ideas. Even though in later life he

was on occasion defensive about the *Social Contract*, which he said
needed redoing, there is plenty of evidence that he was also proud
of it and believed that his 'treatise' (as he liked to call it) faithfully
expressed his thinking on a subject-matter of manifest importance.

That the *Social Contract* absorbed Rousseau's best energies is
indicated in the trouble he took with the title. Only after hesi-
tations did he settle on what is—as will be suggested later—a misleading title. He had even more difficulty with the subtitle and
although the one he eventually chose—*Principles of Political
Right*—gives a better clue as to the real cast of his thinking, perhaps the most accurate description of the *Social Contract* is to be
found in the subtitle *The Formation of the Political Body* which he
eventually chose not to use.

On the title-page Rousseau signed himself 'citizen of Geneva'
and this decision is of more than biographical interest because he
believed that the principles of political right could only be
realized in small compact republics like Geneva, or in those of
ancient Rome and Sparta that he so admired. Only under circumstances that were quite different from the sprawling hereditary
monarchies of eighteenth-century Europe could a political body
be created in which men were first of all citizens and patriots.
Whereas a citizen was a free man who loved the state—the *res
publica*—as his own, the subjects of kings were slaves. Only in republics, where men became the authors of their own laws could
freedom and morality be instituted.

The Formation of the Body Politic

At the very beginning of the *Social Contract* we read that the
'principles of political right' are to be discovered by taking men
'as they are and laws as they might be' (I, ch. I).[1] That the undertaking is problematical is made clear in the sentence which begins
chapter I: 'Man was born free, and he is everywhere in chains' (I,
ch. I). This paradox which lends such effect to Rousseau's famous
declamation is the first example of a style whose power to rivet is
inseparable from the force of his argument. It is a warning that we

---

[1] Jean-Jacques Rousseau, *The Social Contract*, trans. Maurice Cranston (Harmondsworth, 1968). Quotations from the text are to this edition and by book and chapter.

are in the hands of a wordsmith who denied being a philosopher. Instead, this largely self-taught but widely read son of a Geneva watchmaker depicted himself as a 'simple, truthful man'. The truth at issue in the first five chapters is one the author treats as self-evident. Man has been transformed from a condition of freedom to one of servitude. Although Rousseau had offered a speculative account of this movement in an earlier work, the *Discourse on Inequality*, he now disclaims all knowledge of how, historically, it may have occurred. He presents this transformation as a movement of depravation. Because men were born free and independent individuals, there is not, and there cannot be, any such thing as 'natural authority'. First and foremost, men are to be understood in their separate identities as self-sufficient beings. This radical version of individualism deploys the familiar idiom of 'nature' to drive home a conviction that in spite of being everywhere in chains, and irrespective of anthropological considerations, freedom is essential to man. Hence it cannot be given up without violating the 'law' that commands of each the preservation of his 'self'. Since servitude is, as a matter of fact, universal, freedom must therefore have been usurped. Man has been placed in chains by those with power to dupe and coerce. Such rulers are capable of exacting obedience but, no matter what their power, they have no means of transforming 'might' into 'right'. It follows that the moment 'naturally' free men acquire the means of discarding their chains, they have a right to do so. Perhaps they are even bound to.

The predicament of men in chains is, however, more complicated than so far indicated. The rebellion of men against arbitrary power to regain their 'natural liberty' would not be the end of the matter. This Rousseau makes plain immediately following his most famous sentence. He does not know, or much care, how the loss of freedom came about, but adds, disconcertingly:

How can it be made legitimate? That question I believe I can answer (1, ch. 1).

Rousseau's clarification of this comment brings us directly to his first formulation of the principles of political right. We learn that the 'social order is a sacred right which serves as the basis of all other rights' (1, ch. 1), and what this implies is soon explained. The transformation of man away from 'natural freedom' is irreversible. For reasons that Rousseau barely touches upon in the *Social Contract*[2] men come to acknowledge the imperative of belonging to a 'social order' and under these conditions the question is not how once free men can regain their solitary and self-sufficient independence, but rather how can men, each of whom remains condemned to a life of choosing, voluntarily agree to the creation of a social order which though not 'natural' is, or has become, indispensable. 'As it is not a natural right,' Rousseau writes of the necessity of the social order 'it must be founded on covenants' (I, ch. 2).[3] In this view therefore a social order compatible with individual freedom must be created on the basis of choices which embody each person's duty to preserve his self. Between social orders based upon arbitrary power and those issuing from willed covenants, no further possibility is indicated by Rousseau. He does not for example choose to explore whether rule founded in might gradually matures to incorporate the assent of the ruled.

In order to make good the claim that social orders are creations that fulfil man's natural freedom only when grounded in covenants, Rousseau seeks to demolish arguments that, in his view, seek to legitimize servitude. He dismisses the argument—made familiar in his time by Locke's critique of Filmer—that the authority of the father within families is both natural and the model of political right. Once children reach the 'age of discretion', Rousseau says, they regain their freedom which belongs to them 'naturally' as men. Nobody and no circumstances can justify the renunciation of freedom because it belongs to 'one's humanity' (I, ch. 2). The seventeenth-century Dutch author Grotius is attacked

[2] In an earlier version of *The Social Contract*, known as the Geneva Manuscript, Rousseau had included a chapter with the title 'On the General Society of the Human Species' and placed it after the brief introductory chapter. He omitted it altogether from the published version and why he did so has remained in dispute. Rousseau's greatest English critic C. E. Vaughan, whose *The Political Writings of Jean-Jacques Rousseau* remains invaluable, suggests that he did so because the omitted chapter attacks the notion that 'naturally' men form any kind of society. Rousseau did not so much alter his opinion on this matter as realize that to deny any human bonds before the creation of civil society undermined the credibility that any such society could indeed be created. Men would have insufficient in common for the undertaking. Vaughan's surmise is that Rousseau sensed how awkward the whole apparatus of contractualism was for his essential thought. This interpretation has been questioned, notably by Robert Derathé. See *Jean-Jacques Rousseau, Œuvres complètes* (Paris), vol. iii, p. 1410.

[3] Cf. IV, ch. 2, 'every man having been born free is master of himself, no one else may under any pretext whatever subject him without his consent.'

because of his imputed attempt to justify slavery, and thereby a condition in which men, in order to save themselves, may have renounced freedom. Under slavery, Rousseau urges, there is no reciprocity and the terms of the slave's dependence on his master are complete. A man cannot agree to become a slave because a slave is a thing who has ceased to be a man, in the sense that 'If you take away all freedom of the will, you strip a man's actions of all moral significance'.[4] Morality implies Freedom.

For the same purpose and still with Grotius as his butt, Rousseau denies that the condition of war can justify slavery. He denies that the victor has the right to kill the vanquished who is not therefore permitted to purchase life with the sacrifice of freedom. In his view therefore the words 'slavery' and 'right' (I, ch. 4) are contradictory and constitute a 'void'. For men, Rousseau had urged in *Émile*, are born to be self-sufficient with the consequence that all forms of dependence on others is corrupting. It divides them internally between their self-love (*amour de soi*) and the need to live 'outside themselves' in the opinions of others (*amour propre*). Slavery, Rousseau seems to be saying, is the most complete expression of dependence which, however, has its origins in all social orders that bind men together at the expense of freedom. He calls the relation of master and slave an 'aggregation' (I, ch. 5) to distinguish it from the relation of 'a people and their ruler' which he calls 'an association' and it is with this characterization that Rousseau turns towards his central theme.

What marks the crucial difference between an 'aggregation' and an 'association' is that only the latter has 'a common good' and constitutes 'a body politic' (I, ch. 5). Between master and slaves there exists no 'bond of union' whereas a people is already a unity before it becomes 'an association' by acquiring a ruler. The act by which 'people become *a* people' (I, ch. 5) is therefore crucial and is 'the real foundation of society'. The first thing to

---

[4] Cf. IV, ch. 2, 'To assert that the son of a slave is born a slave is to assert that he is not born a man.' But compare this with III, ch. 15, where Rousseau asks 'What? Is freedom to be maintained only with the support of slavery? Perhaps. The two extremes meet. Everything outside nature has its disadvantages, civil society more than all the rest.' His point was however that whereas the civic freedom of Spartans predicated slavery, 'You peoples of the modern world, you have no slaves, but you are slaves yourselves; you pay for their liberty with your own' (III, ch. 15). In this last sentence Rousseau is exploiting a metaphorical sense of slavery in order to lend rhetorical effect to his moral argument. The switch from discussing an actual condition of slavery to its moral equivalent should be pondered. Rousseau's ear for the ability of words to convey overlapping meanings was acute.

notice about this transformation of a multitude of individuals into a unity is that it is an act of the most complete equality because its necessary basis is the unanimous consent of all those who are to form the unity. This act of association is unnatural in the sense that it goes against the grain of man's individually self-sufficient nature, but it has been rendered necessary by the progressive entanglements of 'the state of nature' in which men have unwittingly become dependent upon one another. The profile of this deterioration was drawn by Rousseau in the *Discourse on Inequality* but all that is now said of this corrupt condition is that it has become threateningly terminal (i, ch. 6). The terms in which Rousseau envisages release from this state of affairs are set by his rigorous stress on individual freedom. Freedom may have become problematic, but any solution must preserve this cardinal feature of man's being. The answer to the perilous contingencies of a corrupted state of nature cannot be the chains of fresh servitude. It will however have to be powerful because the predicament has been created by men whose powerful wills are naturally self-centred. These several requirements, of freedom, power, consent, and unity, can be seen in Rousseau's presentation of the essential issue:

How to find a form of association which will defend the person and goods of each member with the collective force of all, and under which each individual, while uniting himself with the others, obeys no one but himself, and remains as free as before (i, ch. 6).

The solution is said to lie in the social contract whose articles of association can be reduced to a demand for 'the total alienation by each associate of himself and all his rights to the whole community' (i, ch. 6). This sentence which has sent alarums through the nerve-ends of liberalism is immediately followed by more detailed description of the three 'articles' by which the social contract creates 'a body politic'. The clue to their significance is perhaps that in all three the relationship being established is not between particular individuals but between individuals, on the one hand, and 'the whole community', on the other. As we have already noticed, Rousseau's prime aversion is to the corrupting influences of personal dependence, and in the articles of the social contract these are excluded. Every individual (i, ch. 6) 'gives himself absolutely' but it is to 'the community' that he does so and under conditions of strict equality. Similarly, the alienation of individual rights is 'unconditional' in order that 'the union is as perfect as it could be' (I, ch. 6). What this is designed to avoid is the strife of individuals who 'in the absence of any higher authority to judge between them and the public' will contest their rights as particulars and thus perpetuate disorder. Unity of the utmost kind is the solution to dependencies of individuals upon one another, and is brought about by the complete identification of individuals with the whole. This is made explicit in article three of the social compact which says that 'since each man gives himself to all, he gives himself to no one' (I, ch. 6). Everyone benefits by a strict reciprocity of equal and mutual dependence—on the unity they create. This wholesale transformation is willed in the social contract whose essence, Rousseau reiterates, is that

Each one of us puts into the community his person and all his powers under the supreme direction of the general will; and as a body, we incorporate every member as an indivisible part of the whole (I, ch. 6).

The self-sufficient unity of the whole replaces the self-sufficient unity of the individual whose 'natural' freedom is, by the act of incorporation, transformed into 'social freedom' and secured by the collective power of the body politic. What is thus brought into being is a state based on the principles of political right. It is however a view of the state whose hallmark is a consciously, and therefore artificially, created unity which is none the less deemed to acquire from the character of the social contract 'its common ego, its life and its will' (I, ch. 6). One must pause here to query what is the persuasive sense of depicting a state as a 'body politic' whose origins are set in multiple individual self-consciousness but whose character is seen as the indivisibility of singular *organic* unity. How can a 'body politic' be created upon the analogy of an individual whose corporate identity is neither made nor willed but biologically given? Perhaps the advent of bio-technology may help to blur this otherwise categorical implausibility. In any case the importance to Rousseau's political ideas of this analogy of the 'body politic' as constituting an 'indivisible whole' cannot be overstated. Just as the individual person is said to have a life and will of his own whose unity constitutes his identity, so also does the artificial and man-made 'body politic'. The state, too, must be a corporate and moral whole. Rousseau seems to take literally this striking analogy but no matter whether or how far he was aware of this, many of his most deeply felt beliefs turn upon it.

The body politic is thus a man-made association of intense, austere, and indivisible unity. It is created in a momentary act of unequivocal self-transformation upon whose consistency its character and continuation is utterly dependent. The bonds of union thus created rest in the civic virtue of men become citizens. In the act of association men negate their 'natural' selves by giving themselves wholly new natures of an artificial and social kind. A citizen is a fresh kind of man whose identity depends on the state.

A citizen is however an equal though indivisible member of the sovereign body, an author whose will and consent is indispensable to the creation of the state. In this sense the social contract which creates the state is the first act of sovereignty. It is the moment at which men become citizens and citizens proclaim their unity as a single body politic. As such, Rousseau argues, the sovereign power is the embodiment of how a multitude ceases to be a plurality of particulars and constitutes itself as a whole. There is therefore nothing in right that can bind or limit the sovereign power. As a source of all law 'there neither is, nor can be, any kind of fundamental law, binding on the people as a body, not even the social contract itself' (I, ch. 7). Similarly, anything that derogates from the original act of association, such as alienating a part of itself or submitting to another sovereign people, voids the act which gives the body politic existence.

There are then only two authentic parties in the body politic—the whole and its individual members. As author-members of the sovereign power men are citizens, but as men obliged to obey the laws they are also (and at the same time) subjects.[5] In their capacity as citizens men have wholly identified themselves with their creation. Henceforth they are inseparable from the political order and since it is *their* creation there can be no clash of interest between citizens and the sovereign power. 'The sovereign', Rousseau writes, 'by the mere fact that it is, is always all that it ought to be' (I, ch. 7). If on the one hand therefore, the citizen needs no guarantee against the sovereign power, this is not true of relations between subject and sovereign. As a subject obliged to obey the

[5] Cf. III, ch. 13, 'The essence of the political body lies in the union of freedom and obedience so that the words "subject" and "sovereign" are identical correlatives, the meaning of which is brought together in the single word "citizen".'

laws of the state, a man retains an individual will which may conflict 'with the general will that he has as a citizen' (I, ch. 7). There
remains then much unresolved tension within the personalities of
men who have become both citizens and subjects. If men were
permitted to enjoy the advantages of being a citizen without fulfilling their duties as subjects, the outcome would be ruinous for
all concerned.[6] In order to prevent this kind of conflict from destroying their creation it is, Rousseau says, 'tacitly implied' in the
social contract that when a man (as a citizen) refuses to hearken to
the 'general will' and seeks (as a subject) to place his 'private will'
before it, this dislocation of a divided self is to be remedied 'by the
whole body'. This, he glosses, in a celebrated phrase typical of his
love of paradox and calculated to incite the dismay of Lockian
individualists, 'means nothing other than that he shall be forced to
be free' (I, ch. 7). Individual men, Rousseau is telling us, who have
willed their own 're-naturation' as social beings cannot rely on
themselves alone to give point and consistency to their new
selves.[7] Their self-transformation into citizens remains fragile and
subject to backsliding. The concerted power and solidarity of the
whole body politic—the state—is necessary to stiffen individual
resolve if private interest is not to destroy the common good. The
general will resides within each citizen and must, if such be necessary, be freed from servitude to our individual wills as subjects.

Once accomplished, this movement from the 'state of nature'
to a 'civil society' can be appreciated as a rebirth. Almost all the
advantages are now seen to lie with civil society. Chapter 8 sets
these forth and leaves us in no doubt that the change is morally
progressive. All the powers of men are heightened and expanded,
but at their kernel is the acqusition of 'civil liberty' which replaces
'natural liberty'. Civil liberty is accompanied by the security of
obtaining legal title to possessions which thereby become property. But before turning in the last chapter of book I to a fuller exploration of property, Rousseau delivers what is perhaps the
central formulation of his political theorizing. 'With civil society',
he says, man acquires 'moral freedom, which alone makes man

---

[6] Cf. III, ch. 15, 'As soon as someone says of the business of the state—"what does it
matter to me?"—then the state must be reckoned lost.'

[7] Cf. IV, ch. 2, 'The constant will of all the members of the state is the general will; it is
through it that they are citizens and free.' And again, 'If my particular opinion had prevailed against the general will, I should have done something other than what I had willed,
and then I should not have been free.'

the master of himself, for to be governed by appetite alone is slavery, while obedience to a law one prescribes to oneself is freedom' (I, ch. 8). With this insight Rousseau does more than take issue with the servitudes of arbitrary political power. Nor is he merely abandoning, once and for all, the vision of man's natural goodness as a riposte to the deprivations of 'living outside oneself'. The antithesis of *amour de soi* and *amour propre* is now revealed as obsolete. Man's self-preservation requires that he raise his self above 'appetite' to a position of moral self-mastery. This, Rousseau says, is a political issue because it necessitates living under law, but the limits which this sets are also the occasion of a new kind of independence for the individual. The citizen becomes, or rather is, a moral person. The price one has to pay for the moral freedom of self-mastery is political life, in the sense that only a citizen who wills the laws for the common good transcends his limitations in a manner compatible with his freedom. Freedom is thus the pre-condition of the moral life. But the free will of individuals is insufficient to create and sustain it. The citizen-centred collaborations of corporate life are necessary to give freedom settled form and steady embodiment. The state as a system of law issuing from the general will of the sovereign people is thus necessary to freedom understood as moral self-determination.

In this reasoning Rousseau is defending a conception of freedom against both Lockian individualism and arbitrary rule, and indeed, for Rousseau there is, ultimately, no distinction for in both circumstances men are reduced to servitude. In the discussion of property which concludes book I he gives plenty of ammunition to liberal theorists. At the moment of the social contract, Rousseau argues, every member gives not only himself but 'all his resources, including all his goods' (I, ch. 9). This increases the dependence of individuals on the state and thereby turns 'their own strength into the guarantee of their fidelity' (I, ch. 9). This does not however deprive a person of his possessions but assures him of their lawful enjoyment because since every owner is regarded as a trustee of the public property, his rights are respected, and indeed better secured, because they are protected by the collective force of the community.

None the less it is clear that individual property is subordinated to the state and this requirement is of great practical importance because without it 'there would be neither strength in the social bond nor effective force in the exercise of sovereignty' (I, ch. 9). Once more Rousseau urges that the creation of a body politic, with its collectivist emphasis on the primacy of the common good, alters everything without disadvantaging anyone. In respect of property, moral and legal equality of ownership replaces the contingent inequalities of nature.

The Legislative Sovereignty of the General Will

In book I it is possible to grasp what Rousseau is advocating by keeping in mind the targets of his hostility. Above all he regards arbitrary rule as incompatible with freedom. His solution is the transformation of 'natural' into 'civil' freedom which in turn comes about only with the creation of a new principle of authority. The general will and the common good of the state must rule over the particular wills of individual interests. In book II Rousseau expands on the implications of this conception of political right and his discussion of sovereignty reveals to what extent he remains the enemy of all so-called authority that does not reside in the body of the people. 'Once there is a master,' he writes, 'there is no longer a sovereign' (II, ch. 1).

The social contract generates a general will and 'a declaration of will is an act of sovereignty and constitutes law' (II, ch. 2). In all his subsequent discussion this line of connection between will–authority–sovereignty–law is insisted upon. All rightful authority resides exclusively in the general will of the body politic. Any tampering with this principle leads directly to the dissolution of the social contract. The act by which a unified and unitary political order was created is destroyed. The preclusively fulsome character of what came, at the time of the French Revolution, to be known as 'popular' and then 'national' sovereignty can be seen in the early chapters (1–3) of book II where the inalienability and indivisibility of sovereignty is emphasized. Whereas thinkers in the liberal style of political thinking habitually sought to buttress individual liberty by treating all authority with caution, Rousseau's prescription is the reverse. Just because the general will 'is always rightful and always tends to the public good' (II, ch. 2), the possibility of its being at odds with the rights and interests of individual citizens is ruled out. It cannot, so long as the general will prevails, arise. Whether this formulation is a 'solution' to the age-old issue of freedom and order or tautological casuistry must be left for later comment. There is at this point of Rousseau's argument another kind of difficulty which arises not through a lack of civic virtue in the general will (something that is inconceivable), but because at the same time as men have become citizens they remain individuals with private interests.

There is often a great difference between the will of all (what all individuals want) and the general will; the general will studies only the common interest while the will of all studies private interest (II, ch. 3).

The resolution of this dilemma, whose ultimate source lies within each person, is to foster the utmost identification of the citizen with the state. The more this dependence approaches the same kind of necessity that men are subject to in their relations with physical nature, the less it can be regarded as a form of those personal and individual dependencies which Rousseau holds responsible for man's moral deformation. In part, the awesome task of reconstituting men as citizen-parts of an indivisible collective identity is one of prevention. Nothing must be permitted to intervene between the citizen and the state. Personal contacts and sectional interests are seen equally as impediments to realizing the general will. As we shall see later, Rousseau's ultimate pessimism with respect to the durability of the general will stems directly from his sense that individual wills cannot finally be transcended, with the consequence that from the moment of its inception the general will is threatened with internal decay. Despite their severity, devices for sustaining the unity of the state can only therefore be temporary. Even so Rousseau wishes to recommend what should be done to sustain the general will, and among these is his stress on the equity of strict equality. 'To be truly what it is,' he writes of the general will,

it must be general in its purposes as well as in its nature; that it should spring from all and apply to all (II, ch. 4).

If, we are being told, the body politic is to prosper, it must be a unity whose wholeness demands that it acts only with respect to the whole. The general will cannot single out particular individuals because were it to do so, it instantly becomes partial, and in becoming so, the common interest is ruptured. Hence the impression Rousseau gives that it is the object of the general will—the common good—rather than its popular or numerical espousal, that is vital.

Citizens must be on the same footing of equality and enjoy the same rights (II, ch. 4) but Rousseau wavers dangerously in seeking to argue that because the civil state is preferable to any other—because it alone frees men to be moral—men make no 'real' (II, ch. 4) renunciation in creating it. It is as if he remained aware that his purported reconciliation of individual rights and the common good remained problematical. That the citizen's life is identified with the state is made clear when we read that a law-breaker who violates the social contract becomes a rebel whose death or expulsion from the state may be necessary. Implications of such dire severity illustrate both the 'sacredness' of the body politic and the erotic energy which Rousseau invests in his conception of the 'bonds of union'. The social contract requires much of the emotional and moral commitment once associated with the contract of marriage.

The state which is created by the social contract is animated and preserved by law. Laws are indispensable to men in general because we are largely deaf to the divine source of justice. Citizens are more particularly in need of law because in civil society 'all rights are determined by law' (II, ch. 6). As we have already noticed, Rousseau considers law as the unique voice of the general will when, but only when, it is considering rules for 'the people as a whole' (II, ch. 6). Once again he stresses that particular individuals or groups cannot be identified by law. It may, and indeed must, designate a particular issue that is to be dealt with but in, for example, laying down that the state shall have a particular kind of government it must not seek to name the individuals who are to compose it. Law in this view is an act of sovereignty[8] and is not to be confused or identified with the activities of government whose sole legitimate function is to administer not make laws. 'A people' we read, 'since it is subject to laws, ought to be the author of them' (II, ch. 6).

The trouble Rousseau now reveals is that 'the people' is unsuited for this crucial task of creating law. As we have already noticed, the dilemma stems from an acknowledgement that the

---

[8] Cf. III, ch. 2, 'Yesterday's law is not binding today, but for the fact that silence gives a presumption of tacit consent and the sovereign is taken to confirm perpetually the laws it does not abrogate.'

general will lacks wisdom. 'Individuals,' he says, 'see the good and reject it; the public desires the good but does not see it' (II, ch. 6). This deficiency of collective insight can therefore only be provided from outside, and Rousseau now presents us (in II, ch. 7) with the figure of 'the Lawgiver'. Much impressed with the image of classical antiquity, he has in mind some such figure as Lycurgus who presented Sparta with an entire constitution. Reputedly of surpassing wisdom, Lycurgus was detached from all personal interest and yet devoted to human welfare. More instructive perhaps than the qualities required of the Lawgiver, is Rousseau's admission of the indispensable need for an agency whose standpoint lies beyond both the subjectivity of the individual ego and the objectivity of the body politic's 'collective "we"'. The absolute standpoint of the Lawgiver has been seen by some critics of the *Social Contract* as evidence of failure to vest political theorizing in the credible reality of human experience. The Lawgiver is a God-like creature. In this view Rousseau's redeeming merit is to have exposed one of the major defects of contractualist thinking. The notion of a social contract envisages the transformation from a 'state of nature' to 'civil society'—but this is divorced from the particularities of historical experience and unrelated to the movements of historical change. And as a result the entire notion of a 'contract' appears arbitrary. Rousseau's summoning of the Lawgiver thus focuses attention on one of the recurrent incredulities of imagining that one can 'set up' a people by an 'act'.

For a newly formed people to understand wise principles of politics, the effect would have to become the cause; the social spirit which must be the product of social institutions would have to preside over the setting up of those institutions; men would have to have already become before the advent of law that which they become as a result of law (II, ch. 7).

Rousseau is, however, doing something more than highlighting an intellectual defect even though it remains unclear how far he realized the full purport of his argument. The figure of the Lawgiver comes as such an intrusion and its implications for the idea of a social contract are so disastrous, that one is led to question whether the true significance of the Lawgiver is perhaps that it signals Rousseau's release from a way of thinking quite at odds with the spirit of his convictions. While remaining attached to the idiom of the social contract, the content of Rousseau's reasoning is surely incompatible with it. For Rousseau the state is a live and active 'body' vested in the passions of its citizens and this is about as far removed from the calculus of interest that typifies a legal contract as one could surely imagine. Support for this interpretation is strengthened by the further description (II, ch. 7) of just what is involved in 'setting up a people'. Although at the beginning of the book Rousseau says that he would treat 'men as they are and laws as they might be', the task of creating a body politic is now described as demanding a change of human nature and the transformation of each individual

into part of a much greater whole, from which the same individual will then receive, in a sense, his life and his being. The founder of nations must weaken the structure of man in order to fortify it, to replace the physical and independent existence we have all received from nature with a moral and communal existence (II, ch. 7).

This super-human task of reformation—of moral, psychological, and social engineering on a collective scale—is so fulsome that Rousseau's Lawgiver is impelled to invoke divine authority in order to give credence to his work. This, too, is significant, for Rousseau is telling us that the 'sacredness' of the state needs the underpinning of transcendent myth. Only wisdom, he says (II, ch. 7) makes lasting bonds.

It is not always clear whether Rousseau believes 'a people' has to be 'created' out of hitherto unrelated individuals, or 're-created' out of men deformed by the servitudes of dependence.[9] He is however clear that wise laws are those that are suited to 'a people' already bound together and identified as a collective whole (II, ch. 8), and in his remaining discussion of law the emphasis is firmly on the latter. The precise configuration of law should be determined by the character and composition of 'a people'.

The wise lawgiver begins not by laying down laws good in themselves, but

---

[9] Cf. IV, ch. 4, 'as peoples are no longer instituted, we have nothing better than conjecture to explain how they were ever instituted.' And *Émile*, bk. 1 (Vaughan, vol. ii, p. 150), 'since, before electing a king, the people is a people, what but the social contract makes it one? The social contract is therefore the foundation of all civil society, and it is in the nature of this act that it is necessary to look for the basis of the society which it gives rise to' (translation provided).

by finding out whether the people for whom the laws are intended is able to support them (II, ch. 8).

Indeed from this point on in the *Social Contract* Rousseau is more and more preoccupied with issues of how laws are to be related to circumstances. C. E. Vaughan noted this shift of emphasis by saying that whereas earlier portions of the book are haunted by the ghost of Plato—the general will as a conception of essential and abiding completeness—it is Rousseau's celebrated near-contemporary, Montesquieu,[10] whose influence is thenceforward present on page after page. This developing stress on what Burke was later to call 'the empire of circumstances' at the expense of abstract and universal propositions about 'nature' and 'man' reaches its climax where, as if bowing to the authority of Montesquieu, Rousseau writes that

Freedom is not a fruit of every climate, and it is not therefore within the capacity of every people (III, ch. 8).

One of the consequences of Rousseau's deepening concentration on the significance of how differing traits and circumstances of 'a people' affect their receptivity to law is that the issue of individual freedom fades from sight. This can be traced in the last four chapters of book II where consideration is given to the principal influences that are said to constitute 'a people'. Nations, we read, 'like men, are teachable only in their youth' (II, ch. 8). On the other hand, 'there is a time of maturity which they must reach before they are made subject to law' (II, ch. 8). Similarly, consideration is given to matters of size and population, terrain and occupation. Rousseau always favours what is small, intimate, unadorned, and 'simple'. These qualities he regards as 'natural' and therefore good. The important thing, however, is that 'a people' already possesses a collective identity but is not so set in its ways as to be ineducable. It is not so much what is to be established, Rousseau says, as what has to be eradicated. Old habits are obstacles to new ways, but the steadfast assumption remains that men, who are not ineradicably evil or corrupt but are made so by

[10] Montesquieu's *The Spirit of Laws* was published in 1748. Its central theme is that the identity of communities is intimately connected with their political institutions and that these in turn are heavily influenced by natural and historical circumstances. Montesquieu's influence on Rousseau is especially apparent in the writings on Corsica, Poland, and Geneva which come after *The Social Contract*.

factors extrinsic to their 'natures', are capable of being remade by the right circumstances. Man's capacity for goodness remains intrinsic, though it is a 're-natured' civic virtue that has to replace the lost innocence of individual natural goodness.

In Europe of the old regime Rousseau detects only one people that satisfies all his conditions for regeneration. In a work that opens with an exploration of the principles of universal political right—'man was born free'—we are not sure how to take it when Rousseau announces that it is the island of Corsica that now appears uniquely suited as the feasible embodiment of his principles. Rousseau was not noted for his sense of humour—few political theorists are—but this oddness, made more enigmatic by the fact that Napoleon Bonaparte was a native of Corsica, should not distract attention from the turn that his thought has now taken. Myriad circumstances, both natural and historical, Rousseau is now arguing, determine the identity of 'a people', and good laws which will educate and instruct (that is change for the better) must reflect the impress of what circumstances have already produced. Laws can transform and redirect provided they also confirm and underpin what has already been achieved. The future, we are being told, cannot be created with only the present in mind. The 'present' is an abstraction, made intelligible only by reference to what has gone before. The future must 'grow' out of the past. History is not to be ignored in the making of laws. And since Rousseau has already connected law and morality, we are now offered the outline, perhaps no more than an intimation, of a connection between history, law, and morality. Laws are, of course, rules of order but pre-eminently they are codes of moral conduct. If we hear less and less that 'a people, since it is subject to laws, ought to be the author of them' and read only that they must give their consent to the provisions of the benign Lawgiver, the heart of the matter for Rousseau is that laws are the articles of civic virtue.

This is elaborated at the end of book II where a 'classification of laws' is presented. The distinctions between constitutional, civil, and criminal laws are made and commented upon, but it is what Rousseau adds that is so important. For what he adds is no mere addition. The fourth 'sort of law' he says is the one upon which the other three depend and is to be found 'in the hearts of citizens'. It is the feature on which the Lawgiver bestows his secret care.

This 'law' which animates and sustains the state is 'morals, customs, and, above all, belief' (II, ch. 12), and it figures in the rightly ordered state at its very centre, as its 'immovable keystone' (II, ch. 12). Morals, it is also noted, 'develop more slowly' (II, ch. 12).

By the conclusion of book II we are in possession of the essentials of Rousseau's political theorizing. The rightly constituted state is a moral order and all else must subserve this fact. This moral order of collective life is the pre-condition and the content of individual moral life. Freedom, as the acquisition of a citizen who is a moral being, has to be understood in this light. The dilemma is that 'morals' must be inculcated by a power—the Lawgiver—who stands detached from the follies of mundane life and yet must inspire and educate the hearts of citizens. This awesome undertaking falls to Rousseau's Lawgiver but one is left with the sense that he has been obliged to summon for his work of redemption a generative power beyond the wisdom of individuals and which history and time can, if at all, alone accomplish. Rousseau does acknowledge that moral instruction takes time and moves 'slowly', but perhaps we are in the presence of a thinker who is struggling to release himself from the static imagery of social contract thinking within which there is scant place for a view of historical development capable of conceptualizing the time-centred movements of moral life. Belief 'imperceptibly substitutes the force of habit for the force of authority' (II, ch. 12) and this is, according to Rousseau, the ultimate bond of union among men whose natures have been transformed into the 'lasting austerities' of civic virtue. The trouble with Rousseau's theory is that this profound insight, into what binds men together and constitutes the basis of law and state, can find no coherent place within the bodice-like constrictions of 'the social contract'. Rousseau is a moralist caught in a rationalist framework and from which only a philosophy of history could have saved him from the necessity of resorting to a 'Lawgiver'. Rousseau bursts the bounds of contractualism without being equipped to transcend them.

Government

Although Rousseau's treatment of government has attracted less interest than his elaboration of the principles of political right, his lengthy discussion of this important matter takes up book III and much of book IV of the *Social Contract*. The cardinal thought is that government should be understood as the creature of the state and not the other way about, but it does not follow that government therefore lacks significance. What Rousseau seeks to demonstrate is that government is directly related to his principles.

In the opening three chapters of book III Rousseau considers the general characteristics of government. Using a variety of metaphors, analogies, and idioms, he underlines his fundamental proposition which he puts most directly in saying that 'the state exists in itself while the government exists only through the sovereign' (III, ch. 1). Members of the government are 'simple officers of the sovereign' and hence there is no 'contract of government' which earlier contractualist writers such as Locke had argued for. It is convenient to keep in mind that Rousseau's target is the rule of monarchs who in his day sought to identify their rule with the very existence of the state. Rousseau argues that government is the legitimate exercise of executive power whose authority derives from—and can be resumed by—the sovereign power not of kings but of 'the people'. Embodied in the general will as the legislative authority, it is this authority which provides the ultimate title to rule. And because sovereignty is inalienable this authority can be neither delegated nor represented. The sovereign legislative body thus declares laws whose instrumental task or 'commission' it is the task of government to administer. This view of government as possessing 'only a kind of borrowed and subordinate life' (III, ch. 1) is of great importance to Rousseau because of his conviction that man's servitude to arbitrary power was expressed in the confusion between sovereignty and government and indeed in their identification.

Once more Rousseau argues by analogy with the individual. If the actions of a man are to be coherent, concurrence is required between will and strength, between our moral and physical selves. Similarly, a 'body politic' has a will embodied in the legislative power and 'strength' vested in the executive power. Because the state is an artificial creation, however, this latter power—which he also refers to as 'the public force'—has to be organized. Only then will it be equipped to act as the instrument of the general will and to perform its other function which is described as 'the means of communication between the state and the sovereign' (III, ch. 1). The unity of the 'public person' depends in large measure on recognizing that both elements—legislative and executive, will and strength, sovereign power and government—are necessary and that their proper relationship is no less so. This relationship which has just been expressed by analogy with 'the union of soul and body' is now depicted in the terms of geometry and physics, and although Rousseau says he is aware that 'geometrical precision has no place in moral calculation' (III, ch. 1), he seems determined to present government as a matter capable of being understood *and practised* as if it shared the quantifiable mechanical certainties of the 'exact' sciences to which the eighteenth century was so attracted. Many of the *philosophes* with whom Rousseau rubbed shoulders in Paris believed that Newton had discovered the methodology of enlightenment. Some of this evidently influenced Rousseau, much of whose thought is otherwise so hostile to its rationalist postulates. His liking for 'mechanics' may therefore be more than an illustration of how thought becomes impaled upon its choice of metaphor, because in his discussion of government Rousseau does seem to believe that once the subordinate relation of government to sovereign power has been established as a principle, what follows, or should follow, is the application of that principle to shifting circumstances. In this sense the subordinate area of government figures as a 'political science' within a setting, however, where the state is conceived of not as a 'mechanical' order but as a moral creation of human will.

Rousseau adopts and modifies the time-honoured classification of government into democracy, aristocracy, and monarchy. Under the former the sovereign places government in the hands of 'the whole people, or the greater part' (III, ch. 3). Aristocracy is government by the few, while monarchy is government by a single magistrate. Each, even monarchy, is 'elastic' in the sense that it may overlap with the others, and each is also capable of being mixed with elements of other types of government. From the opinion that 'the number of supreme magistrates should be in inverse ratio to the number of citizens' (III, ch. 3) it emerges that, in general, democratic government suits small states, aristocracy medium ones, and monarchy large states. What is not to be lost sight of is that providing the sovereignty of the general will is not called in question no form of government is illegitimate.

Discussion of 'the best form of government' ceases to be a matter of principle and becomes one of historical and natural circumstances.

Rousseau is wary of democracy because it threatens the crucial distinction between legislative and executive, and by drawing the former into the realm of particularities undermines its proper concern with the generalities of law-making. And once the general will is corrupted by the pursuit of particular interests, the state is lost. Rousseau's other criticism of democracy is by way of the circumstances which it presupposes. Although some of these—the face to face familiarity of small states, for example—are natural factors and others—such as the absence of luxury—economic and cultural, the most important conditions necessary to democratize government are the civic virtues. Democracy presupposes a 'great simplicity of manners and morals' as well as 'a large measure of equality in social rank and fortune' (III, ch. 4). Rousseau praises Machiavelli for having fathomed that republics are founded in civic virtue, but concludes that the virtues required of democracy lie beyond the reach of men. 'A government so perfect is not suited to men' (III, ch. 4). This rejection of democracy as morally too stringent may surprise those who imagine Rousseau's advocacy of 'popular sovereignty' as meaning the collective self-government of 'direct' or 'people's democracy'. But whatever the merits of democracy on other grounds, Rousseau is here being true to his distinction between the 'very substance' of the state, which is the legislative sovereignty of the general will, and the subordinate modalities of government. He is also being faithful to his pessimism that individual will and interest cannot be lastingly transformed and that therefore the way to defer the corruption of the general will is to separate legislation from administration.

Government, however, remains an important necessity and for these reasons Rousseau prefers an elective aristocracy to other forms of government. This is not, at bottom, a matter of efficiency (numbers and size) but of wisdom. 'It is the best and most natural arrangement for the wisest to govern the multitude' (III, ch. 5). He also believes that the requirement of electing the government will itself assure what hereditary aristocracy cannot, namely that 'honesty, sagacity and experience' (III, ch. 5) are selected. That 'upright and simple men are difficult to deceive precisely because of their simplicity' (IV, ch. 1) was one of Rousseau's favoured beliefs. 'The people' may not be virtuous enough to govern themselves, but citizens are wise enough to elect wise governors to rule them. This makes less demands on citizens than a democracy, but it raises the danger that the 'corporate will' of an aristocratic government will subordinate the general will to its own purposes. This danger, implicit in all government, is compounded by the need for greater inequality of wealth so that the leisured class of governors 'can best give all their time' (III, ch. 5) to government.

The advantage of monarchy is that 'all the levers of the machine' are vested in a single person. Its dangers, however, are directly linked to this because 'everything moves towards the same end . . . but that end is not the public happiness' (III, ch. 6). More than the corporate will of aristocratic government, monarchy threatens the general will because 'Kings want to be absolute'.

Mention was made earlier of Rousseau's developing sense of the importance of circumstances. 'Freedom is not the fruit of every climate'. What accompanies these lines which begin chapter 8 of book III illustrates how far the spirit of Montesquieu had entered Rousseau's thinking. For by the influence of 'climate' he largely means the 'natural factors' which govern agricultural productivity and by reference to which 'one can determine the form of government which that climate necessitates' (III, ch. 8). The assumption that 'circumstances' meant soil and climate is a reminder that whatever his powers of prophecy in respect of other portions of the modern political world, Rousseau had little sense of the impending powers of transformation about to be released by the industrial revolution. For him 'natural factors' and not the forthcoming application of technology to factory production remained the determining considerations. Hence his countryman's view that, in general, the signs of good government was where 'the citizens increase and multiply' (III, ch. 9).

No matter how exactly suited to the natural conditions of a particular people, government does not, however, remain settled. The movements to which, like all else, it is condemned are those of degeneration. 'If Sparta and Rome perished,' he writes 'what state can hope to last for ever?' (III, ch. 11). The source of this 'inherent and inescapable defect' is human will so that 'just as the particular will acts unceasingly against the general will, so does the government continually exert itself against the sovereign' (III, ch. 10). And when government usurps sovereignty this terminates the social pact and citizens recover their natural freedom as men. None the less, a good constitution will buttress the state against the encroachments of time, and at the centre of this sisyphean task stands law and the activities of the general will. To the criticism that the general will can act only when 'the people' is assembled and that this demand lacks plausibility, Rousseau's rejoinder is to cite the experience of the Roman Republic, where regular assemblies of the citizen body did meet. To be a citizen is to have burdensome and active duties without which freedom is merely a slogan. 'Low slaves', he writes, in words that ring true in the fag-end of the twentieth century, 'smile in mockery at the word "freedom"' (III, ch. 12). It is in the assemblies of the people that he sees 'the shield of the body politic and the brake on government' (III, ch. 14), and this fits well with his previous and important precept that the general will cannot be represented. Representation is a sign of the very corruption it is the purpose of good government to withstand. Representation indicates that men serve the state 'with their purse rather than their person' (III, ch. 15). Rousseau considers this venality a modern development of feudal provenance which reflects the commercial and self-interested outlook of sophisticated city-centred life. His contempt for it all is unbounded. In the election of their Members of Parliament the English, he says, fancy themselves free, but in truth 'as soon as the Members are elected the people is enslaved' (III, ch. 15). Deputies can therefore only be 'agents' and not representatives of the people. What stands out from Rousseau's further discussion of government in book IV is how far this 'modern critic' of limited as well as absolute monarchical rule found both defective when measured against the merits of ancient republicanism. Rousseau's knowledge of Rome and Sparta may be partial but his deep admiration of the unifying civic virtues of patriotism is directly related to a theme in the *Social Contract* which has not as yet been adequately touched upon.

We have repeatedly heard how the general will, which aims at the 'sacred name of the public good', is fatally vulnerable to the special pleadings of individual and sectional interests. When these occur, 'the social bond is broken in every heart' (IV, ch. 1), even though Rousseau is at pains to maintain that the general will remains 'indestructible'. The condition where the general will is no longer the will of all is one characterized by 'contradictions and disputes' (IV, ch. 1). 'Long disputes,' we read, 'dissensions and disturbances bespeak the ascendance of particular interests and the decline of the state' (IV, ch. 2). Now this, the articulation of conflicting interests and their mediation within a framework of law, has been widely understood as the very stuff of politics. Within the European traditions, political activity has been understood not as antithetical to the common good but as the principal means by which it finds—however clumsily—civilized expression. Rousseau's aim, however, is not to find precepts and institutions by which a diversity of interests can be housed together, but to envisage their transcendence. He denied that there could be a morality of 'interest' or one based upon the conciliation of interests. His aim is the harmony and wholeness of unity, and in this he is closer to Plato and Marx than to Locke. 'The greater harmony that reigns in the public assemblies,' he writes, 'the more . . . public opinion approaches unanimity, the more the general will is dominant' (IV, ch. 2). Whatever stands in the way of unity is incompatible with the purposes of the state. In a letter, Rousseau likens the 'great problem of political life' to squaring the circle in geometry.

I see no satisfactory median between the most austere democracy and the most perfect Hobbesianism: because the conflicts of men and laws which embroil the state in continual internal war, is the worst of all politics.[11]

Political conflict is civil war.

The Catechism of the Citizen

It is the indelible particularity of separate individual wills which Rousseau identifies as the reason why his vision of republican virtue is that of a buttress raised against the depredations of time. And this understanding of the fragile and impermanent status of attempts to transcend conflicts and transform the state into a

---

[11] Lettre à Mirabeau, Vaughan, vol. ii, pp. 159–62. Translation supplied.

moral order is uncommonly acute. Rousseau believes neither in original sin nor in the perfectibility of man. Civil society is necessary to the flowering of human talents, but he has no theory of historical progress. This is one of the reasons why he was at odds with religious leaders and the *philosophes*. Both correctly identified Rousseau as their enemy.

Perhaps it is because of his belief in the rootedness of individual will that Rousseau resorts to further devices reminiscent of the Lawgiver. Stringent measures are necessary to 're-nature' the endemic wilfulness of individual men and shape them as citizens. And the purpose in book IV of 'The Tribunate' (chapter 5), 'Dictatorship' (chapter 6), and 'The Censorial Tribunal' (chapter 7) is surely to make good the deficiencies of the general will when faced with individual wills. Exceptional wisdom beyond the resources of the general will is necessary if the state is not to founder in divisive conflict. 'The Lawgiver', we learned earlier, 'is the engineer who invents the machine', and it now appears that further expertise is necessary in order to preserve the state from political discord.

Of the aspects of corporate life most in need of 'regulation' that of belief, or opinion, is the most important. In returning to this topic Rousseau resumes the earlier discussion of law. There, it will be recalled, 'opinion' was said to be the stuff of morals and the 'immovable keystone' of the state. We now learn that a public office—the Censorial Tribunal—is needed to 'sustain morals by preventing opinions from being corrupted' (IV, ch. 7), and although the powers of this office and its relationship to the sources of 'public judgment' is unclear, the importance of the matter to Rousseau's thinking is pivotal. The issue is vividly continued in the chapter on 'The Civil Religion'. Said to have been added later,[12] Rousseau here reiterates that the hallmark of the rightly ordered state is unity, and that the unity in question is located in the hearts and minds of citizens. The 'bonds of union' that identify 'a people' are common beliefs and these, like everything in the state, have to be fostered. The inculcation of shared

---

[12] That is, added after the completion of the first version of the *Social Contract*. In the draft of the Geneva Manuscript, it is interestingly placed immediately following the chapter on the Lawgiver. *OC* (Pléiade), vol. iii, n. 3, p. 1427.

beliefs is thus one of public instruction and also one in which the distinction—so important to liberalism—between education and propaganda is necessarily forfeited.

In Rousseau's view Christianity ruptured the unity achieved under ancient pagan rule where religion was regarded as a province of belief subordinate to government. Instead of each state having its own gods, Christianity raised two cities—this world and the next. The result was discord 'where men have never known whether they ought to obey the civil ruler or the priest' (IV, ch. 8). It is the fertile power of religious faith to bind men together that renders it either dangerous or invaluable, depending on what purposes it is directed to serve. 'Communion and excommunication', Rousseau writes in an important note

are the social compact of the clergy, one through which they will always be masters of both people and kings. All the priests who communicate together are fellow citizens . . . This invention is a masterpiece of politics (IV, ch. 8).

Hobbes is credited with having seen that the restoration of political unity required the reunification of religion and state because, 'no state has ever been founded without religion at its base' (IV, ch. 8). Rousseau therefore distinguishes both the 'simple and pure religion of the Gospel, and 'the religion of the priest' (which he identifies, though not exclusively, with Catholicism) from what he calls the 'religion of the citizen' (IV, ch. 8). It is religion of this latter kind that is vital to the moral order and hence to the unity of the state, because 'it joins divine worship to a love of the law' (IV, ch. 8). In this account of civil religion, therefore, we find studied elaboration of the scattered references that appear throughout the book to the *sacred* character of the 'bonds of union' that constitute the state. Just as earlier Rousseau had been willing, in the spirit of Machiavelli, to acknowledge that the Lawgiver needed to summon the mythic powers of the gods, so here he recognizes that civil religion is a necessary dupe 'based on error and lies' (IV, ch. 8). Reliance on the Gospel religion of the private person would 'leave the law with only the force the law itself possesses', and what is necessary is the means of 'attaching the heart of the citizen to the state' (IV, ch. 8). Perhaps this is the best one-line summary the author of the *Social Contract* gives of his political theory. It has little to do with 'contracting'.

If this stress on the 'sacralization of politics' is correct, its importance deserves a further comment. At the very time in the eighteenth century when, in accordance with the *philosophes'* programme of modernity, thought was becoming progressively rational and secularized, Rousseau offers a vision of human redemption that is in keeping with this new spirit. The *Social Contract* is a secular and reasoned response to the issue of man's identity as a moral being. And yet his response contains at its core a view of the secular life of the citizen and the state that turns upon raising civic life to the level of the sacred. The 'bonds of union' have not merely to be sanctified—they must be made and felt worthy of worship. Rousseau invests civic virtue with more than the civic pride of republicanism, but when he resorts to the emotional charge of religious faith he does so on behalf of secular and against theological reasoning. In any case, Christianity is damned as contrary to the 'social spirit' (IV, ch. 8) just because it envisages man rather than the citizen, humanity rather than the patriot. Time and again, as we have seen, Rousseau proclaims that the heart of his theory lies in the identification of citizens with their state. This attachment Christianity cannot foster partly because it has its own preclusive passions set upon the City of God, and partly because it preaches 'only servitude and submission' (IV, ch. 8). True Christians are made to be slaves and cannot be expected to fight tyranny with zeal.

In a masterly feat of looking both ways at once Rousseau, having stressed just how far 'public utility' must go in promoting conformity of opinion, then says that individual belief is a personal matter, 'except when those beliefs are important to the community' (IV, ch. 8). This wish to combine dogma and tolerance sounds like a further example of wanting to square a circle. In any case, Rousseau's argument is that it is for the sovereign body to declare what is to be professed 'not strictly as religious dogma but as sentiments of sociability' (IV, ch. 8). Just as he had earlier favoured few and simple laws, so now the precepts of the civil religion are to be brief. Not surprisingly this 'catechism of the citizen'[13] includes 'the sanctity of the social contract and the law' (IV, ch. 8) whose abuse is punishable with exile or even death. How the tenets he mentions are supposed to move a citizen to

---

[13] *Lettre à Voltaire*, Vaughan, vol. ii, p. 165.

willingly sacrifice 'his life to his duty' is a mystery. The civil religion of nationalism was to have no such difficulty.[14]

Conclusion

In the *Social Contract* Rousseau formulates a political theory around his conception of man. That conception is present in the most famous sentence he wrote. 'Man was born free and he is everywhere in chains.' Although the freedom men have lost is not discussed in the *Social Contract*, Rousseau's sense that men are 'naturally' good and self-sufficient vitiates all his thinking—even though the first is an act of ontological faith and the second little more than anthropological surmise. Even though they disagreed over the political implications of their radically different conceptions of man's condition in 'the state of nature', Rouseau agreed with Hobbes in denying Aristotle's assertion that men were 'by nature' social and political creatures. In the content of man's nature, however, Rousseau stands closer to Plato in the sense that he took men to need wholeness and completeness. Only when men were 'at one with themselves' were they capable of happiness. In *Émile* Rousseau wrote that a man 'to be something, to be himself, and always one, must act as he speaks,[15] and this was the reverse of what he saw all about him. Instead of transparent unity he detected falsehood and conflict, where 'always floundering between inclinations and duties' a man 'will never be either man nor citizen; will be good neither for himself nor for others'.[16] In the name of a wholeness combining virtue and happiness Rousseau thus poses a choice between which there can be no compromise. One is either a 'man' living in accordance with 'nature'

---

[14] There is no place for cosmopolitanism or pacificism in Rousseau's political ideas. 'Patriotism is an exclusive feeling,' Rousseau wrote to a correspondent, 'which makes us view as strangers and almost enemies those who are not our fellow citizens.' Vaughan, vol. ii, p. 160. In various places throughout the *Social Contract* the importance of foreign affairs is mentioned. The establishment of political right, for example, presupposes peace, and federal association, he remarks, is the solution to the individual weakness of small states. Nevertheless, foreign relations receive no sustained treatment and the last chapter of the book only etches a list of topics which should properly complete the consideration of the state.

[15] Quoted in Vaughan, vol. ii, p. 146, translation provided.

[16] Ibid.

or a citizen. The *Social Contract* is an exploration of this latter condition.

At the heart of the *Social Contract* lies the moralists' search for completeness in which the personal dependencies that disfigured the self-sufficiency of 'natural' man are to be overcome by the complete identification of the citizen with the state. It is at this juncture that some readers have become alarmed that the 'contract' by which this transformation is to be achieved is not an individualist charter of Lockian liberties but a recipe for their suppression. And the freedom which Rousseau champions *is* different because he denies that the legally guaranteed pursuit of individual interests deserves the name of freedom. The freedom Rousseau has in mind is not the servile treadmill of sensate pleasures but the moral freedom of self-mastery. And however paradoxical it may at first appear, moral freedom is only attainable within a civil order willed by its citizen-members. Rousseau thus claims to resolve the paradox of identifying individual moral freedom with the active political duties of a citizen by saying that their transformation depends upon the voluntary creation of a state embodying the principles of political right. The *Social Contract* is thus a programme of reformation via political education whose citizen-authors belong to the state as much as it belongs to them. Although Rousseau considered his principles compatible with reason, the 'bonds of union' he has in mind derive their force from moral and emotional sources rather than from legal and prudential calculations. The citizens' attachment to the 'body politic' is thus not a matter of limited interest but constitutes his identity.

The major criticism of Rousseau's political reasoning is not that he advocates an alternative notion of freedom to that of Locke but that he does so by generating a state vastly more intrusive than that contemplated by Hobbes. The *Social Contract* enthrones the principle of popular sovereignty and, in the name of political right, erects unlimited and illimitable power. Might and Right have been reunited. They have been willed and sanctioned in the hearts of men, where the 'chains' that have thus been 'legitimized' as the 'bonds of union' are self-imposed. Rousseau attacks Locke's 'modern' notion of individualism as morally pernicious and he does so in the name of the 'ancient' liberties of classical republicanism. But Rousseau invests his advocacy with a self-conscious fervour which is all his own and whose collectivism is also unmistakably modern. The net beneficiary of his reasoning is neither one notion of freedom nor another, but rather the principle of popular sovereignty. And this, it might be suggested, has turned out to be the cruellest of all modern political ideas.

The persuasiveness of Rousseau's reasoning is also undermined by its separation of will and time. Whereas St Augustine held men to be flawed by original sin, Rousseau urged that men's divisions were extrinsic to their natures. Hence what has been caused by factors external to man's natural goodness can, in principle, be remedied by the reconstruction of alternative and more benign circumstances. It is this belief in the capacity of institutions to remedy human ills that no doubt warmed Rousseau to Machiavelli. Like Machiavelli, however, Rousseau allows no room for history in the task of making men better by creating better laws and institutions. The 're-naturing' of men as citizens is the work of human will—and in the case of the Lawgiver of superhuman will—in which the movements of historical time stand against men's efforts. Rousseau did not share the *philosophes*' confidence in enlightenment as the promise of historical progress, yet his realm of civic virtue needs time in which to develop even if, like all else, it is fated not to endure. In what he has to say about law, Rousseau makes plain that it is the *habit* of sound beliefs that must give consistency as well as unity to the life of citizens. And habits cannot be created by acts of will. They need to have time on their side. Despite his dependence on organic metaphors in the *Social Contract* with their imagery of growth and development, the general will is an apocalyptic and not a historical notion. In Rousseau history is alien to man's nature, whose goodness it relentlessly deforms. 'The march towards the perfection of society', he wrote, 'is as rapid as that towards the deterioration of the species.'[17]

Whereas once it was Rousseau's indictment of tyranny in the name of freedom and popular sovereignty that made his name resound, it is now his 'evolutionary pessimism' that attracts attention. His sympathy for what is small, intimate, and 'natural' places him at odds with the 'big battalions' of mass consumer society where it is neither men nor citizens but rather 'units of consumption' that are to be found.

[17] *OC* (Pléiade), vol. i, p. 935.

Bibliographical Note

The authoritative edition of Rousseau's complete works is *Œuvres complètes de Jean-Jacques Rousseau*, ed. B. Gagnebin and M. Raymond (Paris), vol. i (1959); vol. ii (1961); vol. iii (1964); vol. iv (1969). Vol. iii, which contains Rousseau's political writings, includes *The Social Contract*. This is edited with introduction and notes by Robert Derathé. C. E. Vaughan's *The Political Writings of Jean-Jacques Rousseau* (2 vols.; Cambridge, 1915; reprinted Basil Blackwell, 1962), also remains useful, especially in respect of its introductory essay. A convenient edition of *The Social Contract* in French which incorporates recent textual scholarship is *Jean-Jacques Rousseau, Du* Contrat Social, ed. with an Introduction and Notes by Ronald Grimsley (Oxford, 1962). B. De Jouvenel's *Essai sur la politique de Rousseau* which introduces his own edition of *The Social Contract* (Constant Bourquin, 1957) remains of stimulating value.

The best available English translation of *The Social Contract* is that by Maurice Cranston (Harmondsworth, 1968).

Everything Rousseau wrote and did continues to attract interest, and the large and continuing publications on his political thinking are no exception. Among the less recent works that deal with this topic are: A. Cobban, *Rousseau and the Modern State* (London, 1934; 2nd rev. edn., 1964); J. L. Talmon, *The Rise of Totalitarian Democracy* (Boston, 1952), which envisages Rousseau as a proto-totalitarian; Ernst Cassirer, *Rousseau, Kant and Goethe* (Princeton, 1963); the same author's *The Question of Rousseau* (New York, 1953). More recent interpretations which deserve mention include: J. Charvet, *The Social Problem in the Philosophy of Rousseau* (Cambridge, 1974); Roger D. Masters, *The Political Philosophy of Rousseau* (Princeton, 1968); J. N. Shklar, *Men and Citizens* (Cambridge, 1969); Hilail Gildin, *Rousseau's* Social Contract (Chicago, 1983); James Miller, *Rousseau: Dreamer of Democracy* (New Haven, 1984).

Two important collections of essays in French are: *Études sur le 'Contrat Social'* (Paris, 1964); *Rousseau et la philosophie politique* (Paris, 1965). Maurice Cranston and R. S. Peters (eds.), *Hobbes and Rousseau* (New York, 1972), remains a useful collection of essays, while the 1978 edition of the journal *Daedalus* contains several illuminating essays on Rousseau and the modern world. There is an incisive chapter on *The Social Contract* in J. Plamenatz, *Man and Society*, vol. i (London, 1963). J. Starobinski, *J. J. Rousseau, La Transparence et l'obstacle* (Paris, 2nd edn., 1971), remains the most penetrating exploration of Rousseau's cast of mind.

The many biographical studies of Rousseau seem set to be superseded by the work of Maurice Cranston, whose *Jean-Jacques: The Early Life and Works of Jean-Jacques Rousseau* (London) appeared in 1983.

Index

127017